STUDIES IN HYPERINFLATION
AND STABILIZATION

Studies in Hyperinflation and Stabilization

by

Gail E. Makinen

with

William A. Bomberger
G. Thomas Woodward
Robert B. Anderson
Jarvis M. Babcock

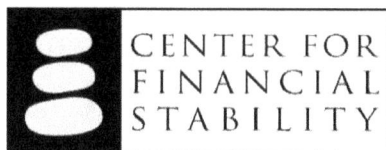

CENTER FOR
FINANCIAL
STABILITY

Dialog • Insight • Solutions

NEW YORK

Chapters are reproduced courtesy of these original publishers:
American Economic Review: "The Greek Stabilization of 1944-46."
Atlantic Economic Journal and Springer Publishing: "Inflation Uncertainty and the Demand for Money in Hyperinflation."
Eastern Economic Journal and Palgrave Macmillan: "The Transition from Hyperinflation to Stability: Some Evidence."
Journal of Economic History and Cambridge University Press: "The Greek Hyperinflation and Stabilization of 1943-1946."
Journal of Money, Credit and Banking and John Wiley & Sons: "The Demand for Money, the 'Reform Effect,' and the Money Supply Process in Hyperinflations: The Evidence from Greece and Hungary II Re-examined"; "The Taiwanese Hyperinflation and Stabilization of 1945-1952."
Journal of Political Economy and the University of Chicago Press: "Economic Stabilization in Wartime: A Comparative Case Study of Korea and Vietnam"; "The Chinese Hyperinflation Re-examined"; "Indexation, Inflationary Finance, and Hyperinflation: The 1945-1946 Hungarian Experience"; "The Hungarian Hyperinflation and Stabilization of 1945-1946."
South African Journal of Economics and John Wiley & Sons: "Some Further Thoughts on the Hungarian Hyperinflation of 1945-46."

Cover design by Wednesday Trotto

Published 2014 by the Center for Financial Stability
1120 Avenue of the Americas, 4th floor, New York, NY 10036
http://www.centerforfinancialstability.org

ISBN 9781941801024 (hardback)

Cataloging data available from the Library of Congress

Library of Congress Control Number: 2013949585

Contents

About the Author and Coauthors

The Author: Gail E. Makinen

Gail E. Makinen is Adjunct Professor at the Georgetown University McCourt School of Public Policy, teaching macroeconomics and international economics. Prior university appointments were at Wayne State University in Detroit and George Mason University in northern Virginia. For nearly twenty years, he was a Specialist in Economic Policy at the Congressional Research Service of the Library of Congress in Washington, D.C. In that capacity, he served as an economic adviser on macroeconomic and monetary policy issues to the Senate Banking and Finance Committees, the House Budget Committee, and the Subcommittee on Domestic and International Monetary Policy of the House Financial Services Committee. Prior to his tenure at the Congressional Research Service, he spent four years as the Principal Macroeconomist for the General Accounting Office (now the Government Accountability Office). He received his Ph.D. from Wayne State University.

Makinen's areas of research interest include hyperinflation, economic stabilization, monetary theory and policy, economic history, and exchange rate regimes. During his career, he has published seven books as well as chapters in edited works, entries in encyclopedias, and more than thirty articles in refereed journals, including *American Economic Review; Journal of Political Economy; Journal of Finance; Journal of Business; Journal of Economic History; Southern Economic Journal; Atlantic Economic Journal; Economic Inquiry; Journal of Money, Credit, and Banking; International Journal of Energy, Environment, and Economics; Economic Development and Cultural Change; Public Budgeting and Finance;* and *Eastern Economic Journal.*

Coauthors

William A. Bomberger

William A. Bomberger is an Associate Professor of Economics in the Warrington College of Business at the University of Florida. Before taking his position at the University of Florida, he held a faculty position at Wayne State University. He has also served as a Visiting Scholar at the Congressional Research Service of the Library of Congress and a Research Associate for the State of Rhode Island. Bomberger has a Ph.D. from Brown University. His research has focused on inflation, in particular episodes of hyperinflation and developing empirical measures of uncertainty regarding future inflation. His published research has appeared in *American Economic Review; Journal of Political Economy; Journal of Money, Credit, and Banking; Economic Inquiry; Journal of Finance; Southern Economic Journal; Economic Development and Cultural Change;* and *Atlantic Economic Journal.*

G. Thomas Woodward

G. Thomas Woodward is now retired from public service after providing economic analysis to the U.S. Congress in various capacities over 30 years. He continues to write and research topics in economic history, taxation, and monetary economics.

Woodward served as an Economist with the General Accounting Office; Analyst and Section Head in the Economics Division of the Congressional Research Service at the Library of Congress; and Chief Economist for the minority staff of the Budget Committee of the House of Representatives. From 1998 until his retirement in 2009, he was Assistant Director for Tax Analysis with the Congressional Budget Office, overseeing its tax studies and revenue projections.

He received his B.A. from the College of Wooster and his M.A. and Ph.D. in economics from Brown University. His work has appeared in the *Journal of Political Economy; International Economic Review; Journal of Money, Credit, and Banking; Southern Economic Journal; Public Budgeting and Finance; National Tax Journal; Journal of Business; Review of Economics and Statistics;* and various conference volumes.

Robert B. Anderson

Robert B. Anderson met Gail Makinen when both were professors of economics at Wayne State University in the mid-1970s. Subsequently, they worked together at the U.S. General Accounting Office in Washington, D.C. Anderson left the General Accounting Office to work on the staff of the Board of Governors of the Federal Reserve System for two years in the early 1980s. From 1983 through 2012 he worked at the Office of Management and Budget, serving on the committee that prepares the Administration's macroeconomic forecast and briefing the organization's officials on economic issues. Anderson's main interests in economics were in economic growth and long-run fiscal policy. For many years, he drafted the sections of the annual federal budget that analyzed budget prospects outside the normal ten-year budget window.

Anderson did his graduate work at Johns Hopkins University. He published papers in *Public Finance; American Economic Review;* and the *Journal of Money, Credit, and Banking.* He died on October 25, 2013.

Jarvis M. Babcock

Jarvis M. Babcock taught economics at Wayne State University, the University of Michigan, and Oberlin College. He served on the staff of the Council of Economic Advisers during the administration of President Lyndon Johnson. He was also a township trustee in his native Rochester, Ohio, where he worked the family farm. He did his graduate work at Iowa State University. He died on May 28, 2012.

Foreword

by Thomas J. Sargent

I worked with Gail Makinen in the Systems Analysis Division of the U.S. Department of Defense during 1968 and 1969. I was a first lieutenant and then a captain in the U.S. Army, while Gail was a civilian employee who had recently concluded his military service and had "re-enlisted" to help out our office. The purpose of the Systems Analysis division, instituted by President Kennedy's Secretary of Defense, Robert McNamara, was to put economics and operations analysis at the service of U.S. national defense.

Among other things, we studied the economy of South Vietnam and the forces fueling the persistently high rate of inflation there. Our attention was of course immediately drawn to the quantity theory of money, and a fiscal theory of inflation, though we didn't call it that at the time. Our office was in charge of administering a system of limitations on the amount of domestic currency that the U.S. Army could spend in Vietnam, a system that some of our predecessors had put in place to try to limit demand. Tracing through the effect of that program through the South Vietnam government's budget constraint led our office to think that the program was counterproductive because it actually fueled domestic money creation. We successfully argued that the program should be terminated, but it took some persuasion.

I suspect that those early Army experiences wrestling with the government budget constraint and monetary disorders set Gail on a productive lifelong quest to explore and understand monetary and fiscal experiments and disorders on a much broader stage. Gail produced a sequence of fascinating studies that succeed in coaxing orderly patterns and basic macroeconomic forces at work in the midst of what at first glance seems to have been chaos.

Personally, I continue to try to make sense of what happened within the United States and Southeast Asia during the years Gail and I served together in the Pentagon. Rereading Gail's papers makes me appreciate how people like Gail picked up the pieces from those years and, by studying mistakes of the past, moved on to shed light on how we can improve things.

Thomas J. Sargent is the William R. Berkley Professor of Economics and Business at New York University, Senior Fellow of the Hoover Institution, and Professor at Seoul National University. He was the co-recipient of the 2011 Nobel Prize in Economics for his research on cause and effect in the macroeconomy, including research on hyperinflations.

Preface

Hyperinflation imposes heavy economic costs and undermines political and social stability. Its often terrible consequences have made it a topic of enduring fascination for economists and public alike. The articles in this volume primarily examine episodes of hyperinflation and the efforts by governments to bring them to an end.

The first reliably recorded case of hyperinflation occurred in France in 1795, during the upheaval of the French Revolution.[1] No subsequent cases were recorded until after World War I. In the political and economic turmoil that accompanied the creation of new nations from what had been parts of the Austro-Hungarian, German, and Russian empires, several episodes of hyperinflation occurred in central and eastern Europe. The public anger that Germany's hyperinflation aroused fueled the early political career of Adolf Hitler, who made an unsuccessful armed attempt to seize power in Bavaria (the "Beer Hall Putsch") in early November 1923, when inflation was near its peak.

The post-World War I hyperinflations prompted inquiry by economists that continues to be read today. Among the early works now regarded as classics are John Maynard Keynes's *Tract on Monetary Reform* (1923), *The Austrian Crown* by J. van Walré de Bordes (1924), Frank Graham's *Exchange, Prices, and Production in Hyperinflation: Germany, 1920-1923* (1930), and *The Economics of Inflation* by Constantino Bresciani-Turroni (1937). Other than Keynes's book, Bresciani-Turroni's work is probably the best-known of the bunch today because of its detailed, compelling eyewitness reporting. The enduring interest in this topic can be seen by the popularity of Thomas Sargent's *The Ends of Four Big Inflations* (1982), which has garnered nearly 1,000 citations by other economists. The League of Nations and the International Labour Organization, both founded soon after World War I, collected data on the hyperinflations that many subsequent

---

[1] Hyperinflation is conventionally defined as beginning in the month the rise in prices exceeds 50 percent. This definition owes its origin to Phillip Cagan (1956).

economists have used.

In the 1930s, economists' interest in hyperinflation waned because the pressing problem of the Great Depression was deflation, not inflation. John Maynard Keynes's *General Theory of Employment, Interest, and Money*, published in 1936, drew economists' attention away from the importance of money and monetary policy. In the 1940s, though, further episodes of hyperinflation occurred in Europe and in East Asia. In 1956, Phillip Cagan published a condensed version of his Ph.D. dissertation, "The Monetary Dynamics of Hyperinflation," as a chapter in the book *Studies in the Quantity Theory of Money*, which was edited by his dissertation supervisor Milton Friedman. Cagan studied seven episodes of hyperinflation, five in the aftermath of World War I (Germany, Austria, Hungary, Poland, and Russia) and two during and after World War II (Hungary and Greece).

Other economists immediately recognized the importance of Cagan's work, and have cited it in nearly every subsequent paper on hyperinflation. Cagan's objective was to demonstrate that even during the turbulence of hyperinflation, it was possible to identify factors that would reliably predict how much money people would hold, or, as economists say, he showed that a stable demand for money existed. For each episode he studied, he estimated a simple demand for money equation in which real (inflation-adjusted) money balances were a function of the expected rate of inflation, with expectations being formed adaptively (that is, on the basis of an extrapolation of recent and past experience with rising prices). Cagan's work had broader implications, for he also inquired into reasons for the increase in the supply of money during these episodes. Cagan's work led to a revival of interest in the study of hyperinflations, the source of money supply growth, and the means that would likely succeed in bringing these chaotic episodes to an end. As a consequence, his dissertation and the studies it inspired helped to restore to macroeconomics a more balanced treatment of the role and importance of money.

About This Volume

The studies in this volume are motivated by the work of Phillip Cagan. They add two more episodes to the seven he studied; they add additional regressors to explain money holdings in hyperinflations; they introduce new data, and, in other cases, reinterpret the data he used.[2] This should not be taken as a criticism of his work. As we said in one of our papers, "It is no reflection on Cagan's careful and exhaustive efforts that subsequent work has occasionally uncovered other time series or questioned some of his assumptions. Indeed, considering the empirical thrust of Cagan's original article, it is puzzling to us that scholars inspired by his work have spent so little time trying to expand and refine his data set. Much more attention has been devoted to econometric techniques than has been applied to improving the data used to test those techniques. In our view, many of the puzzles in these hyperinflation episodes can only be resolved by a further examination of the data." The reader will also note that in most of the papers in this collection the authors gratefully acknowledge the generosity of Phillip Cagan in providing encouraging support and useful comments.

Some of the studies in this volume are primarily concerned with stabilization or the efforts made by governments to reign in the inflation and return to price stability. These too owe a debt to Cagan's work for, as noted above, his dissertation was also an inquiry into the nature of the money supply process.

The articles in this volume are a collaborate efforts. The only person whose name appears on all of the papers is Gail Makinen. He has been joined in various configurations by four coauthors. The research agenda they represent largely began by accident or chance occurrence. The first and most important chance occurrence was that Makinen, early in his career, worked for 18 months with a young Army officer, Captain Thomas J. Sargent. History records that Captain Sargent went on to win the Nobel Prize in economics in 2011. What may not be as well known is how this association changed the focus of Makinen's research interests from international trade and finance to macroeconomics and monetary economics.

The first paper in this volume reflects this new interest. It is a comparison of the stabilization effort made by the United Nations and

---

[2] Recently, Hanke and Krus (2012) have provided an exhaustive list of the countries experiencing hyperinflation according to Cagan's definition. The length of this list suggests that hyperinflation may have been one of the most frequent severe economic problems of the past century.

the United States in Korea and Vietnam, respectively, during the war in each country. The U.S. effort was far more successful in containing the inflation in Vietnam than was the UN effort in Korea. The more successful outcome in Vietnam was due in part to a more effective use of foreign aid to offset the war- induced decline in production and to meet the extra demand resulting from the introduction of a substantial number of foreign troops. In Makinen's opinion, which his later coauthors share, most of the papers in this volume need no revisions except to correct for minor errors, but this first paper might stand some more fundamental changes.[3] The discussion of the velocity of money assumes adaptive expectations. "Rational expectations" theory had not yet entered the literature when the paper was written.[4] The discussion of velocity would likely change somewhat if the treatment of expectations were to be revised. Additionally, Makinen discovered how the disparity between the official and the black market exchange rates in Vietnam was used by American contractors operating in Vietnam and some Vietnamese nationals to expedite the illegal flight of capital from that country. A common pitfall, demonstrated in the studies to follow, was the frequent attempts by authorities to deal with inflation by fixing prices. Such attempts nearly always have undesired and harmful consequences. Expediting illegal capital outflows is one that should be added to the list.

The second paper, on China's hyperinflation of the late 1940s, was also the result of an accidental occurrence. Makinen had come across a study of money demand during the Chinese hyperinflation. The estimating equation modified the original Cagan specification in one important respect. The original specification assumed that the actual and desired money holdings of individuals were identical. That is,

---

[3] Jarvis Babcock, a coauthor of the China paper, died before this project began.

[4] Expectations about inflation are an important determinant of the turnover rate of money and of money spending. If they are "adaptively" formed, it means that individuals extrapolate the current and past history of inflation in deciding what the future rate of inflation will be. If they are "rationally" formed, it means that all relevant information is used in coming to this decision such as the current and expected future position of the government's budget. Since the acquisition of information can be costly, it is possible in some instances for adaptive expectations to be rational.

whenever individuals had cause to change their money holdings it was done instantaneously. The new specification allowed for partial adjustment or an adjustment that occurred over time. Makinen had some concerns about this specification and approached Jarvis Babcock to discuss them. He and Babcock noticed one anomaly in the Chinese study using this new variation. This was the possibility that the inflation could become self-generating.[5] Cagan had raised the possibility. His estimating technique furnished the means to test this notion—he dubbed the crucial parameter "the reaction index." For several high-inflation countries in his sample he obtained a sufficiently large value for the reaction index to suggest that self-sustaining inflation could occur. Even though the rate of inflation in China was on a par with rates in the European countries in Cagan's sample, the reaction index was noticeably smaller. This led Babcock and Makinen to undertake a more comprehensive study of the data for the Chinese hyperinflation. They discovered that the Chinese government had introduced a gold-based currency to restore public confidence in the rapidly depreciating paper money. The data used in the original paper that had sparked Makinen's interest commingled the data from both regimes. Separating these led to a better understanding of what had happened in China and to a reaction index quite in line with Cagan's findings. The new result is the subject of the second article in this volume.

Many of the subsequent papers were set in motion after Makinen found a copy of *Money: Whence It Came, Where It Went* by John Kenneth Galbraith (1975) in a remainder bin of a bookstore in the Durham, North Carolina airport while he waited for a flight. On that flight, he read the chapter on the German hyperinflation. Questions provoked by that reading were to dominate his research interests for the next 35 years. The chapter pointed out that during hyperinflations the composition of the money stock changes—currency displaces checks as the primary means for making payments.[6] Since currency held as

---

[5] This means that once the inflationary process is set in motion, for whatever reason, it will continue indefinitely, even if the money supply growth slows down or stops. This involves an interaction between rising expectations of inflation and a rising sensitivity of money holdings to those expectations.
[6] The reason for this is that it takes time to clear checks—that is, to transfer the ownership of deposits. During this time, the increase in prices will erode

bank reserves supports many times its value as deposits, when currency is withdrawn from the banks, deposit money must fall by some multiple. A rising ratio of currency to deposits is symptomatic of hyperinflation and offsets to some degree the effect on the money supply from printing additional currency.[7] Cagan had noted this phenomenon and had observed that it occurred in six of the seven countries in his sample. The outlier was the hyperinflation in Hungary at the end of World War II ("Hungary II"). An explanation for the cause of this anomaly led to the extension of an ongoing collaboration between Bomberger and Makinen. They discovered that the indexed bank deposits, used by Hungarians as a protection from inflation, were commingled with non-indexed deposits, something not discovered by Cagan even though he knew that Hungary had experimented with indexed money. In a sense, this was China déjà vu. In addition, the Hungarians had experimented with indexed currency during the final two months of their hyperinflation, but these data were not commingled with the non-indexed currency.

The Hungarian research was aided immeasurably by the generosity of Dr. L. László Ecker-Racz, an American military officer and economist who was present at the U.S. Legation in Budapest during the 1945-1946 hyperinflation and who reported extensively on economic conditions in Hungary to the State Department. Dr. Ecker-Racz had kept copies of many of these reports and shared them with Bomberger and Makinen at a time when such information was difficult if not impossible to obtain since both the Hungarian and State Department archives were closed. The use of indexed currency and bank deposits was a unique aspect of Hungary's hyperinflation. Bomberger and Makinen showed how this policy aggravated the hyperinflation. Several years after this paper was published, Makinen presented a paper at a

---

the checks' real value. This is not true for currency. Hence, it becomes the preferred means of payment.

[7] Those familiar with the methodology developed by Friedman and Schwartz in their *Monetary History of the United States* (1963), in which the determinants of the money stock are the monetary base and the money multiplier, will recognize that a rising currency-to-deposit ratio reduces the value of the money multiplier, which slows the growth of the money supply. In a hyperinflation, the growth of the money supply is dominated by the growth of the monetary base.

conference in Spain at which the finance minister of Argentina told him that his government had put aside the implementation of a similar policy after reading the Bomberger-Makinen paper.

Later, a chance discovery by Makinen of an alternative time series on money and prices during the Greek hyperinflation in the *International Labour Review* set in motion his work on that episode—a work made easier by Dr. Gardner Patterson's masterly doctoral dissertation and subsequent interviews with Dr. Patterson, an American military officer and economist. Dr. Patterson was in Greece during 1944-1946 when the hyperinflation was at it peak and, at the youthful age of 30, played an important role in bring it to an end as well as assuring the successful stabilization of the drachma. Makinen found that these alternative time series produced different results from those reported by Cagan (see below).

During the period encompassed by these studies, new ideas and methods of estimation were becoming part of the received doctrine of macroeconomics. Among the most important of these new ideas and methods was rational expectations. Bomberger and Makinen returned to the second Hungarian episode to examine how an assumption of rational expectations would affect their earlier results. Makinen later returned to the Greek episode to see how people responded to changes in government policies that were designed to promote stabilization. The results they obtained were mixed. For Hungary, the new results seemed to suggest rationality, but, in Greece, the public appeared to respond positively to changes in policies that were largely cosmetic, which would be inconsistent with rationality.

The new data on Hungary and Greece also made it possible to deal with a problem that Cagan found in his data. Toward the end of four of the seven hyperinflation episodes, he observed real money holdings that were much larger than implied by his estimated equations given the expected inflation rates—the so-called outlier problem. He excluded these observations from his estimates on the grounds that they likely reflected the anticipations of the public that stabilization was at hand. In the case of post-World War II Hungary, the exclusion of these data was significant since it meant reducing the observations by nearly one-half in a sample that was already very small. With the new data for Hungary and Greece, Anderson, Bomberger, and Makinen showed that this problem disappeared: there were no outliers. This not only added to the robustness of the small samples Cagan had, but the results tended to discount the idea that rational expectations may have played a part in pre-stabilization behavior. Babcock and Makinen also found several outliers at the end of the Chinese hyperinflation and attributed these to the fact that the price index used (it covered only Shanghai) may only have reflected localized inflationary conditions and not those for China as a whole, and that the currency data may have reflected both the amount in circulation and the amount printed but held in the vaults of the central bank awaiting to be put into circulation.

Integral to the study of hyperinflations is the nature of the monetary regime in place when they occur and the subsequent changes that take place in those regimes that yield a successful stabilization. Traditionally, these studies have been largely descriptive, as are several in this collection. Developments in time series analysis during the 1970s, due in large part to the pioneering work of Clive Granger and Christopher Sims, make it possible to see if one time series (such as money) can be useful in forecasting the subsequent behavior of another (such as prices), thereby confirming and enriching the conclusions drawn from the descriptive work. Makinen and Woodward used the method of Granger and Sims to see if, following a successful stabilization, the monetary regime suggested by the data as having generated the inflation had in fact come to an end. Using Cagan's data and subsequent post-stabilization data for these same countries, they discovered this to be largely true. That is, the Granger-Sims estimating technique implied that the post-stabilization data were generated by a different monetary regime. The Makinen and Woodward collaboration was based on their joint view that the extensive literature on the crisis surrounding the French franc in 1926 suffered from a number of shortcomings as did the newly emerging view that interest-bearing debt would, in the absence of legal restrictions, circulate as currency. Their study of the franc crises yielded an unexpected but glaring counterexample to the latter view. This collaboration also expanded the number of hyperinflation episodes by adding the one that occurred in Taiwan during and after the Nationalist government's encampment there in 1949. This additional episode was possible because Taiwan, although a part of China, was maintained as a separate currency area from the mainland.

Finally, Bomberger and Makinen investigated whether inflation uncertainty had any effect on the demand for money in hyperinflations. This built on developments in estimating money demand with U.S. data as well as several studies involving hyperinflations. The studies using U.S. data showed that even with low inflation rates, uncertainty about inflation helped to explain the demand for money. Bomberger and Makinen wondered whether inflation uncertainty could play a similar role in a world with high inflation rates. They found this additional regressor to have a significant positive effect on money demand when added to the standard Cagan estimating equation for the six countries in the Cagan sample (Hungary II was excluded because the small size of the sample imposed what statisticians call a degree-of-freedom constraint). These results linked U.S. behavior with similar behavior in high inflation countries.

Several papers in this volume discuss the shocks that caused governments to pay for their expenditures by printing money rather than by explicit taxes, this being the essence of inflationary finance. The episodes investigated in our papers occurred during and in the immediate aftermath of war, in which the national tax bases of the respective countries were severely compromised and the fiscal needs of governments become subject to extraordinary demands. In Greece, inflation began in 1943 during the German occupation. It is one of the two places in the Nazi empire in which this occurred.[8] The inflation in Hungary took hold after the Nazi army was driven out by the Soviets during 1945. The Chinese switched to inflationary finance in 1937 after the Japanese occupied the major part of eastern China, depriving the national government of a major source of its revenue: the tariff. Taiwan's fiscal difficulties began in World War II when it was a part of the Japanese empire. The island was heavily bombed, which substantially weakened its economy and tax base. It was in this state when it was restored to Chinese sovereignty in 1945. China's ability to improve conditions was hampered by its then ongoing civil war. Wars in Korea and Vietnam also led to inflationary financing of government.

---

[8] The other was in the rump state created in Poland during the 1939-1945 Nazi occupation, known as the General Government.

Lessons

What lessons do we learn from these papers? We offer the following:

(1) Governments must avoid substituting money creation for taxation. We, like others, have identified the cause of hyperinflation as the substitution of money for the tax financing of government expenditures. In an important sense this is only the proximate cause of these episodes. We have not attempted to explain why it occurs—which is, of course, the ultimate cause of the episodes. We leave this investigation to others.

(2) Inflationary finance can only be temporary. John Maynard Keynes famously observed in his *Tract on Monetary Reform* (1923) that governments can live by inflation when they can live by no other means of finance. But we, like others, discovered that inflation only prolongs this life temporarily. Once the public discovers what is occurring it seeks to avoid the inflation tax by shedding money balances. The resulting rise in velocity shrinks the tax base, necessitating a larger increase in the inflationary tax rate to yield the same command over real resources.[9] Ultimately, the tax base becomes so small that even very high tax rates can no longer raise sufficient revenue.[10] At this point, reform is inevitable. Not mentioned by Keynes is the point that governments seldom see inflation as an alternative method of taxation to which the normal analytics of public finance apply.[11] If they did, they would be unlikely to create inflation-protected financial assets to serve as alternatives to money, reducing the tax base for the inflation tax.

(3) One-time measures fail. Government policy makers often seem oblivious to the fact that inflation usually reflects what economists call

---

[9] The *Tract on Monetary Reform* contains a very simple and concise discussion of money creation and inflation as a method of taxation. It should be required reading for central bankers and finance ministers. It is often overlooked that prior to his famous *General Theory*, the monetary writings of Keynes were often in the context of the quantity theory of money.

[10] In the *Tract*, Keynes provides a calculation on how much revenue Germany was able to raise by issuing money in the final chaotic days of its hyperinflation—it is surprisingly high given the small tax base.

[11] The inflation tax may be unique among taxes in the sense that it can be avoided, but not evaded. It also escapes the need for legislation. Perhaps these attributes make it so attractive to governments.

a persistent flow disequilibrium. That is, tax revenue can be thought of as a recurring flow of income to the government, and expenditures as a recurring outflow. A continuing excess of expenditures over tax revenue constitutes a persistent flow disequilibrium. Since government policy makers seldom see it in these terms, they often seek to deal with the disequilibrium by one-time measures such as selling existing stocks of goods or precious metals. If the supply of these stocks is large and if they are priced appropriately, they can provide important budget support of a temporary nature. Nevertheless, the flow disequilibrium must ultimately be dealt with if monetary stabilization is to be achieved, and this involves substituting explicit taxes and other budgetary measures for printing money (the inflation tax).

(4) Monetary control is essential for stabilization. For stabilization to be successful some kind of control must be placed on money creation. This can involve several steps. Of first importance is that the government's budget come into reasonable balance. Second, the monetary authority must be freed from the obligation to finance the deficit. In some instances this may involve turning the monetary authority over to an international body or to foreign nationals, or linking the currency to precious metals or other stable-valued currencies. Whatever the arrangements, the government must adhere to them and must convince the public that they will work.

(5) The costs of stabilization are smaller than the costs of hyperinflation. It is not clear that the costs in terms of lost output and unemployment from successful stabilization of hyperinflation are comparable to what might be expected from stabilizing a much lower rate of inflation. In the hyperinflation episodes, staggered contracts governing the prices of goods, services, and labor eventually vanish. Without these contracts a good deal of the price rigidity that impedes rapid adjustment to decreases in demand vanishes, thereby expediting the return of income to a full-employment path and significantly reducing the costs of stabilization.

(6) Indexation is flawed. Several of the stabilization plans in the episodes we studied involved changes to the monetary arrangements of a country, e.g., indexing bank accounts for inflation and introducing currencies in some way linked to commodities such as gold or silver. Often, these new monies circulated side by side with the existing

monies. Separating these components is often essential to an empirical investigation of the relationship between money and prices, since the new monies are likely to have changed the underlying nature of the data.

(7) People have trouble distinguishing good from bad stabilization plans. While individuals draw information from a variety of sources in forming expectations, it is not clear that, at least over short periods of time, they are able to distinguish genuine reforms that promise success from superficial reforms that will ultimately prove ineffective.

(8) Public policy often worsens inflation. As we note in the studies to follow, governments have had a dismal record in implementing successful policies to stabilize inflation, and often changes in policy actually have worsened ongoing inflations. It should also be noted that governments have sometimes, serendipitously, implemented policies that have unintentionally worked to curb inflation.

(9) Real money balances provide an early signal of successful stabilization programs. We have judged the success of stabilizations by the return of the public's willingness to hold real money balances. After this occurs, governments often have issued large sums of currency. Critics of the money theory of inflation have pointed to this as proof that money issue does not cause inflation. We disagree. Our line of reasoning is that once the public comes to believe that the stabilization will be successful, it will wish to hold larger money balances and the demand for money will rise. This is what would be expected based on a Cagan money demand equation. If the supply of money is not increased following stabilization, the interest rate and, possibly, the foreign exchange rate will have to rise to choke off the increase in money demand. To prevent this, the government has a one-time opportunity to increase the supply of money, and this is the reason why the large increases in money following successful stabilizations can be noninflationary.

(10) Hyperinflation need not directly involve the foreign exchange market. The German hyperinflation occurred during a period when Germany had to pay reparations for World War I and the two came to be causally connected through the effect of reparations on the exchange rate. A line of reasoning held that the payment of reparations caused the German exchange rate to depreciate, increasing the costs to produced

output in Germany and the German mark cost of reparations in the budget (and the budget deficit). The central bank, it was argued, passively increased the money supply to finance the larger deficit and to prevent the cost-induced rise in prices from causing unemployment. Both Greece and Hungary II involved similar budgetary stresses. Both countries had to pay an indemnity and bear the costs of an occupation army. While these additional outlays undoubtedly led to higher budget deficits for both countries, they did not involve feedback through the foreign exchange markets since the indemnities were paid in kind.

(11) The inflation rate is likely to accelerate over time. Hyperinflation does not emerge full-blown. Rather, the inflation rate tends to accelerate over time. At least two reasons explain this. The first we covered in (2) above. The second has to do with the lag between the time taxes are collected and their subsequent remission to the government. During this period their real value falls, forcing the government to substitute additional money issues to pay its bills and accelerating the ongoing inflation rate.

Acknowledgments

There are several people we wish to thank for their assistance in collecting these papers into a single volume. Foremost among them is Kurt Schuler, at whose urging and with whose assistance this project was made possible and came to fruition. We also thank the original publishers of our articles for permission to republish them here; Lawrence Goodman for comments on the manuscript and for his support as the publisher of the book; and LeAnn Yee for help with publication.

1

Economic Stabilization in Wartime:
A Comparative Case Study of Korea and Vietnam*

I. Introduction

This paper will analyze those policies responsible for the successful stabilization of the Vietnamese economy and contrast them with the generally unsuccessful effort to stabilize the Korean economy during the 1950-53 war.[1]

Because of the different nature of the war in Vietnam, the United States has been seriously concerned with economic stabilization lest widespread social unrest and discontent generated by high rates of inflation aggravate a volatile political situation.[2] It is this commitment to control inflation which differentiates Vietnam from Korea.[3] Although it may be premature to discuss the Vietnamese stabilization experience while hostilities continue [*editorial note:* as of 1971, when this chapter was originally published], the main elements in the program have been developed and their results are evident. Not only has

* I wish to thank Professors H. Peter Gray and Michael O'Connor as well as Mr. C. Clifford Tuck and a referee of the *Journal of Political Economy* for their many helpful comments.
[1] By economic stabilization, this paper refers to those policies of a government in a wartime situation that attempt to satisfy the government's military needs without uncontrolled price inflation in an environment where wage and price controls are impractical.
[2] Evidence suggests that the U.S. command believed social unrest could be held within reasonable limits if the rate of inflation could be held to 3 percent or less per year (see *New York Times* 1969b).
[3] It was not until May 1952, almost two years after the war started, that the UN command and the Republic of Korea agreed to a number of policies aimed at combating inflation (U.S. Department of State 1952).

Table 1. Comparative Rates of Price Inflation: Korea and Vietnam

Korea			*Vietnam*		
Date	Price level	Change (%)	Date	Price level	Change (%)
1951	612	512	1966	184	84
1952	1,664	169	1967	250	36
1953	2,167	32	1968	342	37
			1969	393	15

Notes: For Korea, retail prices in Pusan, mid-1950 = 100; index number for each year is that of June. For Vietnam, U.S. Agency for International Development (USAID) Retail Price Index for Saigon, July 1, 1965 = 100; index number for each year is that for the earliest reported date in July.

hyperinflation[4] been avoided, but Table 1 shows that except for 1966, the year of the initial buildup of U.S. forces, relative price stability has been achieved.[5]

This paper will not only explain why this happened, but will provide insights into stabilizing other underdeveloped economies.

II. Some General Observations on the Two Economies

There are many similarities in the economies of these two Asiatic nations. Neither possesses the conditions found necessary for successful stabilization programs in developed nations. Production is of a cottage nature, distribution and exchange is frequently of an open-market or sidewalk variety, and a tax collection infrastructure is not present. Furthermore, the agrarian nature of the economies makes for low supply elasticities, and only a small fraction of gross national product lies outside the barter exchange sector. This makes effective taxation difficult and rationing and price controls virtually impossible

---

[4] Cagan (1956, p. 25) defines hyperinflation as beginning in a month in which the rise in prices exceeds 50 percent and ending in the month before the rise in prices drops below that amount and stays below it for at least a year. Korea also avoided this calamity.

[5] For a discussion of the definitional and measurement problems involved with inflations, see Bronfenbrenner and Holzman (1963), and Johnson (1967b), pp. 104-106.

and, hence, any attempted resource transfer usually results in serious price inflation. Additionally, the conscription of local manpower on a large scale for military use, the introduction of significant numbers of foreign troops, the absence of a developed capital market and banking system, and an initial tax structure relatively inelastic with respect to price and income increases are further similarities which increase the likelihood of failure of any stabilization effort in these two nations.

As discussed below, and shown in Table 1, serious inflation developed in Korea which was not controlled until the last year of the war. Among the factors accounting for a major increase in demand were large currency advances to UN forces, the emergence of large deficits in the operation of private and government firms that sold goods and services at subsidized prices, a sharp rise in money velocity, a lack of concern on the part of the UN command for an effective anti-inflation program, an inadequate tax structure, and the emergence of a substantial deficit in the budget of the central government. Because of a decrease in domestic production and an inadequate and inefficiently managed government import program under which large amounts of goods were either given away or sold at prices substantially under those prevailing in the market, this increase in money demand was not accompanied by a commensurate rise in goods and services available for sale.

The relative price stability achieved in Vietnam stems basically from a firm commitment by the United States to implement a stabilization program and the effective use of an import program, consciously designed to permit the aggregate supply of goods and services to rise to meet the sharp increase in demand. The fact that changes in the velocity of money have not been destabilizing has been favorable to the success of the stabilization program.

Although Korea and Vietnam used markedly different types of taxes, the anti-inflationary impact of the tax structure was weak in both countries. Unlike Vietnam, Korea experienced strong inflationary pressures for the four years prior to the beginning of its war in mid-1950 with prices advancing in the range of 600 percent.[6] Thus, the war aggravated an inflation already in progress.

---

[6] Lee (1968, p. 59).

Table 2. Price Inflation in Korea (index levels)

Date	Wholesale, Pusan	Retail, Pusan	Retail, Throughout Korea
December 1947			100
December 1948			158
December 1949			198
June 1950	100	100	
December 1950	234	260	532
June 1951	480	612	
December 1951	747	860	2,129
June 1952	1,476	1,644	
December 1952	1,511	1,824	5,244
June 1953	1,766	2,167	
December 1953			7,298

Sources: For wholesale and retail prices in Pusan, Korea, Office of Public Information (1955a, pp. 243-244). For retail prices throughout Korea, *ibid.* (1955b, p. 28).

III. The Stabilization Programs

This section will amplify the preceding summary by analyzing the sources of the price inflation in both economies, the weak anti-inflationary effects of their tax structures, the changes in their domestic production, and the size and disposition of imported commodities and their velocity experiences.

A. Sources of the Inflationary Pressure

Korea

The various Korean price indices given in Table 2 show that from the beginning of hostilities on June 25, 1950, until the armistice proclaimed on July 27, 1953, prices rose between 1,400 and 2,200 percent. During

Table 3. Factors Affecting Korea's Money Supply (million hwan)

End of period	(1) Money supply - a, b	Inflationary factors			(5) Counter-inflationary factors: sale of aid goods and foreign exchange (per period)
		(2) Advances to UN forces (per period)	(3) Advances to Korean govt. (per period)	(4) Bank credit expansion	
Dec. 1945	118		1	117	0
June 1950	1,248		838	924	632
Dec. 1950	2,905	547	1,186	-168	-93
June 1951	5,330	1,435	749	638	397
Dec. 1951	7,848	2,189	-753	2,125	1,043
June 1952	10,449	2,324	-1,181	1,852	394
Dec. 1952	15,641	3,229	487	4,273	2,797
May 1953	19,259	2,826	2,464	3,038	4,710
Dec. 1953	34,896	5,196	8,490	15,862	13,911

a-Consists of currency in circulation and demand deposits. The latter is seldom above one-third of the total.

b-Column 1_t = column 1_{t-1} + column 2_t + column 3_t + column 4_t − column 5_t.

Sources: Bank of Korea *Monthly Statistical Review*, April-May 1953 and United States Armed Forces Far East (1953b).

this same period, the money supply increased from 1.248 billion hwan to 24.520 billion hwan, or 1,965 percent.[7]

The behavior of several sources of this rapid rise in prices can be seen in Table 3. The major source on the demand side during the first two years of the conflict was the large hwan advances made by the

---

[7] In a currency reform undertaken in February 1953, the official unit of account was changed from the won to the hwan, with 100 won equaling 1 hwan. This reform is discussed later in the text.

Table 4. Inflation in Vietnam, 1956-July 1965 (1959 = 100)

	Consumer price index for working class	Saigon wholesale price index
1956	105	104
1957	100	104
1958	97	106
1959	100	100
1960	99	105
1961	105	117
1962	107	121
1963	117	124
1964	121	129
1965	146	135

Source: Vietnam, National Institute of Statistics (1966).

Korean government to the UN command. These were made under the agreement of July 28, 1950, which provided that their settlement was to be deferred to a mutually agreeable time.[8] Had stabilization been the goal, repayment for these advances should have been made immediately to provide the Korean government the wherewithal to institute an import program to curb inflation. Not until inflation became very serious in late 1951 was reimbursement made and an import program undertaken.[9]

After June 1952, bank credit expansion and advances to the Korean government played the primary role in the growth of the money supply: the former expanded from 1.8 billion hwan to 15.9 billion hwan while the latter moved from a net deposit of 1.2 billion hwan to a deficit of 8.5 billion hwan (see Table 3). These data relate the amazing fact that

---

[8] The first repayment, totaling $12 million, took place on October 15, 1951. The next, which did not occur until September 4, 1952, was followed by five others culminating in a final payment in June, 1953. These six payments totaled $167 million (see McCabe 1954, pp. 12, 18).

[9] The exchange rate agreed upon for the reimbursement was 60 hwan per dollar which, until the June 1953 revision granting 180 hwan per dollar, was from one-third to one-half the black-market rate (see McCabe 1954, pp. 1-2).

**Table 5. Comparative Price Inflation in Vietnam by Index
and Major Components, 1965-1969 (percent per year)**

Source	Year	General index	Food index	Nonfood index
USAID	1965	44	51	30
	1966	56	60	50
	1967	37	42	24
	1968	30	29	32
	1969	12	14	3
NIS	1965	55	72	29
	1966	59	61	54
	1967	34	43	19
	1968	23	26	22
	1969	n.a.	n.a.	n.a.

Notes: Reference points for the USAID index are January 1, 1965 (= 100); January 3, 1966; January 3, 1967; January 1, 1968; and January 6, 1969. The USAID index, computed weekly by the U.S. Agency for International Development Mission in Saigon, is a subindex of that computed monthly by the Vietnamese National Institute of Statistics (NIS). The USAID index excludes most types of services found in the NIS index. The USAID index shown in this table will show a different rate of yearly inflation from that of Table 8 because of different base dates from which price changes have been measured. The NIS index for working-class families is one of two indices computed for the greater Saigon area. It differs from the middle-class index mainly in that greater weight is given to services.

the Korean government was running a budget surplus until the third year of the war. This was possible largely because the care of refugees and prisoners of war was funded by the UN command. Early in 1953, a sharp increase in defense expenditures prompted the Korean government to seek advances from the Bank of Korea.

Vietnam

Prior to the large-scale American intervention in mid-1965, the rate of inflation was mild. From 1956 until mid-1965, consumer prices

Table 6. Factors Affecting Vietnam's Money Supply (bn piasters)

	1965	1966	1967	1968
(1) Money supply-a	47.6	65.4	82.6	125.8
Change, net	20.2	17.8	17.3	43.2
Inflationary factors				
(2) Advances to U.S. forces	n.a.	38.0	55.7	59.8
(3) Vietnamese budget deficit	34.3	21.4	33.0	60.9
(4) Bank credit expansion	-0.3	21.8	-2.0	-0.2
(5) Other-b	n.a.	8.3	10.8	12.0
Counterinflationary forces				
(6) Imports	n.a.	51.2	78.9	82.3
(7) Other-c	n.a.	20.5	1.3	7.0

Column 1_t = row 1_{t-1} + row 2_t + row 3_t + row 4_t – row 6_t – row 7_t.
a-Consists of both bank notes in circulation and private demand deposits. The latter varies between one-quarter to one-third of the total.
b-Mainly invisible exports.
c-Consists mainly of changes in import margin requirements, time and savings deposits, bank capitalization, and various errors and omissions.
Sources: U.S. Agency for International Development (1966, 1967, 1968) and National Bank of Vietnam (1965, 1966, 1967).

increased 39 percent, or at an annual rate of 1.73 percent. Wholesale prices in Saigon increased 30 percent over the same period, an annual rate of 1.72 percent (see Table 4). However, after American intervention the rate of price inflation increased sharply. During the first six months of 1965 the consumer price index increased only 16 percent. During the last six months it increased 39 percent. The rate of inflation to mid-1969 is documented in Table 5. From mid-1965 to mid-1969 prices increased 307 percent as measured by the USAID all-commodities index. But the peak rise was in 1966. Succeeding years recorded smaller rises, and from mid-1968 to mid-1969 the rate was only slightly in excess of 12 percent. During this same four-year period (mid-1965-mid-1969) the money supply increased from 34.8 billion piasters to 130.5 billion piasters, or 375 percent. Thus, the rate of increase in the money supply has been slightly greater than the rate of increase in the price level.

The magnitudes of the factors affecting demand components in Vietnam and, hence, the relative importance of the sources of excess demand have been somewhat different from those in Korea. The main sources of demand pressure (indicated in Table 6) have been large piaster advances to U.S. forces and the large budget deficit of the Vietnamese government. The expansion of bank credit has been insignificant since 1966. As in Korea, the advances to U.S. forces have been used largely for the employment of local laborers, who number upward of 150,000.

One important difference in the fiscal management of the Vietnamese economy is to be noted. Since mid-1966, the U.S. military has made a concerted effort to limit its piaster spending. While the exact details of this effort are still unavailable to researchers, it is known that the United States has made yearly projections of its expenditures by category (construction, operation and maintenance, etc.) and purpose (labor, heat, light, power, etc.). These projections, when added to forecasts of all other items increasing and decreasing the money supply, yield the so-called monetary gap or net expected new money creation. Depending upon the size of this expected gap, a number of programs have been designed and implemented to lessen expenditures "in country." The most publicized program has been to schedule rest and recreation outside of Vietnam in order to lessen piaster expenditures. As noted previously and implied by the discussion of Korea, this effort to limit piaster spending has differentiated the two stabilization efforts.

B. The Tax Structures

Many criteria might be used to judge the adequacy of a tax structure for stabilization purposes. Two, however, appear of fundamental importance. The structure should effectively depress private consumption without deleterious effects on work incentives, and it should permit the government to maintain, at the very least, a constant command over real resources. It is difficult to specify the most effective combination of income and consumption taxes for depressing

Table 7. Sources of Central Government Revenue in Korea, 1949-1954 (percent per source)

	1949	1950	1951	1952	1953	1954
Direct revenue						
Personal income	26.4	11.8	14.3	12.8	13.8	14.9
Corporate income	2.9	8.8	4.9	3.5	3.9	4.4
Business tax	5.1	9.8	12.6	13.3	14.5	10.0
Temporary land income tax			21.6	30.6	21.8	14.8
Other-a	8.8	39.1	4.8	1.7	1.8	3.0
Total direct	43.2	69.5	58.1	61.9	55.8	47.1
Indirect revenue						
Commodity excise	11.8	6.9	10.3	7.9	8.8	19.3
Customs	10.3	7.9	11.5	14.6	16.3	19.5
Liquor tax	22.1	7.4	10.9	9.9	12.7	9.2
Other-b	12.6	8.3	9.1	5.7	6.4	4.9
Total indirect	56.8	30.5	41.8	38.1	44.2	52.9
Grand total	100.0	100.0	100.0	100.0	100.0	100.0

a-Consists of enterprise, temporary profit, land, inheritance, mining, gifts, travel, registration, and license taxes.
b-Consists of textile, entertainment and restaurant, electricity and gas, admissions, parimutuel, and tonnage taxes.
Source: Bank of Korea (1962).

private consumption in an inflationary situation.[10] Subject to qualification, with unchanged progressive rates and income intervals, tax liabilities rise more than proportionately when money income increases. This is not the case with proportional or regressive taxes. However, if the inflation is severe and the income intervals at which progressive income taxes are assessed lag significantly behind increases

---

[10] This is not to be confused with the question of what type of tax has the greater anti-inflation potential for equal amounts of revenue raised. Musgrave (1959, pp. 449-550) has shown that in this case the consumption tax is generally superior.

Table 8. Real Tax Revenue in Korea, 1949-1953

	1949	1950	1951	1952	1953
Nominal revenue (mn hwan)	136	429	3,921	9,586	21,426
Price index	100	269	1,075	2,648	3,686
Real revenue (mn hwan)	136	159	365	362	581
Percent change		17	230	-1	160

Sources: For nominal tax revenue, Bank of Korea (1962); for real tax revenue, index of retail prices throughout Korea, 1949 = 100.

in wages and salaries, many incomes will rise to the top of the tax range, and from then on the progressive tax takes on a proportional character. It is also possible to posit situations in which a regressive or proportional tax would be more efficient in reducing inflation than a progressive tax (Goode 1952). The second aspect of tax structure, insuring at least a constant command of resources, is important for stabilization, for it lessens the possibility that the government will have to resort to printing money.

Korea

A comparison between Korea's and Vietnam's tax sources is very instructive on this point. In Table 7 it is shown that during the war years over one-half the Korean tax revenue was derived from direct taxes. This has not been the case in Vietnam (see Table 9), where direct taxes have accounted for only about 6 percent on average.

For Korea, the largest single revenue source was the temporary land income tax promulgated in September 1951. It was also the only direct tax with a built-in insurance against revenue depreciation induced by inflation. This was because 95 percent of the tax was paid in kind—mainly rice and barley. The rate schedule was graduated from 15 to 28 percent of physical output according to the amount of the assessed average yield. No tax was required when, as a result of a calamity or abnormal weather conditions, the harvest fell below 30 percent of the

**Table 9. Sources of Central Government Revenue
in Vietnam, 1964-1968 (percent per source)**

	1964	1965	1966	1967	1968
Total direct taxes	7.7	7.2	3.6	5.3	8.0
Indirect taxes					
Indirect	19.1	17.1	9.5	8.8	10.1
Excise	13.9	17.2	11.1	13.9	13.3
Registration	6.8	6.9	5.3	5.4	5.6
Customs	32.8	27.8	21.0	22.3	32.1-a
Austerity	7.1	6.8	6.5	6.7	
Other	12.6	17.0	9.1	7.5	12.0
Per equation			11.1	14.4	16.5-b
Economic consolidation			2.7	7.3	
Exchange equalization			20.1	8.4	2.4
Total indirect	92.3	92.8	96.4	94.7	92.0
Total revenue	100.0	100.0	100.0	100.0	100.0

a-For both customs and austerity.

b-Includes both per equation and economic consolidation.

Source: U.S. Agency for International Development (1968).

rated average yield.[11] Two-thirds of the personal income tax was derived from the net earnings of unincorporated businesses and 30 percent from the taxation of wages and salaries. While the tax rates were graduated the income intervals were not changed during the war years, with the result that the progressivity aspects of the tax diminished. The same was true of the corporate income tax whose graduated rate was from 35 to 70 percent of net income.

The business tax was a transaction tax levied on the gross receipts of all businesses. The law specified thirty-seven rate classifications depending upon the source of business receipts. The tax rates were all a constant percentage.

In evaluating the effectiveness of indirect taxes in a stabilization

---

[11] For a detailed discussion of the Korean tax structure, see Korea, Office of Public Information (1955a, pp. 252-262).

program, several factors are important to consider. First, ad valorem taxes permit revenue to rise in proportion to the increase in prices or, depending upon the volume of goods sold, at a faster rate. Specific taxes also can be effective in reducing inflation if the government is willing and able to make necessary and possibly frequent adjustments in rates. Second, indirect taxes may be unreliable revenue producers if they depend heavily upon imported commodities whose value is determined by a fixed exchange rate. In this case, given an ad valorem rate structure, the increase in revenue will depend upon the relative rates of inflation in the importer and exporter countries, the cross-elasticity of demand of imports and domestic substitutes, and any changes in real income in the importer country. With no inflation in the exporter country, low cross-elasticity of demand, and little change in real income, tariff revenues will remain fairly constant, and a form of monopoly rent will accrue to importers through their ability to buy cheap and sell dear. When flexible exchange rates are introduced, the price of the goods on which the tariff is assessed will depend upon the relative rates of inflation in the exporter and importer countries; and revenue should increase in proportion to the increase in that relative rate. Periodic devaluation provides a further in-between case.

In Korea, the customs, commodity, liquor, and most other indirect taxes were ad valorem, but the rates were not uniform (for example, for commodity excise taxes, the rate varied from 10 to 100 percent depending on seven broad tax classes; the liquor tax varied from 20 to 100 percent of selling price, and the tariff rates varied depending on the import classification). The largest share of revenue derived from indirect taxes came from customs revenue. Its increase over the three-year period basically reflected the implicit devaluation of the hwan. The practice was to grant import licenses on the basis of the official rate (60 hwan per dollar), but to require the importer to buy the foreign exchange and pay duty on the basis of a higher exchange rate (reported to be 190-200 hwan per dollar) (McCabe 1954, p. 18).

As shown in Table 8, the tax structure in Korea was able to triple real tax proceeds from 1950 to 1953. The evidence also would tend to suggest that the elasticity of the original Korean tax structure with regard to money income was close to unity. Even after subtraction of the revenue from the temporary land income tax enacted during the war, total nominal tax revenue increased in every year except 1952 at a rate in excess of the rate of inflation, and in 1952 its rate of increase was close to the inflation rate. Undoubtedly, some of this was in response to tax rate increases. Even in the turbulent year of 1950, in which tax collection was difficult, real tax revenue increased as nominal yield rose 17 percent faster than the rate of inflation.[12]

However, this increase in real revenue did not keep pace with the resource needs of the Korean government. From mid-1952 until the end of the war the government operated with a large budget deficit, which would have arisen earlier had it not been for UN funding of several programs.

An additional question also applicable to Vietnam is whether a revenue elasticity with respect to price inflation of unity implies that the tax structure passes the minimum test of insuring a constant command over resources. This would have been the case if the goods and services purchased by the government had experienced the same degree of inflation as those used in the index to deflate the nominal revenue series. Whether they would have done so is difficult to ascertain. Most of the tax revenue in these two countries has been used to pay wages and salaries; and the evidence, as well as experience, suggests that at least the rates on the official pay tables applicable to the civil service and military have lagged behind the rate of inflation. However, through upgrading of positions and more rapid promotions, the effective rate of

---

[12] In an effort to calculate the revenue elasticity of the tax system with regard to inflation, the nominal tax revenue attributable to the prewar tax structure was regressed on the real value of goods and services available for sale *(B)* and the price index of retail prices throughout Korea *(P)*. The resulting equation and the standard errors of the regression coefficients were:

$$Y = -.21 - .0016B + .00425P$$
$$(.036) \qquad (.00244)$$

which yielded a revenue elasticity with regard to price inflation of 1.22. This is the maximum inflation elasticity of the prewar tax structure, for the rates of some of these taxes were changed during the war and data limitations precluded separating this revenue from that arising in response to the original rate structure in effect at the start of hostilities. The relatively high standard error of the regression coefficient applicable to price changes further reduces the validity of such an elasticity calculation.

compensation may have advanced to keep pace with inflation. It seems probable that such was the case in Korea where prices rose over 500 percent in 1951 and 160 percent in 1952. In Vietnam the wage and salary rates of public sector employees have usually been adjusted with a one-year lag to offset the effects of inflation (*New York Times* 1969a). If such a lag has been reflected in the effective rate of compensation, then unit elasticity implies an increased command over real resources.

Vietnam

As noted above, the structure of taxes in Vietnam is markedly different from that which prevailed in Korea. Over 90 percent of the total central government tax revenue has come from indirect taxes, and some two-thirds of the indirect tax revenue has been in some way related to imports (see Table 9). As discussed below, this is one weakness in the tax structure. A second is that, even though a high proportion of GNP has been related to agriculture, the central government has only two taxes related to agriculture, currently furnishing under 1 percent of the tax revenue (on slaughtering and on rice, the latter collected at the milling stage). The lack of a property registration system has accounted for this situation. A third deficiency of the tax system is that the rates on many highly taxable items, especially petroleum products, are specific, and the government has been loath to change them. Fourth, both Vietnam and Korea have had a lack of trained tax collectors, and many business firms have been run on a cash basis with few records kept.

As Table 9 shows, very little revenue has been raised from direct taxes, which consist of income taxes on business and personal incomes, property taxes, and a patent or business-license tax. While the income tax rates are graduated, they have provided little revenue because evasion has been relatively simple. However, effective January 1, 1967, the government decreed withholding of taxes by employers from workers' wages. For practical purposes this decree affected government employees, those employed by the American sector, and those employed by "large" foreign and Vietnamese firms. Nevertheless, direct tax revenue almost doubled in 1967 over 1966 and increased another 50 percent in 1968. The tax on property has not accrued to the central government but to the village, municipality, or province where the property is located.

While both indirect and excise taxes are listed in Table 9, the distinction is based on which government agency collects them. (Indirect taxes on petroleum products, entertainment, meat, motor vehicles other than motor bikes, paddy rice, ice, precious metals, and dancing are collected by the Directorate of Indirect Taxes, while excise taxes, largely on cigarettes, beer, soft drinks, and various types of production are collected by the Directorate of Excise Taxes.) Many of these taxes are specific rather than ad valorem. However, this has not hampered their effectiveness, for the rates—especially on beer, cigarettes, and soft drinks—have increased faster than have prices. Taxes on these three products have accounted for most of the indirect taxes collected. They have been good revenue producers for two reasons: (1) the inelasticity of the demands for these products, and (2) the fewness of the firms in Vietnam manufacturing them, which has made the levying and collection of taxes relatively easy. Included in excise taxes are the per equation taxes on beer, which are designed to offset some of the comparative advantage of the breweries close to Saigon. (Beer itself is actually subject to five different taxes.)

The registration tax applies to a host of transfers (sale of real estate, motor vehicles, rental contracts, letters of credit, business contracts, etc.), generally at ad valorem rates. The complexity of laws which apply to the tax assessment has made compliance difficult and time consuming.

The other revenue category consists of income collected by various government ministries for services performed or privileges granted to individuals (for example, telegrams, telephone, civil aviation, identification cards, lotteries, forestry contracts, etc.).

Reference to Table 9 shows that over half of Vietnam's tax revenue has been related to foreign trade. This revenue divides itself into two categories: that arising from physical imports and that from the sale of foreign exchange. However, the manner in which foreign trade has been carried on has weakened the tax system as a stabilizing tool. (But since revenue related to imports is relatively easy to collect, taxes based thereon are dependable.) First, the use of a fixed exchange rate has prevented the price of imported goods from rising as fast as domestic

16

prices, thereby reducing the revenue potential of the tax system.[13] Second, while the customs schedules have been revised four times since 1961, the revenue potential of the tariff was long below that possible because of the use of extremely broad classifications. For example, all imported alcohol was charged the same rate whether it was for industrial or human consumption. In 1968 Vietnam adopted the Brussels tariff nomenclature, which, because of its much finer classification system, should raise revenue.

Beginning in December 1961, additional customs duties known as austerity taxes have been placed on "luxury" goods—a category which actually includes a large segment of imports. The austerity taxes were raised in 1965 and again in 1968.

The other taxes related to foreign trade have been based on the sale of foreign exchange and collected by the National Bank of Vietnam instead of the treasury. The first of these is the economic consolidation tax, which represents the difference between the rate at which the United States pays for its advances from the government and the rate at which the National Bank sells dollars to importers.[14] This tax has not been applied to imports financed under the commercial import program (see below). For each dollar of such imports, 118 piasters have been credited to a counterpart account—a rate equal to that paid by the importer.

The exchange equalization tax, which also has been diminishing in importance, was enacted in June 1966 to recover the devaluation profit for the government. All imports licensed under the old exchange rate (60 piasters to the dollar) were taxed in order to equalize the pre- and post-devaluation costs of the goods (the tax was 58 piasters per dollar of imports). In the critical inflationary year of 1966, this tax produced 20 percent of Vietnam's tax revenue.

---

[13] Since 1964 the exchange rate has been subject to one devaluation and revised from an explicit multiple system to a single rate. However, as shown below, because of the tax system an implicit multiple rate system still survives.
[14] The United States was receiving either 80 or 118 piasters per dollar depending upon the purpose of the advance, and the National Bank was selling dollars to importers for 118 piasters. In 1968, an agreement was signed giving the United States 118 piasters for all its purchases and, hence, the economic consolidation tax will diminish to insignificance.

Table 10. Real Tax Revenue in Vietnam, 1964-1968

	1964	1965	1966	1967	1968
Nominal revenue (mn piasters)	13,046	16,442	42,451	54,882	54,212
Price index	100	118	202	297	375
Real revenue (mn piasters)	13,046	13,933	21,015	18,478	14,457
Percent change	n.a.	7	51	-12	-22

Notes: Consumer price index for working-class families, 1964 = 100. The index number for each year is the yearly average.
Source: U.S. Agency for International Development (1968).

The third type of tax related to imports is the per equation tax, whose effect has been to give Vietnam an implicit system of multiple exchange rates. The justification for this tax, instituted in 1966, was to equalize the prices of goods imported from the United States and third countries so that Vietnamese importers would continue to use U.S. import sources. In this case, the goods could be financed under the commercial import program and would not draw down Vietnam's foreign exchange reserves. Of course, such transactions involve a tradeoff between per equation and economic consolidation tax revenue. However, since the rate of per equation tax varies from 5 to 140 piasters per dollar, it generally is a better revenue producer than the consolidation tax. Starting in April 1969, the per-equation tax also has been levied on imports of U.S. origin.

Table 10 shows that while the tax structure has been able to provide the Vietnamese government at least constant real tax proceeds, as an anti-inflation device it has left much to be desired. Had the taxes related to the sale of foreign exchange not been enacted, the rise in nominal tax revenue from 1965 through 1968 would have been less than the increase in prices—despite the fact that the excise and indirect tax rates were increased, as were the customs and austerity rates. In addition, the value of imports for tax purposes was increased by the 1966 devaluation, and withholding of income taxes has been made more effective. Clearly, the elasticity of the prewar tax structure with regard to price and income was less than unity. At least 25 percent of

18

the increase in nominal revenue must be attributed to new taxes and increases in the rates of existing ones.[15]

C. Monetary Policy as an Anti-Inflation Device

That the contribution of monetary policy to the stabilization efforts in both countries has been minimal is attributable to the same set of condi tions: the absence of developed financial markets,[16] an unsophisticated populace reluctant to purchase bonds, legal sanctions against realistic interest rates,[17] a money supply consisting only in small part of demand deposits[18] the reluctance on the part of government to issue constant

---

[15] As in the Korean case, calculations were made to estimate the revenue elasticity of the Vietnamese prewar tax structure with regard to price inflation. The nominal value of tax revenue attributable to that structure was regressed against the real value of goods and services available for sale *(B)* and consumer price index for lower class families in Saigon *(P)*. The resulting equation and standard errors of the regression coefficients were:

$$Y = .100 + .038B + .109P$$
$$(.551) \quad (.017)$$

Using the regression coefficient applicable to prices, a revenue elasticity with regard to price inflation of 0.849 was calculated. As in the Korean case, data limitations precluded separating the revenue applicable to changes in the prewar tax rates from the revenue arising in response to the original prewar rate structure. Hence, the elasticity of 0.849 can be regarded as the maximum inflation elasticity of the prewar tax structure.

[16] This lack of developed financial markets and its implications for open-market operations was anticipated by those who drafted the Bank of Korea Law in 1950. While a provision was made for such operations, they were not expected to be carried out (see Bloomfield and Jensen 1951, p. 51).

[17] In Korea, five-year national bonds were sold whose coupon rate was only 5 percent, while free-market interest rates varied between 60 and 240 percent per year (see McCabe 1954, p. 14). A similar situation prevails in Vietnam. However, I was unable to uncover a reliable estimate of these rates.

[18] In Korea, demand deposits were seldom above one-third of the money supply (see notes to Table 3). In Vietnam the proportion decreased from about one-third in 1959 to one-fifth in 1968 (see Agency for International Development 1968, p. 49). Thus, changes in reserve requirements will not be too effective in restraining total money creation. In Korea, from 1950 until March 31, 1953 the legal reserve ratio on total bank deposits remained at 10

purchasing power bonds, a concept of monetary control different from that prevailing in Western nations[19] and the willingness of the central bank and commercial banks to serve as the handmaidens of the fiscal authorities in creating money to finance the government deficits and foreign trade via bond purchases or advances.[20] However, even within these confines both nations have adopted a device for monetary control which has consisted of an advance deposit on imports. At the time the letter of credit is issued on behalf of the importer, a deposit of from 10 to 30 percent of the cost of the imports must be made. The remaining balance is settled according to the credit arrangements made at the time of the loan. The effectiveness of this restraint depends upon the down-payment rate and the volume of imports. If imports are rising, monetary restraint becomes greater. For an estimate of the effectiveness of this restraint in the Vietnamese case, see Table 6.

---

percent. On the latter date, they were authorized to hold 50 percent of their legal reserves in vault cash instead of at the previous 20 percent level. It was not until June 7, 1953 that reserve requirements were raised to 12 percent and on August 1 to 15 percent (see Bank of Korea 1962, pp. 282, 286). To November 1966, the maximum reserve requirement for Vietnamese commercial banks was 35 percent. From that date until February 1968 the rate was 25 percent on demand deposits and 15 percent on term deposits. After February 1968 the ratio on demand deposits was reduced to 20 percent.

[19] Campbell and Tullock (1957, p. 344) have argued that Western concepts of monetary control have limited applicability to Korea, where the bulk of bank loans have been used to make up losses incurred by the government and other large enterprises who sell their goods and services at prices below cost. As long as the government maintains these subsidies, if bank loans were unavailable, some other equally inflationary way would be found to underwrite them. They feel that it would have been virtually impossible to eliminate these subsidies, as they contributed substantially to the political stability of the central government. In Vietnam such subsidies, especially on rice, have been a source of the government deficit. However, the virtual elimination of this subsidy in 1968 did little directly to undermine the stability of the government.

[20] Because of the conditions enumerated above, it should be obvious that when the central bank and banking system finance the government deficit, the former cannot, in turn, sell securities in the open market to dry up the newly created money. The extent of the purchases of securities by the central bank in the Korean case can be seen in Campbell and Tullock (1957, pp. 348-349). In the Vietnamese case, see Vietnam, National Institute of Statistics (1968, p. 210).

D. The Import Programs

Korea

In underdeveloped nations with low per capita incomes and relative inelasticity of domestic output, a key input in any stabilization program is imports. It is crucial that supply expand as rapidly as demand in order to prevent and/or reduce inflation.

Korea had been the recipient of U.S. aid prior to the war. Since January 1, 1949 the Economic Cooperation Administration (ECA) had been providing aid, the sales proceeds of which were deposited in a counterpart fund for joint United States and Korean use. During 1950 and 1951 most of the goods sold were those imported by ECA or, when ECA was phased out of Korea, with ECA funds transferred to the UN forces. These imports amounted to $45.9 million, of which $32.3 million were sold. During the same two years, the value of aid goods imported by the army, including donations by UN members and goods imported for civilian relief as authorized by Congressional appropriation, totaled $147 million, of which only $15 million were sold. The remainder of these goods were largely given away (McCabe 1954, pp. 11-12).

The net counterinflationary contribution of those goods sold is difficult to determine. Through November 30, 1953 it was estimated to have been 4.6 billion hwan, or about one-fourth of the dollar value of aid goods converted at the rate of 60 hwan per dollar (McCabe 1954, pp. 17-18).

The prime reason for the relatively low level of proceeds from the sale of aid goods was that many were given away, and those sold were priced into the Korean economy at prices considerably below those prevailing in the market. The reason for this practice as it concerns the sale of U.S.-financed aid goods appears to have been the belief that to sell the goods at going prices would cause increased price inflation and upward pressure for wage increase. Johnson (1967a, p. 70) holds that this is both a common belief and practice among underdeveloped countries.

An additional source of imported goods arose when the Korean government sold the proceeds of the reimbursement for its advances to the UN command. This was an especially important counter-inflationary force in 1953 and was largely responsible for the sharp reduction in the rate of price inflation that occurred in that year (see Tables 1 and 3).

Goods imported by the government were generally sold below market prices to its various agencies or organizations. They, in turn, sold the goods at market prices and used the profits to finance their activities. Critics have alleged that this was a sign that the import program was poorly handled and not used as an effective anti-inflation tool. Campbell and Tullock (1957, p. 343) do not support this view. They argue that this practice was simply an indirect way of financing the activities of government organizations and agencies. In its absence, the central government could have sold the goods at market prices, but then, since it would have had to make higher budget allocations to these groups, its overall deficit would have remained the same.

The requirement that licensed importers buy their foreign exchange at rates three to four times greater than the official exchange rate was an additional contribution of the import program to stabilization.

Vietnam

Support for the view that imports have been a critical element in the successful stabilization effort is provided by Table 6. Under the auspices of the Agency for International Development (AID, the successor organization to the ECA which functioned in Korea), a large part of these goods has been supplied from the United States under two programs: Food for Peace (Public Law 480) and the Commercial Import Program (hereafter referred to as CIP). Under these programs, a licensed Vietnamese importer paid piasters into a counterpart fund whose proceeds were divided in various proportions between the Vietnamese government and the United States and used to finance certain on-going U.S. expenses and mutually agreed upon joint programs. In addition, the United States has furnished sizable foreign

Table 11. Import Licensing by Source of Finance
in Vietnam, 1964-1968 (millions of U.S. dollars)

	1964	1965	1966	1967	1968
United States: PL 480	42.8	59.5	93.4	160.0	96.4
CIP	144.6	231.6	321.3	80.3	138.6
Government of Vietnam	92.1	115.3	245.8	291.7	379.8
Total	279.5	406.4	660.5	532.0	614.8

Notes: The amount of imports licensed does not agree with the amount received during the year because delivery is generally from two to six months after the license is granted. Hence, the numbers in this table will differ from those calculated by applying the exchange rate to the figures in Table 6. Public Law (PL) 480 is the Food for Peace program; CIP is the Commercial Import Program.

Source: U.S. Agency for International Development (1968).

exchange for piaster advances.[21] These reserves have been used by the Vietnamese government to fund an extensive import program of its own. The breakdown of these imports by source of financing is shown in Table 11.

These imports, mainly responsible for Vietnam's stability, have been equivalent to approximately 25 percent of the nation's gross domestic product (see Table 16). They have been responsible for the conspicuous absence of austerity in consumption[22] and, as indicated by their size in comparison with the nation's exports, will be unsustainable in the postwar period unless substantial U.S. aid continues.

---

[21] Food for Peace and CIP imports were recorded until June 1966 at the rate of 60 piasters per dollar. Since that date, they have been recorded at 118 piasters per dollar. Reimbursement for advances was, prior to June 1966, at the rate of 73.5 for official purchases and 118 for piasters purchased by the United States for its personnel. From June 18, 1966 until October 1, 1967 the respective rates were 80 and 118. Since that time, all reimbursements have been at the uniform rate of 118 per dollar.

[22] Import licenses financed by the Vietnamese government for motorcycles as a percentage of the total value financed by the Vietnamese government amounted to 10, 20, and 14 percent, respectively, for 1965, 1966, and 1967 (see Agency for International Development 1968, p. 90).

Table 12. Estimated Gross National Product in Korea, 1949-1953
(billions of hwan, 1955 constant prices)

	1949	1950	1951	1952	1953
Primary industry	389	357	301	284	368
Secondary industry	87	57	48	69	110
Tertiary industry	317	268	290	339	391
Total GNP	793	682	639	692	870
Percent change		-14.0	-6.4	8.2	25.7

Notes: This is a value-added concept of GNP. Primary industry consists of agriculture, forestry, and fishery. Secondary industry includes mining, quarrying, manufacturing, and construction. Tertiary industry includes utilities, transportation, mercantile, finance, imputed value of the ownership of dwellings, public administration including defense, services, and net foreign expenditures.
Sources: Bank of Korea (1952-1955, 1963).

The ability of imports to absorb local currency was significantly aided by the nearly 100 percent devaluation of the piaster in June of 1966. This act raised the exchange rate from 60 to 118 piasters per dollar, thereby doubling the anti-inflationary impact of each dollar's worth of imports.[23] The devaluation and the import program taken together constitute the primary reason for the success of the stabilization program and evidence the conscious stabilization effort which was absent in Korea.

E. Domestic Production

Korea

The impact of the war on domestic production is shown in Table 12. As measured in constant 1955 hwan, production fell during the first

---

[23] The rate of exchange proper went from 60 to 80 piasters per dollar. To this was added the economic consolidation surtax of 38 piasters per dollar, making an effective exchange rate of 118 piasters per dollar. However, for tariff purposes, the 80 per dollar rate was used.

Table 13. Index of Domestic Production in Vietnam, 1964-1968

	1964	1965	1966	1967	1968
Agriculture, forestry, hunting, fishing (1957-59 = 100)	125.1	116.5	104.6	109.2	105.8
Mining and manufacturing (1962 = 100)	132.0	158.0	171.0	190.0	201.0

Source: U.S. Agency for International Development (1968).

two years of the conflict but revived after the authority of the central government had been restored in most of South Korea.

Vietnam

Since GNP statistics for Vietnam after 1965 do not exist, it is difficult to describe accurately the effect of the war on domestic activities. However, the breakdown in Table 13 provides some indications of the impact of domestic production on the stabilization problem. The two categories of domestic production, accounting for over 40 percent of gross domestic product by industrial origin, present a mixed picture. Agriculture, accounting for over 30 percent of GDP, has declined since hostilities started on a large scale. The decline in agriculture is largely accounted for by the decrease in rice production, which is still below its 1964 level even though it increased in 1967. Since manufacturing is largely in the protected urban centers, it has continued to expand during hostilities. Nevertheless, overall domestic production has decreased since American intervention in 1965, and this has had an adverse impact on stabilization.

F. An Additional Stabilization Tool

The attempt to stabilize prices by instituting what John Gurley (1952) has classified as a type-three currency reform was applicable only to Korea. In February 1953 the money supply was reduced directly by instituting a new unit of account worth 1/100 of the old unit. A portion of the money supply, measured on a progressive scale according to the total amount of an individual's or company's holdings, was then blocked and could not be used. The immediate effect of these actions was to reduce the price index slightly during April and May. But, because little had been done to curb the excess demand, the inflation continued. Moreover, "such a severe stringency developed in funds for the conduct of current industry and business that the Bank of Korea was authorized by the Monetary Board to take exceptional measures and provide considerable loans to enable some firms to continue operations" (United States Armed Forces Far East 1953, p. 7). It was further reported that "paralysis of some business operations because of lack of funds necessitated granting of loans to large firms of amounts not exceeding blocked deposits but nevertheless, in such volume as to almost negate the reduction in note issue brought about by the currency conversion" (United States Armed Forces Far East 1953, p. 9). It was estimated that about 8 percent of the money supply outstanding at the time of conversion remained frozen as of June 30, 1953. This was more than offset by a 23 percent increase in the money supply from December 1952 to June 30, 1953 (Korea, Office of Public Information 1955a, pp. 251-252). Any wealth effect from this reform appears to have been limited, and since the conversion occurred at the concluding stages of the war, the stabilization effort did not benefit. It did, however, aid the government in the collection of back taxes and the investigation of tax evasion, and it reduced the bulkiness of money needed for everyday transactions.

G. The Experience with Velocity

An important variable in any stabilization program and one over which authorities exercise only indirect control is the velocity of money. As shown by Cagan (1956), velocity is crucially dependent upon expectations of price changes. Changes in velocity can hamper severely any attempts to curb inflation. Despite data limitations, the evidence below indicates that, while velocity did change significantly in Korea, it has not been a problem in Vietnam.

Korea

The Korean velocity experience (see Table 14) corresponds to the explanation given by Cagan (1956, pp. 73-77, 86-88). In the early part of the war, the expansion of monetary demand and the fall in domestic output caused the rate of price increases to rise above that experienced

Table 14. Velocity Index Estimate for Korea, 1949-1955

	1949	1950	1951	1952	1953	1954	1955
Billion current hwan							
GNP	12.6	16.3	102.0	238.0	374.0	505.0	950.0
Imports	3.1	1.5	7.1	13.2	43.4	45.9	61.5
Total	15.7	17.8	109.1	251.2	417.4	550.9	1,011.5
Less: Exports	0.1	0.3	0.5	0.6	1.0	1.4	2.5
G&S for sale	15.6	17.5	108.6	250.6	416.4	549.5	1,009.0
Index, 1949 = 100							
G&S	100	112	696	1,606	2,669	3,522	6,468
Money	100	200	512	1,117	2,405	4,567	7,476
Velocity	1.0	0.56	1.36	1.44	1.12	0.77	0.87

Notes: Imports and exports include goods and services ("G&S"). Imports and exports are converted from dollars to hwan at the official rate of exchange. "Money" is the money supply.
Sources: Bank of Korea (1952-55, 1963); Korea, Economic Planning Board (1962). Index number represents the average money supply for the year.

in the prewar period. However, it is sometime after a change in the actual rate of price inflation before individuals expect the new rate to continue long enough to make adjustments in their cash balances worthwhile. The longer it is expected that the new rate will continue, the more likely it is that cash holdings will be considerably reduced. It is during this period of revised expectations that actual cash balances run ahead of their desired magnitude. This will initially cause velocity to fall as it did in Korea during 1950. However, once people revise upward their expectations of future price inflation based upon what actually happened, the lag in adjusting actual cash balances to the desired level is generally of short duration. When such an attempt to restore equilibrium is made, velocity will rise and further destabilize the situation. There can be little doubt that this was the course of events in Korea.[24] The sharp increase in prices from mid-1950 to mid-1951 was

[24] An additional factor in Korea which might have explained the flight from money was the precarious nature of the military situation. The UN command was almost expelled from the Korean Peninsula early in the war, and the entry of the Chinese forces in 1951 caused a marked retreat below the thirty-eighth

almost as great as the rise in the previous five years. It surely caused expected prices to increase and was of such a magnitude that the inducement to adjust cash holdings to a lower level was great.

Unlike the cases documented by Cagan, hyperinflation did not develop in Korea during the war. Accounting for this favorable experience were the reduction in the rate of money creation which accompanied the completion of the military buildup by the UN command, the implementation of the import program in late 1952, the decrease in the rate of decline in domestic output in 1951 and its revival and expansion in 1952 and 1953, and the restoration of confidence following the stabilization of the military situation.

In order to estimate the expenditure velocity index shown in Table 14, the value of goods and services available for sale in current prices must first be calculated. In Korea this has been accomplished by taking gross national product in current hwan, adding to it the value of goods and services imported in current prices, and subtracting the current value of goods and services exported. An index was then constructed showing the net value of goods and services available for sale at current prices. This index would represent the price-real income portion of the familiar equation of exchange. Once the money supply index was constructed, division of the former index by the latter yielded the index of expenditure velocity.

Vietnam[25]

While no GNP series exists past 1965 [at the time of writing], it will be possible, by making several reasonable assumptions, to arrive at an index of goods and services available at current prices from which an estimate of velocity can be made. This is done by first obtaining an estimate of gross domestic product (GDP), to which is added the excess of imports over exports. Since values for the money supply are readily available, it will then be possible to deduce what has happened to expenditure velocity.

---

parallel. The uncertainty of the military situation could have caused the flight from money to goods.

[25] The work in this section owes a great deal to the imaginative thinking of Dr. William Perkins and Mr. David Hemenway.

Table 15. Estimated Gross Domestic Product in Vietnam, 1963-1968 (billions of piasters)

	1963	1964	1965	1966	1967	1968
1. GDP at current prices	101	115	142	239a	364a	475a
2. GDP at 1960 prices	90	100	106	105b	110b	114b
3. GDP implicit price deflator, line 1 / line 2	112	115	134	228c	331c	417c
4. CPI, lower-income Saigon families, 1959=100	117	121	143	244	357	454
Ratio of line 4 / line 3	104	105	106	107d	108d	109d

a-Derived by multiplying line 2 by line 3.

b-Assumed numbers based upon inspection of domestic production (see Table 13) and real government expenditures, which constituted over 62 percent of the industrial origin of GDP in 1964.

c-Derived by dividing line 4 by line 5.

d-Extension of the series based upon the assumption that the existing pattern continued from 1966 through 1968.

Sources: Vietnam, National Institute of Statistics (1967, 1968).

The GDP in both current and constant prices is available for 1963 through 1965. From personal inspection of the data on agricultural and industrial production (see Table 13) and government expenditures in constant prices, which constituted the industrial origins of over 62 percent of GDP in 1964,[26] it was concluded that real GDP probably decreased a little in 1966 and rose modestly in both 1967 and 1968. Based upon this, best-guess piaster values were assigned in order to complete the GDP constant-piaster series for 1966 through 1968.[27]

---

[26] The first two categories were 32 and 11 percent, respectively, with government expenditures accounting for 19 percent of the total.

[27] Crucial to the assignment of these values was the method used to measure real government expenditures. A suitable price index for accomplishing this does not exist. However, since most of these expenditures were for wages and salaries and, as noted above, these have lagged behind price increases, the consumer price index for lower-class families (used in Table 4) was converted to serve as the deflator. This was done by keeping the rate of increase in that index to one-half the actual average annual increase. Applying this index to the current piaster expenditures of the government yielded a real value time series

Second, advantage was made of a relationship between the GDP deflator and the consumer price index for lower-class families in Saigon. When the former series is divided by the latter for the years 1963 through 1965, the respective quotients are 104, 105, and 106.[28] Assuming this relationship to hold in the following three years, the series was extended at values of 107, 108, and 109. Dividing this series into the CPI for lower-class families completes the GDP implicit price deflator series for 1966 through 1968. The GDP implicit price deflator series is then multiplied by the GDP at constant prices to yield the GDP at current prices series (see Table 15).

The excess of imports over exports was added to the series of GDP in current prices to yield an estimate of goods and services available for sale (Table 16).

From Table 16 it can be concluded that changes in velocity have not been destabilizing in the Vietnamese case. While this conclusion rests on several shaky assumptions, several other pieces of evidence tend to support it. First, there has been an almost one-to-one relationship between changes in the money supply and changes in the price level. Given an almost unchanged real GDP over the 1963-68 period, the net difference between imports and exports appears to have been offset by changes in velocity making the near-proportional relationship possible. Second, if people had expected runaway inflation, they could have shifted into dollars or gold, which are freely available on the black market. Yet, AID weekly price quotations for these two stores of value have been remarkably steady from the 1966 devaluation through 1968, with some of the observed upward movement being accounted for by developments in the world price of gold and its substitute relationship

---

which rose in 1965, declined slightly in 1966, and rose again in both 1967 and 1968. These increases in real public sector expenditures and manufacturing output, when weighted by the approximate importance of each sector, were taken to offset the rather significant decline in the important agricultural sector (see Table 13). It also must be remembered that the large increase in the Vietnamese armed forces during the 1965-68 period was not in the regular forces but in the militia-type regional and popular forces, which were paid almost nominal amounts. Thus it was possible to add significant numbers of the military forces at a very modest increase in the government budget.

[28] For 1960 through 1962, the respective numbers were 101, 102, and 103.

30

Table 16. Velocity Index Estimate for Vietnam, 1963-1968

	1963	1964	1965	1966	1967	1968
Billion current piasters						
GNP	101	115	142	239	364	475
Imports	41	44	52	89	107	109
Total	142	159	194	328	471	584
Less: Exports	16	15	24	57	64	61
G&S for sale	126	144	170	271	407	523
Index, 1963 = 100						
G&S	100	114	135	215	323	415
Money	100	119	179	265	349	499
Velocity	1.0	0.96	0.75	0.81	0.93	0.81

Notes: For derivation of GDP in billions of current piasters see Table 15. Imports and exports include goods and services ("G&S").
Sources: U.S. Agency for International Development (1967, 1968).

developments in the world price of gold and its substitute relationship with the dollar. Third, recent work on demand for money in Vietnam by Stroup and Frazer (1969) shows that at least with 1964 data, the income elasticity of demand for money was greater than unity.

Last, Cagan's explanation also has relevance to this situation. Accompanying the initial U.S. buildup was a rapid expansion of the money supply, and the rate of price increase in 1965 was markedly above that previously experienced. During the period of expectation formation, actual cash balances ran ahead of desired balances and velocity fell (see Table 16, figures for 1965). However, the prompt implementation of the import program and the confidence created by the U.S. troop presence that the piaster would not be repudiated were factors which convinced many Vietnamese that the price increases of 1965 were transitory and that the rate of price increase would fall in the near future. This decline in the rate of increase was no doubt responsible for the fact that while velocity rose in 1966 and 1967, it only returned to approximate what it had been prior to the U.S. intervention.

Of final interest is the relevance of the classical price-specie flow doctrine to these two stabilization efforts.[29] According to this doctrine, in an open economy relatively high rates of inflation induce balance-of-payments deficits. Persistent deficits reduce the reserves of the banking system, thereby shrinking the money supply by some multiple which, in turn, reduces the available financing of the excess demand. This ultimately decreases the rate of inflation and serves as a means of restoring external equilibrium. The inapplicability of this mechanism to Korea and Vietnam arises from the fact that large and persistent balance-of-payments deficits have not served as a constraint on domestic policies. This is because the size of the deficits has been largely continued for stabilization purposes and their financing, especially in the Vietnamese case, has been consciously and continuously provided for by the United States. Thus, bank reserves and the money supply have been largely immune from balance-of-payments considerations and relatively high rates of inflation can continue.

IV. Summary

The purpose of this paper has been to show how significantly the United States could control inflation in two underdeveloped nations during wartime. As such, it involved an inquiry as to the sources of the inflationary pressure, the important stabilizing role of imports in augmenting a diminished domestic production, the inconclusive role of the tax system in each nation as a stabilization tool, the limited assistance offered by monetary policy, and the problem posed by velocity changes.

---

[29] Most inflation models are developed in a closed economy context (see Bronfenbrenner and Holzman 1963 and Johnson 1967b).

2

The Chinese Hyperinflation Re-examined

(with Jarvis M. Babcock)[*]

I. Introduction and Summary

In an article in the *Journal of Political Economy*, Hu (1971) presents three related distributed-lag models of the demand for real cash balances during hyperinflation and applies them to Chinese data covering the period from the autumn of 1945 to the fall of Shanghai in May 1949.[1] Like most of us, Hu tends to emphasize the extent to which his results conform to received doctrine and previous empirical findings. Several such similarities are noted by Hu in the discussion of his empirical results and in the conclusion to his paper.

Because of the apparent accord between the Chinese hyperinflation and those analyzed by Cagan (1956), we were struck by an anomaly: the sample value of the reaction index reported by Hu is approximately 0.2,

---

[*] We gratefully acknowledge the constructive comments of the referee and the computer assistance provided by Wayne State University.
[1] For the sake of brevity we will concentrate in this note on the basic adaptive-expectations model. In our case this consists of two equations, a demand function and an expectations generating function,

$$(1) \quad \log (M/P) = \gamma + \alpha P^* + u$$

$$(2) \quad P^* = \beta \log (P/P_{-1}) + (1 - \beta)P^*_{-1}$$

where M and P are, respectively, indices of the stock of nominal cash balances and the price level, P^* is the expected rate of change of prices, and u is a random disturbance. The important parameters of this model are α—the long-run elasticity of demand for real cash balances with respect to the current rate of change of prices; β—the coefficient of expectations regarding the rate of change of prices.

or only about one-half as large as the smallest estimate recorded by Cagan.[2] A value as small as this seemed to us to be inconsistent with the severity of the inflation relative to the increase in nominal cash balances (Hu 1971, p. 187, Table 1). To put it another way, given Hu's estimate of the reaction index, we would expect the holders of cash balances to have exercised a substantially greater restraining effect on the course of the inflation than is evident from the data.[3]

As a first step toward solving this puzzle, we attempted to reproduce Hu's results. During the course of assembling and processing the data, however, it became clear that certain outside information had to be taken into account if we were to avoid misspecifying the demand function and selecting an inappropriate sample of observations with which to estimate the parameters of that function. The purpose of this note is, then, to offer some alternative findings based on a more discriminating use of the Chinese data. The main thrust of our analysis may be summarized as follows:

(1) The unsuccessful monetary reform of August 1948 was accompanied by, if in fact it was not the cause of, an apparent shift in the demand function.

(2) During the last 2 months for which there are published data, outlying observations occur which are at least superficially similar to those found in four of the seven hyperinflations studied by Cagan.

---

[2] Cagan (1956, pp. 66-69) labels the product $\alpha\beta$ the "reaction index." In our adaptive-expectations model, this index may be interpreted as the short-run elasticity of demand for real cash balances with respect to the current rate of change of prices. That is, it is a measure of the responsiveness of short-run behavior to changes in the rate of inflation. The larger the index, the greater the contribution of such behavior to further intensification of an accelerating inflation. Although both α and the reaction index are algebraically less than zero, we will avoid some cumbersome phrases by referring to them in terms of their absolute values.

[3] In an amendment to his article, Hu (1975) indicates that his initial formulation of the adaptive-expectations model is analytically different from Cagan's. However, his revised findings are perhaps even less plausible than are his original results. For, in addition to a reaction index of the same order of magnitude as that which originally piqued our curiosity, the coefficient of expectations is now reported as being smaller than any found by Cagan and not significantly different from zero.

34

(3) If, for purposes of functional specification and sample selection, one accepts the two preceding points, estimates of the reaction index are obtained which are some three to four times as large as reported by Hu. This places the Chinese hyperinflation much closer to the "self-generating" category and more nearly in line with those European inflations of greatest duration.

(4). However, points (1) and (2) above also raise issues regarding the behavior of the demand for money during the period in question which are at best only partly resolved by our analysis.

The remainder of this note elaborates on the items listed above, assesses evidence from outside the sample, and discusses empirical results of somewhat lesser importance.

II. Discussion

Figure 1 is a scatter diagram in which we have plotted, for the period January 1946-May 1949, an index of real cash balances against expected rates of change of prices. The expected rates were calculated by assigning to β the value 0.30.[4] Two features of the diagram alert one to the possibility that more than a single structure may have been responsible for generating the entire set of observations. First, the data from January 1946 to March 1949 fall into two nearly linear and parallel subgroups, the breaking point occurring at the time of the reform. We designate these subperiods, for convenience if not with precision, the China National Currency (CNC) regime and the gold yuan (GY) regime.[5] Second, the observations of April and May 1949 lie well to the

---

[4] This is the same value Hu originally reported as maximizing R^2 for the adaptive-expectations model. The use of 0.30 in Figure 1 is arbitrary in the sense that the essential features of the pattern observed there are consistent with a wide range of values of β.

[5] More precisely, the latter regime lasted from August 1948 until July 1949 when, in another ineffectual reform, the gold yuan was replaced by the silver yuan. The postwar CNC regime began ostensibly at the end of World War II. However, we start our sample in January 1946 rather than, as Hu did, three or four months earlier because of complications attributable to the presence of wartime puppet currencies which were still legal tender during the late months of 1945. The nominal money series excludes such currency, being limited to notes issued by the Central Bank of the Nationalist government. Somewhat

right of linear extrapolations based on a regression (see regression A, Table 1) using pooled deviations from respective means of the CNC and GY regimes.

Despite the well-known difficulties associated with alterations in specifications, we have incorporated in our empirical work the modifications in functional form and sample coverage suggested by an inspection of Figure 1. The overall quality and plausibility of our results tend, in an *ex post* fashion, to justify this decision. Further, extrasample information, although neither as plentiful nor as unambiguous as we would like, lends some support to our contention that the entire sample period should not be considered as a homogenous unit. In this connection a shortcoming of the data from which Figure 1 is constructed should be reemphasized. Neither the price nor the money data are as comprehensive as is desirable for our purposes, and, furthermore, the series are restricted in different dimensions. The former is an index of wholesale prices pertaining only to Shanghai, whereas the latter omits bank deposits. Such geographic and definitional limitations increase the difficulty with which aberrations caused by inadequacies of the data are disentangled from the effects of structural change. We can claim to be only partially successful in this task.

Consider first the abortive monetary reform of August 1948 in which the CNC dollar was replaced by the gold yuan at a ratio of 3 million to one. Although in many aspects this was little more than a

---

paradoxically, the price series is affected at least as seriously. This is due to the fact that the set of regulations under which the puppet notes were exchanged for CNC notes proved to be highly inflationary in the formerly occupied areas. Shanghai was in one of these areas and, as a result, the Shanghai wholesale price index, which must be regarded as a surrogate for an index representing prices in China's entire money economy, registered a rate of change during the fall of 1945 grossly different from that found in "Free China." During the period in question (August-December 1945), the Shanghai index rose 259 percent while the All Free China wholesale price index fell 13 percent. On the problems posed by the presence of puppet currencies, see Chang (1958, pp. 69-70) and Chou (1963, pp. 1-3, 23-24, 214). The All Free China index may be reconstructed, primarily on a semiannual basis, from information given in various tables by Chang (1958, pp. 26-52).

Figure 1. Real Cash Balances and Expected Rate of Price Change in China, January 1946-May 1949

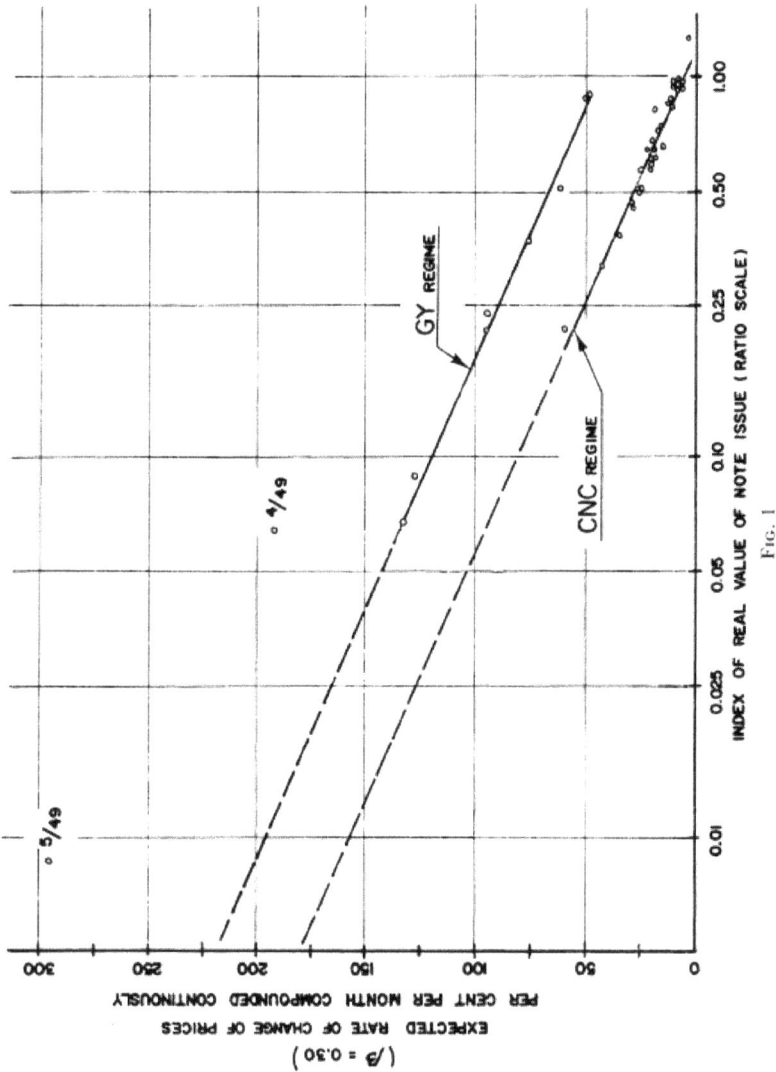

[*Editorial note:* The figure is an image of the original. We no longer have the underlying data to generate a graph from scratch.]

change in the unit of account, Figure 1 shows a definite and sizable positive shift between regimes. To what extent can the increase in demand be explained in terms of identifiable forces and why did this shift apparently persist throughout the GY regime?

In the first place, a substantial proportion of the initial shift can be attributed to the requirement that private owners of gold, silver, and foreign exchange surrender to the Central Bank these assets, as well as their CNC holdings, in exchange for gold yuan.[6] That is, the forced alteration of the composition of private wealth is manifested in the monetary data as an abrupt increase in the stock of currency. However, this explains neither the full extent of the initial shift nor, since the ban on private ownership of gold was removed before the beginning of 1949, the persistence of that shift. On these matters we can offer only some informed conjectures. One possibility is that, as military and political conditions deteriorated, the public chose to hold a larger proportion of the money stock in the form of currency as opposed to demand deposits.[7]

That is, the upward shift in the demand for real note issue, shown in Figure 1, may have as its counterpart a reduction in the demand for real bank deposits. Finally, there is the likelihood that, as the government itself began to anticipate future inflation, a peculiarity of official accounting practice caused published data on the stock of nominal currency to continuously and increasingly overstate the amount actually in circulation.[8]

---

[6] The conversion decree was part of the currency reform. By September 6, 1948, it was reported (*New York Times* 1948) that the population had converted the equivalent of approximately US$57 million in bullion and foreign currencies. At the prevailing GY-to-dollar exchange of four to one, this amounted to GY228 million which more than doubled the original authorization for CNC conversion. The amount of bullion and foreign currencies ultimately converted amounted to US$170 million (see Chang 1958, p. 80).

[7] Data presented graphically by Chou (1963, p. 216) show that the amount of deposits in private banks relative to the note issue declined fairly sharply after October 1948. However, since data on deposits in government banks are absent, no firm conclusions may be drawn.

[8] Chou (1963, p. 18) notes that the Department of Issue of the Central Bank, which compiled the data on note issue, did not adjust its statistics for the

Table 1. Empirical Results on the Chinese Hyperinflation

Re-gres-sion	Sample period	In-ter-cept	α	β	Reaction index	R^2
			Parameter estimates			
A	CNC + GY	2.38 2.88	-3.027 (.076)	0.30	-0.908	.985
B	CNC regime	2.44	-4.178 [-3.64, -5.07]	0.174 [.12, .23]	-0.727 [-.61, -.84]	.979
C	GY regime	2.83	-2.826 [-2.47, -3.33]	0.325 [.24, .41]	-0.918 [-.80, -1.01]	.995
D	1/1946- 6/1948	2.53	-4.478 [-3.73, -6.10]	0.247 [.12, .37]	-1.106 [-.73, -1.38]	.889

Notes: (1) The observable variables upon which the regressions ultimately depend are measured in logarithms to base 10. Estimates of α, β, and the reaction index are invariant with respect to the particular base employed. However, since the intercept serves as a scale factor, the sample values of the intercept recorded above reflect the fact that common logarithms are used. (2) In regression A, β is treated as if it were a given constant. For that reason the sample standard error of the estimate of α was calculated according to the conventional least-squares formula. (This standard error appears in parentheses.) (3) In regressions B, C, and D, β is considered an unknown constant to be estimated from the sample. An iterative routine was employed which sought the sample value that minimized the residual sum of squares for a given equation. Approximate 95 percent confidence intervals were constructed by means of the likelihood ratio method described by Cagan (1956, pp. 93-96). (These intervals appear in brackets). (4) The dependent variable in regression D differs from those of the other regressions (see text for explanation).

---

amount of notes held in bank vaults except those within the department itself. Thus, if, as is likely, the government in anticipation of future inflation "stockpiled" an ever-larger quantity of gold yuan in order to meet its commitments, the recorded stock of issue would run increasingly over the amount actually in circulation. If the commitments were roughly constant in real terms, then the overstatement of issue in real terms would also tend to be constant.

The interpretation of the observations for April and May 1949 is also open to question. At first sight these observations are akin to several found by Cagan (1956, pp. 44, 46, 50, 52) in the German, Greek, Polish, and second Hungarian hyperinflations. That is, at extremely high actual—and, for fixed β, expected—rates of inflation, observed real cash balances are much greater than estimates derived from previously well-behaved regressions. In the cases explored by Cagan, such observations appear in the terminal months of hyperinflation and are at least tentatively explicable in terms of abrupt structural discontinuities as the prospects for reform and relative price stability in the near future suddenly improve. In the present instance the outliers occur during the final two months for which our data series are published, the termination of which coincides not with the end of hyperinflation in China but, rather, with the end of the Nationalist control of Shanghai. Our inclination is to simply claim that due to extraordinary local conditions the Shanghai wholesale price index was no longer representative of prices of the larger geographical area in which the gold yuan circulated. Whether this is true or whether a more sophisticated interpretation is correct, we are in either case persuaded to exclude April and May 1949 from the sample used to estimate the parameters of the demand function.[9]

Turning now to our empirical results, reference has already been made to the regression appearing in regression A of Table 1. The CNC and GY regimes are constrained in the regression to have a common slope and, in order that the regression might be graphed in Figure 1, β is taken as given and equal to 0.30. The estimate of the reaction index turns out to be nearly 300 percent greater than that reported by Hu

---

[9] Only in retrospect, of course, is it known that the inflation would continue for some time thereafter. At the time, the imminent change in political regimes may have been interpreted as an omen of price stability in the near future. In this connection it is worth noting that the outlook was for a 10:1 conversion of gold yuan into units of People's Currency rather than for confiscation (*New York Times* 1949). Other possible rationalizations of the outliers for which there is fragmentary evidence, include: (1) given the institutional arrangements, an increase in the velocity of circulation above that attained in March was difficult; (2) the flight of holders of large amounts of currency caused the recorded amount of nominal note issue to further overstate the amount effectively circulating.

and, we believe, captures more effectively than the latter the widespread and diligent efforts to "get out of money and into goods" described, for example, by Chang (1958, pp. 232-233). A comparison of the sample intercepts for the two regimes shows that, for any given expected rate of change of prices, real cash balances during the GY regime are estimated by regression A to be about three times as large as during the CNC regime.

There is no compelling reason to require, as is the case in regression A, a single value of either the coefficient of expectations or α to hold for the time period spanned by the combined CNC and GY regimes. In fact, in five of six cases for which there are adequate data, Cagan (1956, pp. 58-60) found that β increases over time during hyperinflation. To see whether the Chinese experience conforms to this pattern, we relax the restrictions on the demand function, allowing all three parameters (α, β, and intercept) to vary between regimes. The estimates, recorded on regressions B and C of Table 1, reveal that the sample value of β did indeed increase, nearly doubling between the CNC and GY subperiods. Concomitant with this increase in the rapidity with which the public incorporated current inflation rates into future expectations, the reaction index rose from 0.73 to 0.92. That is, the monetary reform was accompanied by a change in the short-run marginal behavior of cash balance holders which abetted, rather than dampened, the volatility of the inflation. Although many other factors undoubtedly were involved in the deterioration of confidence implied by the increase in value of this index, the superficial nature of the "reform" itself may well have played a part. For instance, Chang (1958, p. 79) indicates that at the time of the change some financial advisers warned that, in view of the government's unwillingness to tackle the more basic causes of inflation, the new gold yuan might prove to be less acceptable to the public than the much-depreciated but familiar CNC issue. There is an apparent paradox in this result. A comparison of intercepts would indicate that the prospects for stability were improved by the reform, whereas a comparison of reaction indices indicates the opposite. The resolution of this conflict may lie in the fact that the money series is confined to the stock of note issue. The gold yuan were less desirable than the old CNC issue (hence, the larger reaction index) but, nonetheless, were preferable to contemporary bank deposits (hence, the larger intercept).

The dependent variable in each of the preceding regressions is based on an index of real currency issue. The dependent variable of our final regression, appearing in regression D of Table 1, is based on an index of the sum of such currency plus deflated bank deposits. The period covered lacks only July 1948 of being coincident with what we call the CNC regime. In comparing regressions D and B it is evident that the inclusion of bank deposits worsens the quality of fit as measured by R^2. This is due, at least approximately, to several rather abrupt changes in the deposit-to-currency ratio.[10] We also note that the point estimate of the reaction index is about 1.1. However, the 95 percent confidence interval is so wide that a hypothetically true value of considerably less than unity cannot be rejected. The inclusion of deposits causes us to revise upward our view of the explosiveness of behavior during the CNC regime, but the statistically imprecise nature of the results leaves some doubt as to just how great this revision should be.

III. Conclusion

The purpose of this note has been to present alternative evidence within the context of the basic adaptive expectations model. Given that framework, we have shown that a more discriminating use of the Chinese data leads to estimates of the important parameters which, both in terms of their absolute values and changes in these values over time, are quite reasonable in comparison with results for the European hyperinflations. At the same time, the very process of selective estimation generates ambiguities which we have been unable to completely resolve. As a minimum, though, we believe the regressions

---

[10] In an extreme case, the deposit-to-currency ratio rises in a single month from 0.97 to 1.54. The abruptness of change is of some interest in itself, for it is contrary to the assumption made by Cagan (1956, pp. 49, 51) when interpolating annual deposit data. Chou (1963, p. 212, Table 6.5b) gives the reciprocal of the deposit-to-currency ratio. The (currency + deposits) series can be constructed from a knowledge of Chou's ratios and the data on note issue. Chou is not explicit as to the exact nature of the bank deposits. However, in his own analysis he treats them as if they were mainly or entirely demand deposits. Published data on deposits in all banks, government as well as private, are apparently unavailable subsequent to June 1948.

confined to the CNC regime (regressions B and D) can stand on their own merit.

Ideally, one would like a model capable of satisfactorily explaining the entire sample taken as a homogeneous unit. The pursuit of this objective is severely restricted by the weakness of the data at hand and by the paucity of information on other variables. We have experimented briefly with adding to the model a partial adjustment feature and by considering a nonlinear argument in the demand function. The results are only modestly promising. We must, therefore, conclude that, although we believe our results are superior to Hu's, they hardly represent the last word on the demand for money during the Chinese hyperinflation.

3

Indexation, Inflationary Finance, and Hyperinflation: The 1945-1946 Hungarian Experience

(with William A. Bomberger)[*]

Many recent studies have examined the benefits of altering contractual and accounting procedures in order to insulate economic agents from the effects of persistent and sometimes unpredictable inflation. Proposals have been made for "indexing" in labor and debt markets in order to avoid inflation-induced redistributions of income (Tobin 1971; Friedman 1974). More recently it has been proposed that tax laws be indexed to avoid distortions produced by accounting procedures which are based on the assumption of price level stability (Feldstein, Green, and Sheshinski 1978).

A major drawback to such proposals which is usually mentioned is the possibility that the symptomatic relief which indexing provides may decrease the incentive to affect a cure for inflation.

While partial wage indexation is now common, and debt indexation is being used in some countries, most indexation proposals seem exotic. It is, then, rather surprising to discover that an ingenious scheme for indexing in both the tax system and the banking system was instituted in Hungary after World War II. Curiously, the program was put in place to protect the purchasing power of government tax revenue, even though government is the traditional beneficiary of inflation-induced income redistribution. Paradoxically, the scheme not only failed to insulate government revenues from the effects of inflation but also provided the decisive mechanism whereby the 1945-

---

[*] The authors gratefully acknowledge the helpful comments of their referee, Phillip Cagan.

1946 Hungarian hyperinflation became the most severe in recorded history.

I. Hyperinflation and the Supply of Money

The cause and dynamics of hyperinflation are well known, at least in general outline. A weak government is forced to rely on the issue of new money as the principal source of its revenue. The proceeds may be thought of as an "inflation tax" on real money balances. An increase in the rate of money growth increases the "tax rate" and, to the extent that the resulting increase in the rate of inflation is perceived and expected to continue, induces money holders to avoid the tax by reducing their real money balances. In so doing they reduce the "tax base" and force the government to increase the tax rate (rate of new money issue) if it is to finance the same level of real expenditures. The process can become cumulative and lead to a breakdown of the monetary system.

The differences in the intensities of the episodes of hyperinflation which have been recorded presumably depend upon differences in the characteristics of government needs and private behavior among the countries in question. Among the relevant characteristics should be (a) the relative sizes of the required real government revenue and real money balances held by the public, (b) the elasticity of demand for real money balances with respect to expected inflation, and (c) the speed with which money holders adjust their expectations when actual inflation differs from previous expectations. In a terminology consistent with the inflation-tax concept, these characteristics represent (a) the relative sizes of the required tax receipts and the tax base, (b) the willingness and ability of taxpayers to avoid payment of the tax as the tax rate rises, and (c) the difficulty (for the government) of circumventing tax avoidance with unperceived increases in the tax rate.

The Hungarian experience, which includes two episodes of hyperinflation in less than four decades, provides at least a minor puzzle for traditional theories. The first Hungarian hyperinflation, from March 1923 to February 1924, proceeded at an average rate of 46 percent per month. The maximum increase in the price level for a single month was 98 percent. Each figure is the smallest recorded for the six European hyperinflations first examined by Cagan (1956). For the second Hungarian hyperinflation, from August 1945 to July 1946, the average and maximum monthly rates were 19,800 percent and 4.2 × 10[16] percent, respectively—by far the highest inflation rates ever recorded.

Martin Bailey (1956, p. 108) has suggested a reason for the contrasting intensities of the Hungarian inflations: "The share of national income that government could get...was far smaller in the second hyperinflation than in the first. One possible explanation for this is that a second hyperinflation within a single generation found people far better prepared to reduce their cash balances than they had been when they had no such previous experience." Hence, when the Hungarian government attempted to extract a comparable fraction of national income from post-World War II Hungary (hereafter Hungary II) an explosive inflation resulted.

This conjecture can be interpreted in two ways: (1) money holdings as a fraction of national income were smaller at the outset for Hungary II than for Hungary I (i.e., velocity had risen permanently as a result of the previous episode) or (2) the demand for money was more elastic with respect to expected inflation for Hungary II (i.e., money holders quickly rediscovered methods of avoiding the inflation tax which they had learned in the previous episode).

Barro (1972, p. 984) has estimated the inflation tax base as a fraction of national income at low inflation rates for Hungary I and Hungary II. The estimates are comparable, casting doubt on the correctness of Bailey's conjecture according to the first interpretation.

Support for Bailey's conjecture according to the second interpretation should take the form of an estimated demand for real balances for Hungary II, which is more elastic with respect to expected inflation than a comparable estimate for Hungary I. Cagan (1956, p. 43) finds the Hungary I estimated money demand more than twice as elastic at every level of expected inflation as the Hungary II estimate. Barro and Jacobs have attempted to improve upon the original Cagan estimates by using more complex functional forms and more sophisticated estimation techniques. Although both their procedures and their results differ substantially, each study yields an estimate of the demand for real balances for Hungary II which is virtually identical with that for Hungary I (Barro 1970; Barro 1972, p. 996; Jacobs 1977, p. 298).

Barro and Jacobs also examine the formation of expected inflation. Both use variations of the adaptive-expectations model. Although the functional forms are different in each study, the resulting estimates of the speed of adjustment are virtually identical within each study for Hungary I and Hungary II. Cagan arrived at a speed-of-adjustment estimate for Hungary II which is somewhat higher than that for Hungary I. However, the predicted levels of real balances provided by his estimates for the early Hungary II period seriously understate the levels of real balances held in the later part of the episode. He is forced to exclude the last 6 months of Hungary II from his estimates. He mentions the possibility that adaptive expectations provide an overestimate of actual expectations because of the anticipated possibility of an imminent monetary reform (Cagan 1956, pp. 55-57).

In short, there seems to be little evidence that the explosiveness of the Hungary II episode was caused by money holders who (a) held less money per unit of income to begin with, (b) adjusted their money holdings more rapidly as perceived inflation rose, or (c) adjusted their expectations of inflation more rapidly to observed changes in inflation.[1]

The source of the contrast between the two Hungarian inflations is, we feel, not to be found in shifts in private behavior or government revenue requirements. Instead, an institutional change in the nature of bank deposits occurred midway in the Hungary II episode which had a decisive effect on the subsequent intensity of the hyperinflation.

---

[1] Another possibility is that the government attempted to extract a larger fraction of national income in Hungary II than in Hungary I. Jacobs (1977, p. 300) seem s to imply this. Bailey (1956, p. 99), Cagan (1956, p. 82), and Barro (1972, p. 985) agree that the actual fraction of national income extracted was smaller from Hungary II. How much the government wished to extract is, of course, difficult to measure. Contemporary observers were apt to look elsewhere for the source of the contrast. Kaldor (1946) felt that attempts by workers to achieve prewar levels of real wages constituted an important factor. Nogaro (1948, pp. 535-536) pointed to speculation in foreign exchange (principally the dollar) as the crucial factor.

II. The Hungarian Tax Pengö

While governments are often identified as a major beneficiary of inflation-induced redistributions of income and wealth, inflation itself can cause tax revenue to lose a great deal of its purchasing power between the time the tax is assessed and the revenue collected and expended by the state. This is especially likely to occur during hyperinflations and was characteristic of the situation confronting the Hungarian government in 1945. It responded on January 1, 1946, with a decree designed to index the nominal tax liabilities of its citizens.[2] The decree required all taxpayers to pay the treasury the amount specified on their tax notices multiplied by the rate of currency depreciation, as measured by the official price index published daily. The decree served to create a new unit of account called the tax pengö, which was a form of noncirculating money (i.e., it was not a medium of exchange).

While the indexed method of assessing taxes was a desirable innovation from the viewpoint of the Hungarian government, it did little to safeguard tax receipts from further depreciation once they were collected and deposited in banks awaiting future disbursement.

In an effort to provide such a safeguard, the government, on January 10, 1946, obliged commercial and savings banks to open accounts denominated in tax pengö. The decree also permitted individuals to deposit currency in the banking system and receive interest equal to the rate of inflation. That is, upon withdrawal, customers were to receive regular pengö notes in an amount determined by the movement in the price index from the date of deposit.[3]

To preserve their capital and profits, banks were then permitted to make loans denominated in tax pengö. Moreover, the government

---

[2] Descriptive treatments of this period can be found in Kaldor (1946), Nogaro (1948), and Falush (1976).

[3] For 3⅔ months, the tax pengö deposits were immune from inflation. However, on April 19, 1946, for technical reasons, the index number used for conversion was changed to that prevailing at the close of business on the day prior to withdrawal. This one-day lag led to a subsequent depreciation of the tax pengö.

actively encouraged the use of tax pengö deposits by the public because, among other things, it supposedly reduced the demand for dollars and other foreign currencies. This served to slow the rate-of-exchange depreciation of the pengö and, the government believed, the internal rate of inflation.[4]

Once the banks were forced to offer tax pengö deposits, the Hungarian government unwittingly created two classes of money: One, currency notes, was subject to massive depreciation while the other, bank deposits, was not.

Such a system may be treated in two ways. The indexed deposits may be considered a newly created alternative to money (notes). Money (note) demand is reduced, thus decreasing the inflation-tax base. Increases in expected inflation will now cause a more severe reduction in the tax base as money holders switch into deposits.

Alternatively, money may be defined broadly as notes plus deposits. No inflation tax may be collected (by the government or the banks) on the deposits since the depositors' "tax payments" are returned upon withdrawal. Increases in expected inflation will increase the fraction of money which is "nontaxable."

According to either concept the result is the same. The indexing of deposits forces the government to achieve a higher percentage rate of growth of notes in order to extract a given amount of revenue. Increases in the growth rate of notes will, via the increases in inflation and expected inflation they generate, produce more than proportional increases in the growth rate of broadly defined money. Both effects should intensify the acceleration of inflation.

---

[4] Governments are apt to blame inflation on external causes, especially if the depreciation in the rate of exchange exceeds the internal rate of inflation. Their reasoning makes reference to an often observed tendency that as inflation continues sellers begin to calculate costs and prices in terms of a stable unit of account. Thus, as the exchange rates depreciate (usually attributed to speculators) internal prices are pushed up. Apparently, the Hungarian government, observing such practices among Hungarian sellers, sought ways to reduce this demand for foreign currencies in the belief it would moderate the course of the inflation. The prevalence of this view of inflation is widespread. For its appearance in Germany, see Graham (1930) and Bresciani-Turroni (1937); and for Austria, see Walré de Bordes (1924).

Table 1. Quarterly Deposit/Note Ratios:
European Hyperinflations

	Austria	Germany	Poland	Hungary
1920 Q4	3.13	2.08		
1921 Q1	3.70	2.22		
1921 Q2	5.00	2.22		
1921 Q3	5.56	2.13		
1921 Q4	3.33	1.82		
1922 Q1	4.00	2.78		
1922 Q2	4.76	4.00	1.25	0.34
1922 Q3	2.33	4.17	0.85	0.30
1922 Q4	2.78	1.69	0.76	0.43
1923 Q1	2.94	2.78	0.83	0.28
1923 Q2		4.00	0.51	0.37
1923 Q3		2.70	0.30	0.28
1923 Q4			0.26	0.56
Average monthly inflation, %	47	322	46	81

Note: the time periods shown for each country correspond to the period of hyperinflation as designated by Cagan (1956).

Sources: The above computations are based on data taken from the following League of Nations publications: *Memorandum on Currency 1913-1922, 1913-1923; Memorandum on Currency and Central Banks 1913-1914, 1913-1925.*

That the institution of indexed deposits led to this result is indicated in Tables 1 and 2.

In Table 1 we show the quarterly movements of the deposit-to-note ratio for four European hyperinflations. In Table 2 we demonstrate the effect of the two-class money system on the monthly pattern of note issue, the composition of the money supply, and the course of the inflation rate for Hungary II.

In none of the countries examined in Table 1 did the respective governments introduce indexed bank deposits.[5] Thus, for the post-

---

[5] Deposit data are unavailable for Greece. No deposits existed in the Russian hyperinflation.

World War I hyperinflations, the effect accelerating inflation rates had upon money holders' demand for notes versus deposits depended largely upon the efficiency of the banking system. If checks were cleared slowly, accelerating inflation would likely increase the portion of money held as notes at the same time as the public was reducing its demand for money in general. This tendency to hold notes is evident in the Hungary I data, whereas no definite trend is as evident for the other countries shown in Table 1.

Variations in the deposit-to-currency ratio have never played a prominent role in theories of the hyperinflation process. For all cases other than Hungary II this omission is appropriate. While the variations over time shown in Table 1 are substantial by modern standards, they could certainly be disregarded as sources of the 17-fold to 7-billion-fold increases in broadly defined money over the periods in question. For Hungary II the picture changes. From June 1945 until December 1945, the Hungary II experience paralleled Hungary I, as shown in Table 2.

As inflation gathered momentum, the deposit-to-note ratio declined steadily. The average monthly inflation rate over this period was 199 percent. This was higher than the average inflation rates experienced by most other countries shown in Table 1 but was of a comparable order of magnitude. Quite clearly the decrees in January 1946 creating and institutionalizing the tax pengö dramatically reversed the trend in the deposit-to-note ratio. As the inflation intensified, the indexed deposits became increasingly attractive relative to the depreciating notes. Accordingly, note holdings declined relative to deposit holdings until notes virtually ceased to be held by July 1946.[6]

The effect which the changing deposit-to-note ratio had on the time path of inflation was decisive. At the end of December 1945, the real value of the broadly defined money supply was less than 9 percent of the June 1945 figure and consisted of more than 90 percent notes.[7] The institution of indexed deposits in January 1946 increased the demand

---

[6] Other factors, such as widespread black markets and the fear of an imminent communist takeover, should have encouraged the use of currency. One must presume that the deposit-to-note ratio would have continued to decline in the absence of the tax-pengö deposits.

[7] The price index used to arrive at the 9 percent figure and other estimates of real balances below is taken from Cagan (1956, p. 110).

Table 2. Outstanding Notes and Bank Deposits: Hungary

	Notes	Deposits	Deposits to note ratio	Inflation rate, % per month
Notes and deposits in pengö				
December 1944	10.7 bn	3.0 bn	.28	2
June 1945	14.5 bn	3.2 bn	.22	-8
July	16.3 bn	3.9 bn	.24	19
August	24.4 bn	4.7 bn	.19	63
September	41.9 bn	6.2 bn	.15	122
October	110 bn	9.6 bn	.09	541
November	360 bn	28 bn	.08	435
December	770 bn	64 bn	.08	219
January 1946	1.6 trn	151 bn	.09	74
February	5.2 trn	1.1 trn	.21	503
March	34 trn	12 trn	.35	329
April	430 trn	350 trn	.81	1,820
May	6.6×10^{16}	1.1×10^{17}	1.67	31,400
June	6.3×10^{21}	1.7×10^{22}	2.70	8.44 mn
July	4.7×10^{25}	2.4×10^{35}	5.1 bn	4.19×10^{16}
Notes and deposits in forints (1 forint = 400 octillion, or 4×10^{29}, pengö)				
August 1946	356 mn	51 mn	.14	n.a.
September	607 mn	110 mn	.18	-6
October	843 mn	172 mn	.20	6
November	937 mn	245 mn	.26	7
December	968 mn	280 mn	.29	-3

Note: The forint was introduced on August 1, 1946.
Source: United Nations Statistical Office (1947).

for real balances and temporarily slowed inflation. Although notes and deposits increased in January by 108 and 136 percent, respectively, prices rose by only 74 percent. However, as money holders switched into deposits in increasing amounts the government was faced with a shrinking "taxable" portion of the money supply. Notes accounted for 83 percent of broadly defined money by the end of February 1946 and an increasingly smaller portion thereafter.

This erosion of the effective tax base forced an increase in the rate of growth of notes to 225 percent in February 1946 and to increasingly higher levels thereafter. As the increase in the rate of new note issue produced increased inflation, the flight into deposits continued. Very likely more and more notes were concentrated in the banking system as reserves supporting the more attractive deposits. Possibly they supported an increasingly larger amount of deposits as banks had an increasing incentive to economize on their rapidly depreciating cash reserves.[8] Thus, the rate of growth of deposits reached 628 percent in February 1946 and was followed by increasingly higher levels. The rate of broadly defined money growth consistently exceeded the rate of growth of notes after January.

By July 1946 the already astronomical rate of note issue was transformed into a rate of money expansion which led to a money supply 5 billion times larger than the note issue. This explosion of deposit creation had a decisive effect on the inflation rate which averaged over 1 million percent per month from January to July 1946, after having declined steadily from October to December 1945.[9] It seems likely that the tax pengö and its institutionalization in the deposit accounts of the banking system was the crucial factor in converting severe hyperinflation into total monetary chaos.[10]

---

[8] Unfortunately, due to the absence of data on bank reserves, the possibilities raised here must remain unsupported.

[9] The broadly defined money supply at the end of June 1946 was almost equal, in real terms, to its level at the end of January. Inflation, then, roughly kept pace with the growth of broadly defined money. Over the month of July the real value of broadly defined money fell to 2½ percent of the June figure. At the intensive rate of inflation in July the incompleteness of the indexing (see note 3 above) was probably quite apparent.

[10] In December 1945 all deposits were nonindexed. We have implicitly assumed that the post-December deposit figures include nonindexed deposits

III. Conclusion

It is our belief that the difference between Hungary I and Hungary II did not arise from differing patterns of private behavior. Rather, in Hungary II, the government instituted a banking practice which forced it to share the proceeds of the inflation tax with depositors. This arrangement required a greater tax rate (rate of new note issue) in order to achieve a given rate of real revenue extraction from a given level of broadly defined real balances. As the tax rate rose the taxable portion of real balances fell and the rate of growth of broadly defined money (and prices) exceeded the tax rate. The tax rate which money holders sought to avoid (i.e., the inflation rate) exceeded the tax rate at which the government collected funds, further exacerbating the government's difficulties.

This episode may provide a warning to contemporary governments attempting to deal with persistent inflation. In the 1950s Finland, France, and Israel, among other countries, indexed savings and time deposits. Brazil has done the same as part of an ambitious and extensive indexing strategy.[11] Not surprisingly, Albert Fishlow (1974, p. 275) reports that the ratio of (indexed) time and savings deposits to

---

plus the current "flat" pengö value of indexed deposits. While this would seem to be a sensible accounting procedure for the banks, contemporary observers were frustratingly silent on this point. The sources themselves provide no explanation of accounting procedures (consistent deposit numbers are available from Hungary, Central Statistical Office (1946) and the United Nations Statistical Office (1947). After examining these sources, Cagan felt that indexed deposits were not included in the published figures. We do not share his belief because the real value of deposits behaved in a manner consistent with what would have been expected if the published data had included the indexed deposits. They declined steadily from June 1945 to December 1945, and then in a dramatic reversal rose steadily to June 1946. By way of illustration, the real value of deposits was 1,250 percent greater in June 1946 than it was in December 1945 and was even 20 percent greater than it was in the relatively "stable" period of September 1945. The real value of notes in June 1946 is 40 percent of the December figure and less than 7 percent of the figure for the previous September. It is hard to believe that the current value of indexed deposits is not included in the published deposit figures.

[11] For a discussion of the Brazilian experience, see Fishlow (1974).

monetary assets subsequently rose by 1,200 percent between 1966 and 1973. These deposits provided a much-needed channel for household saving and have been followed by falling rather than rising inflation.

The example of the tax pengö suggests, however, that a further extension of indexation to demand deposits would be unwise regardless of its potential for increasing financial intermediation. This is at least true for countries in which a substantial amount of government revenue is collected from new money issue.

4

The Hungarian Hyperinflation
and Stabilization of 1945-1946

(with William A. Bomberger)

From July 1945 until August 1946, Hungary experienced the worst hyperinflation on record. In this brief period of 13 months, the price level rose by a factor of 3×10^{25}. When stabilization was achieved on August 1, exchange of old for new currency was at a rate of 400 octillion to one. This contrasts with the conversion in Germany's famous hyperinflation of a trillion to one.[*]

---

[*] Any attempt to study this era is fraught with difficulties. Hungarian state archives are in reality closed. Because this period is now 36 years in the past, few individuals associated with it are still alive, outside Hungary. Fortunately, we located several strategically placed officials in the U .S. and Hungarian governments who provided us with information that made it possible to conclude our study. We were able to locate these individuals through the assistance of Professor Joseph Zrinyi, S.J., of Georgetown University; Aladar Szegedy-Maszak, Hungarian Minister to the United States, 1945-46; and Professor William Fellner. With their assistance, we traced Dr. Arthur Karasz, president of the National Bank of Hungary (the central bank of Hungary) from August to December 1945, and a member of its board of directors until June 1946. Dr. Karasz provided us with a great deal of information on the inflationary process, the unique Hungarian experience with indexed money, and institutional details surrounding the successful stabilization. Dr. L. László Ecker-Racz, economic counselor to the Allied Control Commission (the allied occupational authority in Hungary) and later economic counselor at the American Legation in Budapest, made available two extensive statistical and economic analyses of the Hungarian economy and state finances during and after the hyperinflation. The data used in these studies were provided to the U.S. Legation by the government of Hungary. Many of these data have been hitherto unavailable to researchers. We were unable to inspect the Hungarian archives, but Dr. János Fekete, currently first deputy president of the National Bank of Hungary, was responsive to our written requests seeking clarification

4. The Hungarian Hyperinflation and Stabilization of 1945-1946

Every hyperinflation offers insight into the inflation process and anti-inflationary policy. Aside from its severity, Hungary's 1945-46 experience is unique in a number of respects. First, of all the countries after World War I experiencing an episode of hyperinflation, only Hungary had the misfortune to suffer a second hyperinflation after World War II. Second, in Cagan's (1956) seminal study of the demand for money in hyperinflations, Hungary stands out as posing the most formidable data problems. Third, Hungary is unique in its extensive experiment with indexed money.

It is remarkable, in the light of the magnitude of this hyperinflation, that it has yet to receive a systematic treatment.[1] We propose to fill this gap. We are able to do so because of newly uncovered data on the Hungarian money stock and public finances and the use of resources unavailable or unexploited by other researchers.

Our paper has three goals. First, we will discuss the origin and magnitude of this hyperinflation in terms of the state of Hungary's public finances, the depressed level of national income, and the use of indexed money. Second, using new money data, we are able to explain the anomalous movement in the deposit to note ratio described by Cagan (1956). Third, we will describe what we believe to be the crucial elements in the Hungarian stabilization program and draw appropriate lessons for contemporary stabilization strategies along lines consistent with rational expectations.[2]

---

of some of the data on the money stock during this period. We are especially grateful to Professors Zrinyi and Fellner, Doctors Karasz, Ecker-Racz, and Fekete, and Mr. Szegedy-Maszak for the time they shared and the useful data they furnished. We wish to offer special thanks to Professor Phillip Cagan for his encouragement and useful comments on an earlier draft. Finally, we gratefully acknowledge the assistance of James Harris, Vincent Marie, Thomas Woodward, and Eileen Mauskopf as well as the useful comments of an anonymous referee.
[1] The best partial accounts available in English are to be found in Kaldor (1946), Nogaro (1948), Cagan (1956), Falush (1976), and Bomberger and Makinen (1980; chapter 3 in this book). See also Kemény (1952), Ecker-Racz (1954), Eckstein (1955), Helmreich (1973), and Berend and Ranki (1974).
[2] In this endeavor, our work is complementary to a recent study by Sargent (1980).

I. The Hyperinflation of 1945-46

A. The Depressed Level of National Income and the State of Public Finances

It is frequently asserted that the cause of hyperinflation rests in a government whose political survival is so precarious that it cannot levy sufficient explicit taxes. It is, therefore, forced to rely on the issue of new money as the principal source of tax revenue. This is an apt characterization of the situation in Germany, Austria, Hungary, Poland, and Russia following World War I. It has an element of truth when applied to Hungary after World War II, but it is not the whole truth. In Hungary in 1945, unlike post-World War I Hungary, the prevailing political party (the Smallholders) commanded an absolute majority in the National Assembly, having received 60 percent of the vote in the November 1945 election. Hungary was, however, governed by a coalition that included the Communist party. This government appeared to enjoy wide popular support. The coalition was agreed on before the election as a means of achieving political unity during the difficult postwar reconstruction period.

Because Hungary had been one of the lesser Axis powers, its government did not enjoy complete sovereignty. In most matters, especially foreign affairs, the decisions of the government were subject to the approval of the Allied Control Commission, a group dominated by the Soviet Union (in accord with the Yalta agreement). We describe below the role of the Control Commission in the hyperinflation.

In addition, unlike the countries experiencing hyperinflation after World War I, Hungary was a major battleground in World War II. For six months beginning in October 1944 the front line moved across Hungary, accompanied by heavy fighting. Budapest was liberated only after a long siege and heavy street fighting. As the German army retreated, it pursued a policy of removing much of the portable capital stock to Germany and destroying much that remained (e.g., the railroad system).[3] A great deal of the remaining physical capital was

---

[3] For a detailed account of war damage, see Berend and Ranki (1974, pp. 180-182).

systematically removed by the Soviet army.[4] It is estimated that World War II destroyed some 40 percent of the nonhuman wealth of Hungary (Commercial Bank of Pest 1947). The mass deportation and extermination of Hungary's Jews and the prisoner-of-war status of many of the young men who formed the basis of the Hungarian army deprived the country of badly needed human capital. While precise calculation of the national income for 1945 is questionable, it is estimated at 40-50 percent of the prewar level.[5]

When Hungary signed the armistice on January 20, 1945, ending its state of belligerence against the Allies, it consented to pay reparations of $300 million.[6] For the first reparations year (ending on January 20, 1946), Hungary was obligated to furnish to the Soviet Union $33 million in goods, exclusive of any costs for preparation and shipment. Should she fail to meet the scheduled payments, an interest penalty of 5

---

[4] Under the Potsdam Agreement, the Soviet Union was entitled to the possession of all German property in Hungary. They interpreted this right broadly and removed much equipment that, while not German owned, had been produced in Germany. There is no doubt that this equipment removal was extensive, for German economic penetration of Hungary was substantial (see Kemény 1952, pp. 169-176). The U.S. government strongly protested this policy (see *New York Times* 1946c).

[5] The Hungarians did not compile their national income accounts according to methods used in the United States. For a detailed discussion of their procedures, see Eckstein (1955) and Spulber (1973). Ecker-Racz (1946b, p. 145), reporting data furnished by the Hungarian Institute for Economic Research, gives national income for 1945-46 as 2,541 million pengö compared with 5,192 for 1938-39 (both in 1938-39 prices). While no figure is available for 1944-45, it might reasonably be set at 55-65 percent of the 1938-39 figure, or from 2,860 to 3,375 million pengö. The United Nations Relief and Rehabilitation Agency (UNRRA) estimated that the real wage declined from a monthly high of 54 percent of the 1938 average in August 1945 to a low of 12.8 percent in July 1946. The monthly average during the hyperinflation was 28.3 percent (UNRRA 1947, p. 77).

[6] Of this sum $200 million was to go to the Soviet Union, $70 million to Yugoslavia, and $30 million to Czechoslovakia. In millions of dollars, the Hungarian reparations payable to the Soviet Union in goods were industrial machinery 36.1; ships 12.9; railway equipment 46.4; metals 70.3; grains and seeds 9.0; animals 17.3; and all other 8.0. The real burden of these payments is discussed below. As the indemnity was to be paid in kind, no transfer problem of the kind discussed by Keynes and Ohlin was to emerge.

percent per month was to be imposed. In addition, she agreed to pay the full cost of the Soviet army transiting through Hungary to and from Germany. The size of the Soviet garrison was estimated to vary from 500,000 to 700,000 men (see Ecker-Racz 1946b, p. 149). This combination of reparations and occupation costs accounted for 25-50 percent of monthly expenditures by the Hungarian government during the hyperinflation (see Table 1).

The revenue and expenditures of the Hungarian government are reported in Table 1 on a monthly basis for all except the final two months of the hyperinflation. These data show that, for all but three months, less than 10 percent of expenditures were covered by revenue.[7] It is estimated that for the final 2 months of the hyperinflation less than 5 percent of expenditures were covered by tax revenue (*New York Times* 1946a). In Table 2 we show the issue of treasury bills necessary to finance the budget deficits.[8]

---

[7] Revenue collection in Hungary suffered from many problems. First, the tax administration system was badly disrupted. Many experienced tax administrators fled Hungary with the Nazi government in early 1945. Of those remaining, many were removed by postliberation political committees and replaced by large numbers of inexperienced tax collectors. Second, the war caused a massive destruction of public records. Third, the tax base was seriously eroded, in part because of the land reform policy. In early 1945 the government broke up the large estates, which reduced both output and tax revenues. The tax base eroded also because of the cessation of foreign trade, the sharp reduction in the level of economic activity, and the widespread growth, especially as inflation accelerated, of what we now call the underground economy. In 1945, approximately 75 percent of tax revenues came from the turnover tax and from the state monopolies on alcohol and tobacco (see Ecker-Racz 1946b, p. 71). To our knowledge, this is the first time these data on state finances and treasury bill issues have been published.

[8] An important distinction between the second Hungarian hyperinflation and the first was the limited role played in the former by credit granted to the private sector by the central bank. The overwhelming proportion of the bills discounted by the central bank (over 90 percent) were those of the Hungarian treasury. This resulted from the presence of a credit allocation system operated by a body called the Economic High Council. Thus, even though the central bank's discount rate remained at only 3 percent throughout the second hyperinflation, the private sector could not obtain unlimited funds at negative real interest rates.

Table 1. Expenditures and Receipts of the Hungarian Government, July 1945-May 1946 (regular pengö)

Million pengö	July 1945	Aug. 1945	Sept. 1945	Oct. 1945	Nov. 1945	Dec. 1945
Expenditures						
1) Ordinary	1,726	4,231	8,903	29,143	132,427	304,437
2) SOE deficits	896	1,713	3,703	13,756	54,757	108,198
3) Reparations	569	2,293	2,256	8,149	49,318	224,627
4) Occupation	148	590	1,348	3,915	29,355	46,656
5) ACC	64	179	349	1,635	5,999	24,997
Total of (1)-(5)	3,403	9,006	16,559	56,589	271,857	744,916
Revenues	231	746	1,210	3,222	17,973	53,047
(3)-(5) as % of expenditures	23	34	23	24	31	40
Revenues as % of expenditures	6.8	5.3	7.3	5.7	6.6	7.1

Trillion pengö	Jan. 1946	Feb. 1946	Mar. 1946	Apr. 1946	May 1946
Expenditures					
1) Ordinary	0.689	2.48	17.00	189.5	31,900
2) SOE deficits	0.194	0.72	3.50	36.4	7,500
3) Reparations	0.318	1.50	13.00	222.0	24,500
4) Occupation					
5) ACC					
Total of (1)-(5)	1.191	4.70	33.50	448.0	63,900
Revenues	0.169	0.68	4.35	43.8	4,700
(3)-(5) as % of expenditures	26	32	39	50	38
Revenues as % of expenditures	14.2	14.4	13.0	9.8	7.3

Source: Ecker-Racz (1946b, pp. 58, 60).
Notes: (2) SOE means state-owned enterprises. (3) In 1946, reparations, occupation and control commission costs are combined and reported in the reparations row. (4) Soviet occupation. (5) ACC is the Allied Control Commission.

Since Hungary has the distinction of having had two hyperinflations, we were curious to learn what role the earlier post-World War I experience played in the actions of the central bank and government. We were told by Arthur Karasz (1981) that the central bank did not believe that it was operating under any kind of real-bills doctrine or that the inflation was due to speculative movements in the foreign exchange rates. Rather, the central bankers were monetarists in the sense that they knew that the policy of discounting treasury bills to finance a large deficit would lead inevitably to a repetition of the earlier episode. The officials of the central bank continually warned the Allied Control Commission of the consequences of this policy. The Soviets, who dominated the Commission, turned a deaf ear to these warnings, which led some to conclude that the hyperinflation was designed to achieve a political objective—the destruction of the middle class.[9]

In summary, even though Hungary was stable in the political sense that one party commanded a majority in the parliament, the very depressed level of national income in 1944, 1945, and 1946 and the fact that the actions of the Soviets indicated that they wanted inflation made it very difficult for any government to raise sufficient taxes to cover expenditures. Resort was made, therefore, to the inflation tax which governments impose when they can impose no other.[10] This was done, one suspects, although it was quite well known what the ultimate result would be.

---

[9] The Hungarian central bank was nominally independent of the central government. Article 50 of its statutes forbade granting direct credit to the state. This statute was suspended before World War II and remained suspended during the hyperinflation. On May 7, 1946, the government extended its direct control over the central bank through a decree giving it the power to appoint a commissioner who was to ensure that the work of the bank accorded with the laws of the land, the general economic interests of the country, and the government's credit and foreign exchange policy. The powers of the commissioner were so broad that he became, in effect, the central banker.

[10] Initially, money issue was hampered by a lack of paper and the removal of plates to Germany by the Hungarian Nazi government. Dr. Karasz (1981) told us that when he returned to the bombed-out central bank, Hungary did not possess sufficient foreign exchange to pay for the imported ink which had been used for note printing; this money had to be borrowed.

**Table 2. Treasury Bills Issued by the Hungarian Government,
July 1945-June 1946 (billions of pengö)**

July 3, 1945	5	January 8, 1946	500
July 20	5	January 30	800
August 11	5	February 12	2,000
September 3	15	February 25	4,000
September 15	15	March 6	10,000
October 5	20	March 18	25,000
October 24	25	April 1	100,000
October 30	50	April 15	500,000
November 10	80	May 2	2,000,000
November 19	200	May 11	10,000,000
December 4	350	May 24	100,000,000
December 20	400	June 3	300,000,000
		June 8	2,500,000,000
Total late 1945	1,170	*Total early 1946*	2,912,000,000

Source: Ecker-Racz (1946b, pp. 74, 76).

B. The Hungarian Tax Pengö

In an earlier paper (Bomberger and Makinen 1980) we discussed the link between indexed deposits supplied by Hungarian banks (at the insistence of the government) and the severity of the hyperinflation. The existence of these deposits decreased the tax base against which the inflation tax could be levied.[11] To obtain the same real resources, the government was forced to accelerate money growth and the rate of

---

[11] Our early impression that all bank deposits were indexed by the decree of January 10, 1946, was incorrect. Deposits at the Postal Savings Bank, mainly in provincial areas, were not indexed until July 9, 1946, some three weeks before stabilization. Quantitatively, these deposits were significant, varying from 16 to 54 percent of total bank deposits. On January 31, 1946, they made up 48 percent of total deposits declining to a low of 16 percent at the end of May. After they were indexed, they rose to a high of 54 percent of total deposits on July 31.

inflation rose dramatically.[12]

As inflation intensified, the popularity of the tax pengö accounts grew. This is shown in Table 3 by the very sharp rise in the deposit to note ratio January-April 1946 (the subsequent decline is explained below). By June 1946, it was virtually impossible to find regular pengö currency in circulation in Budapest and other cities, especially after 2 P.M., the hour the banks closed. Businesses and individuals would deposit practically all their currency in banks and withdraw a scaled-up sum the following morning with which to conduct business.[13] It should be noted that the tax pengö itself did not remain immune from

---

[12] Although indexed deposits were instituted to protect state revenues from depreciation, they were extended to the private sector to reduce the velocity of money by providing an attractive alternative to commodities and foreign currencies. In this regard the tax pengö had an interesting but ill-fated antecedent. On February 25, 1924, the Hungarian government attempted to curb the earlier hyperinflation by introducing the saving crown (or sparkorona). Regular paper crowns (the unit of account) could be deposited in saving crown accounts, which were indexed. The index was computed daily on the basis of the crown rate in Zurich and Vienna, the dollar exchange rate of the Foreign Exchange Office in Budapest, and the price of six arbitrage securities traded between Budapest and Vienna. This experiment came to an end on May 31, 1924, at which time the regular crown had depreciated by 25 percent relative to the saving crown. It ended because the adjustment formula tended to rise faster than domestic prices. For a discussion of this earlier effort at indexed money, see Humphrey (1924), Donaldson-Rawlins (1925), Mitzakis (1926), and Ecker-Racz (1933). For its possible effect on the currency-to-deposit ratio, see Makinen (1981). Dr. Karasz (1981) related that the tax pengö system was proposed by individuals who remembered the experiment with the saving crown. Others in the government opposed the extension of the tax pengö to the banking system. They feared that indexed accounts would have an adverse psychological effect by convincing the public that the government was not serious about curbing inflation.

[13] Dr. Ecker-Racz (1981) drew our attention to this phenomenon, which was confirmed by a report in the *New York Times* (1946b). The desire to get rid of currency by 2 p.m. caused serious problems in exchange and distribution. To deal with these, the government on July 8 was forced to decree that food stores and the like remain open until 5 p.m. However, after 2 p.m. they were not required to accept regular pengö notes. The decree also specified that any wage earner could refuse his wages if they were tendered later than 2 p.m. and could insist on being paid the following day at that day's quotation for the tax pengö.

Table 3. Deposit to Note Ratio in Hungary (end of month)

June 1945	.32	January 1946	.18
July	.33	February	.30
August	.27	March	.49
September	.22	April	1.03
October	.13	May	.29
November	.10	June	.31
December	.13	July	.00000009

Source: Authors' calculations.

depreciation. It did, however, depreciate at a more modest rate than the regular pengö.[14]

In addition to the tax pengö deposits supplied by banks, tax pengö notes were also printed. On May 21, 1946, 2 months before stabilization, the minister of finance was authorized to issue tax pengö notes. They made their appearance the following week. Originally they could be used only for the payment of taxes, and in this regard they correspond to tax anticipation notes issued by the U.S. government. Thus, individuals who had future tax liabilities could purchase these notes and use them to discharge their tax liabilities when they came due. The notes had a term of 2 months and were to lose their value on the date of expiration, without obligation on the treasury for reimbursement.

On June 13, the minister of finance extended the use of tax pengö notes to cover payment for such things as public utility bills, rail fares,and other services supplied by the state or state enterprises. In addition, the government could make payments with these notes for

---

[14] At its inception on January 1, 1946, the value of the price index used for scaling up was that prevailing two days earlier. On March 1, it was advanced to the index number for the preceding day (the government announced the value for the coming day by radio at 6 p.m.). Beginning April 19, 1946, the government scaled up the tax pengö by arbitrary values that fell short of the actual increase in the index. The reason for this change in policy is unclear. Ecker-Racz (1946a, p. 4) states that it was to comply with the somewhat obscure price policy of the Economic High Council (the price-setting authority).

produce delivered to it under the system then in place, which obligated farmers to furnish a portion of their output to the state.

In May, when the tax pengö notes were introduced, the government was experiencing great difficulty in finding individuals or businesses who would accept regular pengö notes. In the face of this massive repudiation of the regular currency, the government decided to extend the use of tax pengö notes further. On June 23, five weeks before the hyperinflation ended, it began to disburse all of its expenditures in these notes. In this regard, the notes functioned much like emergency issues of scrip made by U.S. cities during the 1930s or like the greenbacks issued during the Civil War. In Table 4, we show the magnitude of this issue in the final weeks of the hyperinflation.

Because it issued its own money, the government had little need to discount treasury bills with the central bank. Discounting ceased on July 9 and on July 12 the central bank issued its last pengö notes— these bearing a denomination of 100,000,000 trillion regular pengö (10^{20}). The data on notes outstanding published for the week ending July 15 reveal that the issue of ordinary pengö notes reached their peak of 76×10^{24}. By July 31, the note issue had fallen to 47×10^{24}. At the official rate of exchange, the total note issue could have been purchased for \$23,245 (or approximately \$2,300 on the black market).

On July 9, the tax pengö notes became legal tender and their printing and distribution were taken over by the central bank. During the few remaining days of hyperinflation, these notes became the sole medium of exchange in Hungary. In the August 1 reform, provision was made for the conversion of the tax pengö notes. They were, however, allowed to circulate after stabilization as an auxiliary and fractional currency. They were gradually withdrawn from circulation during 1946 and early 1947.

Once tax pengö notes were introduced, the government was theoretically returning most of its inflation tax revenue to the public. The portion it kept was determined by the fraction of the rise in the price index that it did not allow to be reflected in the scale-up of the tax pengö.

The effect of the notes was the same as if the tax base had been reduced in the absence of their issue. To obtain the same real revenue it

Table 4. Hungarian Tax Pengö Notes Outstanding (millions)

May 29, 1946	4,447,810
July 15	11,427,723
July 23	276,698,900
July 31	2,798,667,900

Source: Ausch (1958, p. 116).

would have been necessary to increase further the rate of regular note issue, aggravating the rate of inflation. Thus, the issuance of tax pengö notes served only to accelerate the rate of inflation by reducing the inflation tax base. These notes also drove the remaining regular pengö notes into the banking system, where they served to increase the rate of deposit creation.

It is hard to avoid the conclusion that tax pengö deposits and notes were anything other than a major contributing factor to the severity of the hyperinflation. Clearly, the lesson is that when governments attempt to raise their revenue from inflation taxes, instituting indexed money may be counterproductive.

II. The Tax Pengö and the Deposit to Note Ratio

Movements in the deposit to note ratio have played the major role in cyclical movements in the money multiplier. Cagan (1956, p. 111) drew attention to this ratio in his examination of the hyperinflation episodes. He observed that, except for the 1945-46 Hungarian episode in which it rose astronomically, this ratio declined as inflation increased.

It was the movement in this ratio that (in our earlier work) caused us to question Cagan's interpretation of the available data. He was aware that both indexed deposits and notes had been issued in Hungary, but he assumed that the data on both notes and deposits reported only the unindexed components. Unfortunately, the data sources available to him (see Hungary, Central Statistical Office 1946 and United Nations Statistical Office 1947) were silent on the important issue of the degree to which indexed and unindexed monies were commingled. We can now state with certainty that the data on deposits do commingle indexed and unindexed components. By July

67

31, 1946, all deposits were indexed.[15] The currency data used by Cagan (1956) report only the note issue of the central bank. They exclude the indexed currency issued by the Hungarian treasury shown in Table 4. The deposit to note ratio was, therefore, computed using indexed deposits and unindexed notes.

The issuing of tax pengö notes and their emergence as the dominant medium of exchange raise the question of their effect, if any, on the deposit to note ratio. We show in Table 3 the movement of this ratio incorporating indexed currency. In making these computations, we have used a more complete data set than was available to Cagan. In particular, we have uncovered monthly data on the deposits of the Postal Savings Bank, which were of considerable importance, and, of course, data on the stock of tax pengö notes.[16]

As shown in Table 3, the ratio rose after indexed deposits were introduced, reaching a maximum in April. The introduction of the tax pengö notes in May caused the ratio to decline once again, indicating that the Hungarian experience corresponds to the others studied by Cagan.[17]

---

[15] Several sources confirm this conclusion. Our primary reference is a work by Ausch (1958), available only in Hungarian; we have had portions translated into English. Ausch provides information on the proportion of bank deposits which were indexed (p. 116) and the extent to which indexed currency was issued (p. 119). To learn more about his data sources, we wrote to Ausch (using the good offices of János Kornai, Hungarian Academy of Sciences); but, unfortunately, he had died in 1974. However, János Fekete of the Hungarian central bank was able to answer many of our data questions through correspondence. Additional confirmation was provided by Karasz (1981) and Ecker-Racz (1946b, p. 86).

[16] The only money data still missing are monthly observations on the deposits in provincial banks. Data for these banks are available on a monthly basis for the post-stabilization period (August 1946 until the series ends in 1948). These data reveal that the deposits in provincial banks varied between 4 and 10 percent of the total deposits in the Budapest banks and the Postal Savings Bank.

[17] Strictly speaking, the note component of this ratio should measure only currency in circulation outside the banking system. The available data do not allow such a computation. For the July observation, however, the stock of tax pengö notes is so large relative to regular pengö notes that it would make no difference if all regular pengö notes were held by banks. Tax pengö notes were converted to regular pengö using the established conversion ratios in the

III. The Stabilization Program

Contemporary views on the success of stabilization efforts generally follow one of two lines. For one group, inflation is generally held to depend on the trend growth of per unit labor costs. This trend growth is frequently called the core or underlying rate of inflation. According to this view, any attempt to bring down the core rate will not be successful in the short run. Rather, a prolonged period of high unemployment is necessary to accomplish a significant reduction in the core rate. The cost of such a policy in lost output is often judged to be too high when fiscal and monetary policy are used alone.

This view is discounted by advocates of rational expectations. They claim that major regime changes lead to major behavioral changes on the part of market participants. That is, once the public believes the government is sincere in reducing inflation, as evidenced perhaps by substantial reductions in budget deficits and moderation in the rate of growth of money, it will modify its behavior accordingly and stabilization will occur without the necessity of a prolonged period of high unemployment. To provide evidence that discriminates between these alternative views, the stabilization phase of hyperinflation episodes has recently attracted attention (Sargent 1982).

We conclude this paper with two sections that examine the Hungarian experience. Although our approach is basically descriptive, we construct our account with the controversy above in mind. In discussing the design of the stabilization program, we emphasize the attempts to provide not only the substance but also the appearance of a regime change. In describing the results of this policy we focus on events that may be used to discriminate between alternative views. The Hungarian experience not only adds another observation to the sample collected by Sargent but also provides an opportunity to examine the effect of the severity of the hyperinflation on the success of the subsequent stabilization.

National Bank of Hungary *Monthly Bulletin* (September 1946, p. 81). The ratio for June is only an approximation as no data are available on the outstanding tax pengö notes for June 30. As a point of interest, the ratio in the post-stabilization period (August 1946-April 1948) rose gradually from 0.23 to 0.71.

A. Preliminaries

A basic goal of a stabilization program is the restoration of the public's faith in the value of money so that monetary exchange will take place once again. The essential ingredients usually include a complete overhaul of the fiscal system designed to achieve a balanced budget both in the near term and over the longer run. Frequently, stabilization programs also involve the additional step of restoring the convertibility of domestic money into gold or stable-value foreign currencies. This step imposes an additional constraint on fiscal policy and serves to reinforce the belief of the public that a serious attempt is being made to balance the budget.

Monetary and fiscal reform may be aided by the availability of foreign loans. On the other hand, it may be made more difficult if the nation in question must pay an indemnity whose amount or amortization schedule is uncertain. Uncertainty here makes individuals uncertain about the resources the government has available for fiscal stability and for currency convertibility.

We have already mentioned several aspects of the Hungarian situation relevant to stabilization: the very depressed state of the economy, the great imbalance in the state budget, the indemnity of $300 million,[18] and the cost to provision the Soviet army of occupation.

---

[18] Of relevance is the real magnitude of foreign claims to Hungarian resources. Under the armistice concluded on January 20, 1945, Hungary promised, in addition to reparations and occupation costs, to restore all legal rights and interests of the United Nations and their nationals as they existed before the war and also to return their property in complete good order. The $300 million indemnity was to be paid over a period of 6 years, with $33 million due to the Soviet Union during the first year. Other claims by the United Nations and their nationals were to be determined at a later date. The sum of $300 million did not include packaging, transportation, and insurance. These additional costs were estimated to add 15-20 percent to the total. Moreover, if Hungary were late in making deliveries, a 5 percent per month interest penalty was to be imposed. The real burden was greater than the nominal sum might suggest. According to the annex to article 12 of the armistice, products delivered for reparations were to be calculated in 1938 prices with an increase of 15 percent for industrial equipment and 10 percent for other goods, to reflect changes in world prices. In interpreting this annex, the Soviet Union determined what 1938 prices should be. Naturally, they were set quite low.

Of additional uncertainty was the geographic area of Hungary and the population that was to bear the reparations burden. Under the Treaty of Trianon signed on June 4, 1920, Hungary lost 71 percent of her territory and 60 percent of her population. Hungary's support of the Axis powers during the 1930s led to a restoration of a portion of these so-called lands of the crown of St. Stephen. These territories almost doubled the geographic area of Hungary and increased her population from 9 million to 14.6 million. When Hungary signed the armistice on January 20, 1945, she agreed to evacuate all her troops and officials to within the limits of her frontiers as they existed on December 31, 1937 (the Trianon frontiers). The armistice did not, however, settle the question of the size of Hungary. It remained an issue pending a formal treaty.

B. The August 1 Reform

On August 1, 1946, the Hungarian government introduced an ambitious stabilization program prepared in large part by the Communist party.[19] The government undertook the program on its own initiative. It did not occur at the instigation of the United Nations or the Allied Control Commission, nor was it based on large foreign loans.[20] Our discussion of the reform is to be organized in terms of its key elements:

(1) proposals designed to increase the general acceptability of money;

(2) the drastic reform of the fiscal system; and

Using prices relevant to Hungary, it was estimated that $300 million was, in fact, two or three times that amount. The national income of Hungary for 1946-47 was estimated to be approximately $1 billion (see Commercial Bank of Pest 1947, p. 3).

[19] The architect of the reform was Professor Eugene Varga of the University of Rostov, a Hungarian who immigrated to the Soviet Union after World War I. It is a curious fact that a Marxist should have drawn up a stabilization program so much in agreement with modern monetary theory. Perhaps this supports the contention that monetary theory does not have an ideological basis.

[20] By contrast, the Hungarian stabilization effort in 1923 was prepared with the active aid of the League of Nations and based on a substantial foreign loan.

(3) the availability of foreign gifts and loans, the rescheduling of the reparations payments, and the fixing of Hungary's borders.

C. Measures to Increase the General Acceptability of Money

Apart from monetary and fiscal policies, three measures were designed to increase the general acceptability of the monetary unit.

(1) A new unit of account was introduced to replace the badly depreciated pengö. This was the forint (Hungarian for florin, the old stable unit of account of the Hapsburg monarchy).[21] The regular pengö was exchanged for the forint at a rate of 400 octillion to one, while the conversion rate for the tax pengö was fixed at 200 million to one. The forint was given a gold content and the law provided that it was to be covered by gold to 25 percent of its face value. During the first 6 months after the reform the gold cover averaged in excess of 50 percent. However, the forint was not convertible into gold or foreign currencies.[22]

(2) The Hungarian government recovered from the United States the $32 million in gold reserves of the central bank removed to Germany by the Nazi government. The gold was returned to Budapest on August 6, amid great press publicity.[23] Another $12 million in gold and foreign exchange (largely in U.S. dollars) was produced from domestic sources during the grace period before laws went into force forbidding such holdings subject to draconian penalties. This combined sum of $44 million, equal in value to 517 million forints, provided a

---

[21] Again by way of contrast, the pengö itself was not introduced until January 1, 1927, several years after the successful stabilization following Hungary's first hyperinflation.

[22] In the Hungarian stabilization program worked out with the assistance of the League of Nations in 1924, the Hungarian crown was pegged to the British pound, which did not then enjoy gold convertibility. When the pound was made convertible in 1925, the crown was returned to a gold base, although it was not itself convertible. This was also true of the pengö when it was introduced as the new unit of account. The practice of pegging the Hungarian unit of account to the British pound ended in September 1931 when Britain abandoned the gold standard.

[23] The gold weighed 22 tons and was brought to Budapest in the private train of Adolf Hitler (*New York Times* 1946e).

gold cover in excess of 100 percent for the notes of the central bank on the day the forint was introduced.

(3) Article 50 of the statutes of the central bank was reimposed, forbidding the central bank directly or indirectly to lend to the government except on deposit of gold or foreign exchange in equivalent sums for the notes advanced (i.e., the practice of discounting treasury bills was ended). To give the treasury a breathing period before new taxes yielded sufficient revenue to cover expenditures, the law permitted an initial advance of 300 million forints.[24] The law also specified that prior to July 31, 1947, not more than 1 billion forints in notes could be issued by the central bank.

(4) To control the supply of demand deposits, 100 percent reserve requirements were placed initially on commercial banks.

These changes in the nature of the currency unit were more than cosmetic. They accomplished a rather fundamental change. At the margin, the forint was backed by gold, foreign exchange, and commercial bills. The promises of the government did not enter as a factor determining the acceptability of money.[25]

The issue of forint notes proceeded at a faster pace than the formulators of the stabilization program envisioned. By December 1946, the issue of notes came close to exceeding the 1 billion forint limit. It was held below the ceiling only through rigid credit controls and deflation. In January 1947, the authorities waived the ceiling.[26]

---

[24] This extraordinary advance was not sufficient to cover the budget deficit during 1946 (see Table 5). The government borrowed 60 million forints from the Postal Savings Bank and received 450 million forints from the profits of the revaluation of the gold reserves of the National Bank and the sale of goods obtained within the framework of UN relief and U.S. aid (see below).

[25] We do not claim that a successful stabilization program must rest on central bank adherence to the real-bills doctrine. Forcing a central bank to pursue such a discount policy remains controversial. We do suggest that the success of this stabilization program is in good measure due to the fact that the government was forced to place its interest-bearing debt with the private sector or with foreign parties whose acceptance depended on the government's fiscal policy.

[26] The original limit seems to have been imposed for psychological reasons. On December 31, 1946, 968 million forints in notes were outstanding, of which 339 million were created in exchange for gold and foreign currencies

However, throughout 1947, the 25 percent gold cover was maintained. New notes were advanced only on discount of commercial paper, and the government lived within the limits of article 50 in that no new treasury borrowing was made.

D. Reform of the Fiscal System

A comprehensive reform of the tax system was undertaken. Rates of taxation were raised considerably over those in force prior to the war. Income taxes were imposed at a rate of 2 percent on incomes exceeding 1,200 forints (about $100), rising to a maximum of 60 percent on income from work and 80 percent on income from property. The maximum rates applied to incomes exceeding 84,000 forints. The gross rent on houses was subject to a tax ranging from 60 to 80 percent. The purchase tax was raised from the prewar rate of 2-5 percent to 3-10 percent. The company tax had to be paid according to turnover, irrespective of profit. All taxes in arrears were subject to a monthly penalty rate of 10 percent.

Expenditures were also subject to severe fiscal discipline. Just before stabilization, the number of civil servants was reduced in each ministry to 90 percent of the number in the 1937-1938 fiscal year. The regular army was reduced to 20,000 and the members of the state police to 5,000 (see National Bank of Hungary, *Monthly Bulletin*, January-June 1946, p. 21). Drastic economies were effected after stabilization. The civil service was reduced further and government salaries and pensions were cut to less than 50 percent of those received in 1937-38. The magnitude of this reduction in administration costs can be seen in the fact that the 1946-47 budget was approximately equal to that for 1937-38, but with reparations and occupation costs not found in the earlier budget accounting for some 40 percent of the total (see Commercial Bank of Pest 1947, p. 7; Hungarian General Credit Bank 1946, p. 7).

The results of the fiscal reform were dramatic. In August 1946, only 21 percent of expenditures were covered by tax proceeds. This rose to 33 percent in September and 96 percent in October. For the fiscal year

---

and 495 million in exchange for commercial bills. The remainder represented notes advanced to the state.

**Table 5. Public Finances of Hungary for Fiscal 1946-47
and 1947-48 (millions of forints)**

	1946-47	1947-48
Expenditures		
Goods and services	2,265	3,758
Reparations and occupation costs	1,436	1,707
Planned investments		833
Total	3,701	6,300
Revenue		
Current tax receipts	2,891	6,047
Borrowing and extraordinary sources	812	359
Total	3,703	6,406

Source: Kemény (1952, p. 138).

1946-1947, Table 5 shows that tax revenue covered 78 percent of expenditures, and for fiscal year 1947-1948 it covered 96 percent. The budget data also reveal that reparations and occupation costs continued to be a heavy drain on state finances, amounting to 39 percent in 1946-47 and 27 percent in 1947-1948.

These dramatic fiscal results could only have served to reinforce the belief of market participants that a major regime change had taken place.

E. Other Elements

The stabilization program contained or benefited from at least four other provisions that furnished additional financial wherewithal, reduced uncertainty, or provided psychological support.

(1) On May 2, 1946, the U.S. government provided Hungary with a $10 million credit to purchase surplus American property. On June 19, this sum was increased by an additional $5 million. The UN Relief Agency provided about $4 million in food supplies. These were sold by the Hungarian government and provided an extraordinary source of revenue.

(2) On July 29, 1946, a peace conference was convened in Paris to

deal with the lesser Axis powers. On that date, the text of the U.S. peace proposal was published together with comments by the USSR and the United Kingdom (see *New York Times* 1946d). The treaty left no ambiguity about the frontiers of Hungary. They were to be identical to those fixed by the Trianon treaty with the exception of several small villages opposite the Czech city of Bratislava, which Hungary was to give up. The text also provided for the continued occupation of Hungary by the Soviet army.

(3) The amortization schedule for reparations was firmly fixed. The period of payment was, however, extended from six years to eight years. The annual payments to the USSR were fixed, in millions of U.S. dollars, at:

  1945: 10.2   1946: 21.8   1947: 23   1948: 25   1949-1952: 30

(The 1945 figure represents the amount actually delivered.) Similar relief was granted by Czechoslovakia and Yugoslavia. Moreover, the $6 million interest penalty for nondelivery of goods in 1945 was canceled,[27] and the Soviet Union consented to take shares of the Petrosani Colliery Company (the most important coal mining company in Romania, a majority of whose share capital was Hungarian owned) as partial amortization of the 1946 and 1947 reparations payment. This transfer discharged a large fraction of the $21.8 million due in 1946.

(4) The government selected August 1 as the date for stabilization because it corresponded to the time when the summer harvest would be brought to market. In addition, a purposeful effort was made to stock the stores of Budapest with imported merchandise to give the impression that goods were plentiful.[28]

---

[27] After the Communist takeover of Hungary, the Soviet Union suspended the remaining reparations payments. They were used from time to time to persuade a somewhat reluctant Hungary not to deviate too far from the Soviet line.

[28] To obtain some of these goods, Hungary concluded a series of barter treaties during early 1946, with Romania (April 13), Switzerland (April 27), Austria (May 13), and Poland (June 26). Ecker-Racz (1981) provided details of the actual barter transactions, which involved a clever arbitrage of markets. Large quantities of Hungarian tobacco products, e.g., were sold in Vienna, where their price was high in dollars. The dollars were used to purchase cheap Polish sugar. The sugar was sold in Bucharest where its price was high in

IV. The Results

An effective stabilization should bring an abrupt end to inflation. An entirely successful stabilization should be accompanied by an abrupt reduction in expected inflation of equivalent magnitude. A reduction in inflation is easily documented. An accompanying reduction in expected inflation leaves two forms of indirect evidence. First, real money balances should abruptly rise as the public shifts away from foreign currency and barter. The magnitude of the increase should reflect the rate of inflation expected prior to stabilization. Second, unemployment should not rise as wage bargains are struck with the new (lower) rate of inflation in mind.

The results of the Hungarian stabilization effort were dramatic. From August 1 through December 31, 1946, the cost of living rose 6 percent. During 1947 the rise was approximately 19 percent. This modest rise in the price level was achieved in spite of a much more substantial increase in the money supply. The latter increased 221 percent between August 31 and December 31, 1946, and 132 percent during 1947.[29]

A. Inflation

The low post-stabilization inflation rate is consistent with an effective regime change, although it is slightly higher than those reported by Sargent (1982). Before we take these inflation data at face value, we should note a peculiarity of the Hungarian price system that raises a question about whether what the index reported was representative of price movements.

Prior to stabilization the Hungarian authorities concluded that inflation had distorted relative prices. They therefore set out to recast the entire structure of relative prices. The relative price structure of

---

broken gold. The gold was taken to Budapest where it was struck by the Hungarian mint into gold Napoleons. These gold coins were then used to buy imported goods from Switzerland.

[29] Money is measured as the sum of National Bank of Hungary notes and all deposits at commercial banks and saving institutions (mainly the Postal Savings Bank).

1938 was largely accepted for farm prices. The price of wheat was then arbitrarily fixed at 40 forints per quintal, or 2.1 times the pengő price. On this basis the price of other farm products was determined. Because of the heavy loss of livestock during the war, a price multiplier exceeding that for grain (2.1, as noted above) was given to livestock. Finally, the relation between farm prices as a whole and industrial prices was set in favor of industry.[30]

The intention of the planners was that the forint price level should be on average (as measured by wholesale prices) four-fold the price level expressed in 1938 pengő.[31] As one might expect, these "scientifically" determined prices did not stand the test of time. From the outset they were on the whole quite contrary to those dictated by market forces; that is, agricultural prices were set too low. By July 1947, farm prices were some 70 percent above their December 1946 level, whereas industrial prices had risen on average less than 5 percent.

Not only were prices set artificially, but through the early months of stabilization they were subject to substantial state control, though cost pass-throughs were allowed. The official price index soon after the stabilization may understate the true level of prices and, thus, lead to an overstatement of subsequent inflation as the controls were eased. The degree of understatement is difficult to assess. However, while we do know that a black market functioned, especially in foreign exchange, its extent was insignificant, which indicates that the official prices may roughly reflect the actual movement of prices.

---

[30] On the basis of 1938 = 100 for each respective price, the mandated price levels were: agricultural products, 270; animal products, 420; farm products (total), 330; industrial products, 460; all products, 400 (from Kemény 1952, p. 14).

[31] The four-fold increase was arrived at in the following way. Originally the pengő had been defined as 1/3,800 kg of fine gold. The devaluation following the international monetary crisis of 1931 reduced the pengő to 1/5,757 kg of fine gold. The monetary reform of 1946 set the forint equal to 1/13,210 kg of fine gold, producing a ratio of pengő to forint of 2.29 to 1. In setting the new price level, the planners assumed that world prices had risen 75 percent between 1938 and 1946 ($2.29 \times 1.75 = 4$).

B. Money Growth

Table 6 documents the dramatic increase in the notes outstanding, which, in the presence of relative price stability, represented an almost equal increase in real balances.[32] The 17-fold increase in notes outstanding by the end of 1947 with little inflation certainly suggests a perceived regime change. Nevertheless, the data are not entirely consistent with an instantaneous change to expected price stability on August 1. As with other stabilizations the increase in the money supply was large but somewhat protracted.

One explanation is that the stabilization program was not entirely credible to all market participants. Only after they had been convinced by several months of stable prices did some individuals revert to holding the level of money balances commonly maintained in noninflationary times. Alternatively, there may be adjustment costs involved in adjusting one's payments practices and average money balances, leading to a gradual increase in money holding after a sudden change in expectations. Neither explanation seems entirely satisfactory.[33]

---

[32] Note issue is, of course, not the only measure of the money supply (see note 29). However, it has the advantages of being available weekly for 1946 and of being more comparable across countries than other measures. Other measures of the Hungarian money supply do not show a significantly different monthly pattern.

[33] These explanations spring from the traditional analysis of the demand for money. Alternatively, one could view the post-reform period as one of reintermediation, rather than remonetization of the economy, and explain matters in terms of the demand for credit. Sargent and Wallace (1982, pp. 1225-1227) analyzed the behavior of an economy with private borrowing and lending facilitated by central bank intermediation. Note issue is generated by an accommodative discounting of private debt (consistent with a type of real-bills doctrine). They find that in such a model movements in the supply of money and the price level may not be closely related. One could take the Hungarian experience as evidence in favor of this prediction. As credit markets were re-established, the central bank accommodated private borrowers by discounting their debt and issuing notes, while refusing to do the same for government. The resulting increase in the supply of money was not associated with comparable inflation, though the pre-reform increase in the supply of money to finance government deficits led to a different result. In

STUDIES IN HYPERINFLATION AND STABILIZATION

Table 6. Note Issue in Hungary after Stabilization (mn forints)

August 7, 1946	114	December 7, 1946	926
August 15	227	December 15	988
August 23	294	December 23	956
August 31	356	December 31	968
September 7	416	January 31, 1947	1,017
September 15	460	February 28	1,093
September 23	526	March 31	1,173
September 30	607	April 30	1,258
October 7	656	May 31	1,408
October 15	719	June 30	1,468
October 23	745	July 31	1,592
October 31	843	August 31	1,754
November 7	821	September 30	1,834
November 15	879	October 31	1,869
November 23	852	November 30	1,829
November 30	937	December 31	1,992

Source: National Bank of Hungary, *Annual Report* (1946, p. 17; 1947a, p. 28).

It is interesting that the post-stabilization increase in money is larger in this case than in any of the four cases examined by Sargent, perhaps because of the much greater severity of pre-stabilization inflation. This explanation is made plausible by the fact that the positive relationship between the magnitude of pre-stabilization inflation and the rate of post-stabilization money growth holds within Sargent's group as well.[34]

---

such a model no stable demand for money (notes) exists, which is independent of the asset side of the central bank's balance sheet (see Sargent and Wallace 1982, especially p. 1226, n. 11).

[34] If we take the month in which prices stabilized as the month of stabilization, we can use the note issue as of the end of that month as a base for calculating post-stabilization money growth (weekly data are not available for most countries). For the post-World War II Hungarian case, the ratio of notes on August 31, 1947, to notes on August 31, 1946, is 4.93. Comparable ratios for the other cases are given in the continuation of this footnote on the next page.

C. Unemployment and Output

Evidence on the effect of stabilization on output and employment is spotty and unclear. Stabilization was accompanied by a measurable rise in unemployment. Unemployment among trade union members stood at 10,498 in July 1946 (its monthly average in 1938 was 17,796). It rose to 40,698 in December 1946, reached 81,548 in June 1947, declined through August, and rose to a high of 103,687 in December 1947. For the first 6 months of 1948 (at which time the series ends) it averaged about 116,000 (with a very small deviation).[35] This increase in unemployment is substantial but in no way comparable to the amount of unemployment sometimes alleged to accompany each percentage point drop in inflation in the United States. In addition, the highest unemployment seems to occur in late 1947 and 1948, by which time the most skeptical observer should have been convinced of the success of the stabilization program. The extent to which these data are representative of total unemployment is impossible to ascertain. In evaluating their significance, it should be remembered that in early 1947 some 250,000 prisoners of war and deported civilians were returned to Hungary.

Data on output provide an opposite indication, but they, too, are clouded by the extraordinary circumstances. From August 1, 1946, to July 31, 1947, real national income rose by 20 percent and continued to rise dramatically throughout 1947 and 1948 (the years for which data are available).[36] Since the country was recovering from the devastation

	Hungary	Austria	Poland	Germany
One-year money ratio	2.66	2.73	3.18	3.91
Inflation rate (percentage increase in monthly prices)	46	47	81	322

The comparable inflation rate for post-World War II Hungary is 19,800 (Cagan 1956, p. 26).

[35] See National Bank of Hungary *Monthly Bulletin,* October-December 1946, p. 132; May-December 1948, p. 165. It is doubtful whether these data are seasonally adjusted.

[36] This large rise in output was a minor but possibly significant factor in the ability of the Hungarian economy to absorb a large post-stabilization increase in the money supply without substantial inflation.

of a major war, the rise in output is to be expected and the effects of the stabilization may be concealed in this more massive "supply" effect.[37]

The longer-run implications of the August 1 stabilization cannot be told, for Hungary soon moved from a market to a command economy. In June 1947, the Communists managed what was in retrospect a coup d'état.[38] Thereafter, the economy was progressively nationalized and subjected to central planning.

V. Conclusion

This paper has had two general purposes. The first was to discuss the role played by indexed money, the depressed state of national income, and the condition of public finances as factors influencing Hungary's hyperinflation. This discussion was made possible by the use of data and other information hitherto unavailable or unexploited. Its second purpose was to discuss the stabilization effort in order to isolate its key elements, to offer evidence that this is the type of regime change that will change the behavior of market participants, and to see if the severity of an inflation has any implications for the success of stabilization. We tentatively conclude that at least for the Hungarian case it did not.[39] Price level stability was achieved rapidly, without a period of prolonged massive unemployment.

---

[37] Sargent found incomplete and mixed results in this area too. Unemployment rose substantially after the Austrian stabilization, possibly because of dislocation effects following the war; output rose and unemployment fell after the German stabilization (1980, pp. 11, 22).

[38] In May 1947, while the Prime Minister of Hungary, Ferenc Nagy, was on vacation in Switzerland, he was accused by the Communists of complicity in a conspiracy to re-establish the Horthy regime. He was forced to resign and the government passed to the left-wing elements in his party. By 1948, these persons were replaced by Communists.

[39] Phillip Cagan offered the interesting observation that the more severe the hyperinflation, the fewer may be the obstacles to a successful stabilization. This is because of the effect of inflation on fixed-interest-rate contracts. When the inflation becomes severe, such contracts disappear, making the public much more accepting of the sudden transformation required for an abrupt stabilization (personal communication from Professor Cagan, January 4, 1981).

5

The Greek Stabilization of 1944-46[*]

It is a matter of great contention among economists whether economic stabilization programs can be instituted without imposing high real costs. Those believing in the core or underlying rate of inflation hypothesis argue that relying only on conventional monetary and fiscal policies will impose high costs. The rational expectations proponents, on the other hand, argue that a convincing anti-inflation program will likely minimize these costs as economic agents respond to a genuine regime change or change in the rules under which monetary and fiscal policies are conducted.[1] A way of discriminating between these contending views is to examine the stabilization phase of the world's episodes of hyperinflation. Thus far, the work of Thomas Sargent (1982) on the post-World War I experiences in Austria, Hungary, Poland, and Germany, and William Bomberger and myself (1983) on post-World War II Hungary have adduced evidence in support of the rationalists' view. Price level stability was achieved rapidly without a prolonged period of high unemployment. The Greek stabilization of 1944-46 is not so straightforward and, as such, provides an interesting contrast to the other episodes. Its unique feature is that price level stability took over a year to achieve following the initial reform of November 11, 1944. It was not achieved until, in a third reform in early 1946, the Greek government put in place those features identified by the other studies as essential to the successful stabilization efforts they examined. Price level stability followed immediately in an environment

---

[*] This study has benefited from constructive comments by Phillip Cagan, Gardner Patterson, Thomas Woodward, Robert Anderson, William Bomberger, and two anonymous referees. My understanding of the stabilization effort was substantially enhanced by reading Patterson's dissertation.
[1] The "core" or "underlying inflation" view of stabilization is best identified with Arthur Okun (1978), James Tobin (1980), and Otto Eckstein (1981).

Figure 1. Price of the Gold Sovereign and Note Issue in Greece, January 1943-March 1948 (end of month data)

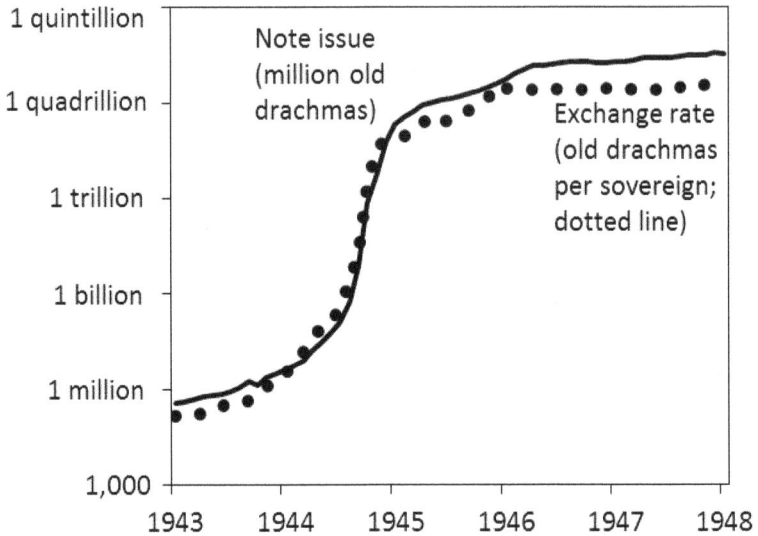

where unemployment apparently declined. The Greek episode thus provides a good setting for evaluating the alternative views on stabilization as well as elements of successful and unsuccessful stabilizations.

To give some perspective to the period to be studied, in Figure 1 data on the money stock (measured as notes of the Bank of Greece) and the market price of the gold sovereign are recorded for the period 1943-1948, a period both before the hyperinflation and after the successful stabilization. (The source for Figures 1 and 2 is Delivanis and Cleveland 1949.) The market price of the sovereign was selected to reflect prices in general for two reasons. First, no price index exists on a monthly basis which covers the 1943-48 period. Second, it is the least encumbered by prices which were either frozen (rents) or set by government decree (as were many food prices).

I. Stabilization

While the particulars of the various stabilization efforts differ, the prior

Figure 2. Real Money Balances in Greece, Deflated by Various Measures, December 1944 (= 1) to December 1946 (end of month)

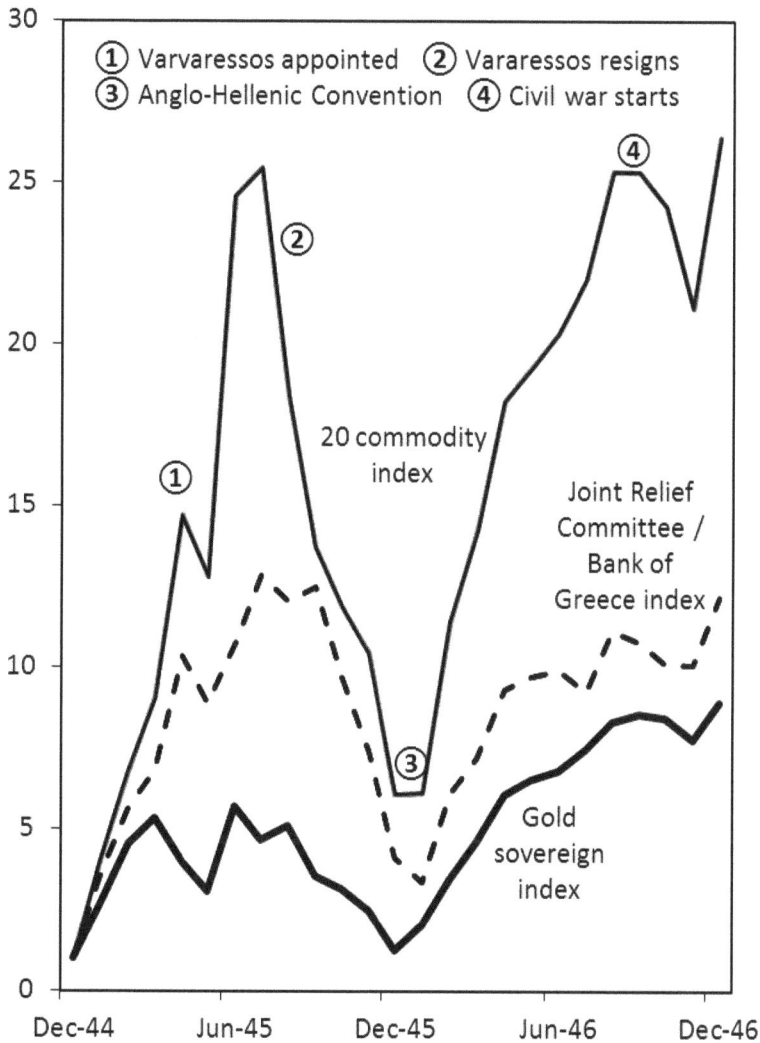

studies identified two specific measures as essential to their success. First, an independent central bank was reconstituted with the power to refuse the government's demand for unsecured credit. Second, fiscal policy was substantially overhauled so that through a combination of tax increases and expenditure reductions, the government budget in the near term and over the longer run was brought into reasonable balance (if not surplus).

To the extent that these changes are convincing, rational economic agents will perceive a regime change and revise downward their expectations of future inflation, and a phenomenon associated with successful stabilizations will be observed: a substantial increase in high-powered money occurs without a parallel movement in prices (i.e., real money balances rise). Supposedly, these same forecasts of inflation should lead to a moderation in wage demands so that unemployment need not rise during the stabilization.[2]

The stabilization phase of the Greek hyperinflation will be discussed in terms of the initial event which occurred on November 11, 1944, the second attempt, the Varvaressos Reform, in June 1945, and, finally, the third effort, the Anglo-Hellenic Convention concluded on January 24, 1946. This will be followed by an analysis of the behavior of unemployment and real balances.

A. November 11, 1944

This initial effort at reform had but two essential features. The first limited the government to an overdraft of 2 billion drachmas at the Bank of Greece. The second involved a massive conversion of old drachmas for new at a rate of 50 billion to one.[3] The new drachma was

---

[2] In his study, Sargent notes that the foreign exchange rates also stabilized as well. Data on these rates were not available to Bomberger and me.

[3] By way of contrast, only in Germany and Hungary II did the initial reform coincide with the introduction of a new unit of account. In Poland the introduction was delayed several months and in the cases of Austria and Hungary I by several years. In all of the other episodes the reform legislation forbade the governments from borrowing from the central bank on an unsecured basis. However, in the cases of Germany, Poland, and Hungary II, the governments were allowed an initial limited overdraft in order to finance expenditures until the new taxes yielded revenue. Finally, in both Germany

then made convertible into British Military Authority (BMA) pounds at the rate of 600 to one (but only in lots larger than 12,000 drachmas).[4] Old and new drachmas and BMA pounds were made legal tender, although the latter was not legal tender in Britain. No changes were made in the tax system nor were expenditure cuts announced. However, Greece expected to be the recipient of massive amounts of foreign aid that was to be sold and the revenue used for budget purposes.[5]

The results of this first stabilization effort were less than promising. Within the first two months the government had exceeded its legal overdraft at the Bank of Greece and thereafter operated in disregard of the law. During the first seven months after stabilization, prices, as shown by the cost of living index in Table 1, rose 140 percent (measured as May over November). Since this index contains commodities and services (principally rent) fixed or controlled by government edict, it likely understates price movements in general. As a substitute, if the price of the gold sovereign, the principal alternative to commodities as an inflation hedge, is used, the rise is over 800 percent.[6] Taxes yielded less than one-sixth of total revenue and, while the sale of aid goods yielded almost 45 percent of total revenue, their distribution

---

and Hungary II, an absolute ceiling was initially placed on the amount of notes the central bank could issue.

[4] This convertibility placed no effective limit on the fiscal activities of the Greek government. By secret treaty, the British had agreed to advance a maximum of 3 million BMA pounds. This ceiling was never reached (see Patterson 1948, pp. 58-60). In essence, this convertibility was analogous to the relationship of the U.S. Treasury to the Federal Reserve in determining the composition of the U.S. money supply.

[5] At the time of the reform, the British were furnishing substantial aid to the Greeks. On April 11, 1945, the aid program was taken over by UNRRA. From April to December 1945, UNRRA spent $350 million which, if one disregards price level changes, was equal to about one-half of the 1938 national income of Greece. No other stabilization effort benefited from this type of aid. In Austria and Hungary I, stabilization was supported by foreign loans and, in the case of Germany, the Dawes Commission suspended her reparations payments and rescheduled the remainder so to reduce their burden.

[6] The foreign exchange rates did not stabilize, the black market rates continued to rise, and the gap between them and the official rates widened over this period.

Table 1. Selected Greek Economic Data,
December 1944-December 1945 (percent per month)

	Rate of inflation	Rate of note issue	Rate of rise in the price of sovereigns	Expenditures covered by receipts
December 1944	63.2-a	990.0-a	47.6	n.a.
January 1945	-8.1	270.0	35.5	2.3-b
February	5.3	78.0	7.1	6.5
March	6.7	42.0	20.0	30.5
April	1.6	65.0	122.2	36.4
May	40.0	22.0	58.3	51.7
June	-38.5	17.4	-36.8	47.2
July	5.4	9.2	33.3	75.0
August	69.5	22.4	12.5	57.5
September	55.0	15.9	66.7	52.3
October	51.6	31.3	46.6	50.9
November	42.1	25.1	59.1	55.5
December	126.3	31.3	160.0	37.7

a-Percentage for December calculated from November 11, 1944.
b-The 2.3 percent represents the total for the months of December 1944 and January 1945.
Source: Delivanis and Cleveland (1949, p. 188).

costs were high. So high, in fact, that for all of 1945, the aid program yielded no net revenue (gross revenue was 16.4 billion drachmas while distribution costs were 16.8 billion).

The failure of the economy to revive and the acceleration of the inflation rate in April and May convinced the Greek government that a new reform was needed. On June 3, Kyriakos Varvaressos, a prominent economist, was named as a sort of economic czar.

B. The Varvaressos Reform of June 4, 1945

As Varvaressos saw it, the failure of the Greek economy to recover was due to a lack of effective state control over the economy and inadequate assistance from abroad. To remedy affairs, the government:

(1) devalued the drachma (the official rate was still under the black market rate); (2) accelerated the arrival and distribution of foreign aid; (3) raised wages, especially at the lower level; (4) imposed wage and price controls; and (5) reduced by one-half the prices at which aid goods were sold. As provisions 3, 4, and 5 adversely affected the Greek budget, a large tax was imposed on the occupants of rented dwellings (rents having been frozen in Greece since 1940).

Varvaressos did not succeed largely because he antagonized a politically powerful group with his rent tax and the government could not guarantee supplies of those items subject to price controls. He resigned on September 1.

During his three months in office, prices fell in June, rose slightly in July, and sharply in August (see Table 1). The gold sovereign price shows a similar movement. State finances recorded some improvement. Once the potency of the rent tax was reduced, the fiscal situation deteriorated during the remainder of 1945 and inflation accelerated.

In December, the British initiated a major effort to stabilize the Greek economy. The result was the Anglo-Hellenic Convention of 1946.

C. The Anglo-Hellenic Convention, January 24, 1946

The provisions of this convention, embodying the reforms common to the other successful episodes, contributed substantially to a final and successful stabilization.

First, British experts helped to revamp the fiscal system by (a) preparing a realistic budget, (b) improving the tax assessment and collection administration, (c) adjusting many specific taxes for past inflation, and (d) increasing substantially the prices at which aid goods were sold. Had it not been for the outbreak of civil war in September 1946, the budget would have been balanced.

Second, while an independent central bank was not reconstituted, a five-member Currency Committee was created whose unanimous consent was required before the Bank of Greece could issue any notes. The Committee came to exercise a pervasive control over the Greek economy and public finances.[7]

Third, to enforce fiscal and monetary austerity, the Bank of Greece pledged to maintain a fixed exchange rate vis-à-vis the dollar and pound sterling through open market operations in gold sovereigns.

This restored the gold convertibility of the drachma for Greek citizens.[8]

Fourth, to provide the financial wherewithal to carry out this program, the British cancelled their loan of £46.5 million made to Greece in 1940-41. This unencumbered over one-half of the reserves of the Bank of Greece. In addition, they made a loan of £10.0 million to serve as a cover for the note issue.[9] The United States furnished credits of $80 million.[10]

The effect of policy based on the Convention was immediate. The Bank of Greece commenced open market sales of gold sovereigns and maintained the drachma-pound-dollar exchange rate. The price level as shown in Table 2 not only stabilized but a mild deflation set in. While state receipts covered only 45 and 36.5 percent of expenditures in January and February, they rose to over 50 percent in March. The fiscal picture improved markedly thereafter. This is demonstrated by the fact that whereas the government borrowed 204 billion drachmas from the

---

[7] The Committee contained an American (Patterson) and a British member. While it abridged the sovereignty of Greece, both Austria and Hungary I had had to admit a League of Nations supervisor to ensure that the provisions of their stabilization programs were being carried out.

[8] At this time, the drachma was devalued and set at rates closely approximating those on the black market. Greece was then one of the only countries in the world with an internal gold standard. In no other stabilization program was gold convertibility restored.

[9] This reserve was more superficial than substantive since these notes had no gold reserve requirements or other specific backing. This is not true of the other stabilizations.

[10] Since the British were very instrumental in stabilizing the economies of Austria and Hungary at the end of World War I and, at the time the Committee was functioning, Hungary was busy stabilizing its own monetary system, I was interested to learn the ways these experiences were being used in Greece. I was told that the British may have used them in their plans made in London, but they were never mentioned in the deliberations of the Currency Committee (Patterson 1983).

Table 2. Selected Greek Economic Data, 1946 (percent /month)

	Rate of inflation	Rate of note issue	Rate of rise in the price of sovereigns
January	32.7-a	33.6	-17.6
February	-13.6	61.6	-4.5
March	2.1	27.5	-4.1
April	2.1	30.4	n.a.
May	1.3	7.1	-0.9
June	0.2	5.8	1.7
July	-0.2	7.8	1.7
August	-3.1	11.6	n.a
September	3.2	3.2	0.5
October	3.1	-1.2	n.a
November	3.7	-7.4	0.4
December	-5.7	14.8	n.a

a-The inflation rate for January is computed using the old price index. Data for subsequent months using this index are unavailable.
Source: Delivanis and Cleveland (1949, p. 188).

Bank of Greece for the first two months after the Convention, it only required 196 billion for the final nine months of 1946.

II. Evidence Bearing on a Regime Change

A. Unemployment and Output

Any interpretation of the unemployment and output effects of stabilization in each of the episodes is clouded by individual real dislocations or shocks that each economy suffered. After World War I, Austria and Hungary emerged as independent countries greatly reduced in size with the need to realign their economies accordingly. Poland was newly created and Germany lost substantial territory in the east and west. Both Hungary and Greece were major battlefields during World War II. Greece, in addition, had to readjust her foreign trade as her major prewar trading partners were Axis countries and those in the newly emerging Soviet sphere of influence.

The data assembled by Sargent show that while unemployment rose substantially in Austria, it was not as serious a problem in Hungary; that while it rose substantially in Poland it was no worse than in some months before stabilization; and that in Germany unemployment decreased.[11] Bomberger and I found that unemployment rose in Hungary II, but not by a magnitude or duration that would be suggested by those adhering to the concept of a core rate of inflation.

Unfortunately, no data on unemployment were ever collected on a systematic basis at this time in Greece. Two observations do exist, however, for the period following the Anglo-Hellenic Convention. A survey undertaken in the summer of 1946 fixed the Greek population at 7.257 million and the labor force (14 years and older) at 2.663 million, of whom 197,000 or 7.4 percent were unemployed.[12] On December 31, 1947, the Greek Ministry of Labor reported unemployment at 122,000.[13] Whether the two methods of estimating the unemployed are comparable is unknown. Reinforcing the conclusion that unemployment fell are data on the real national income of Greece: it rose 5.5, 62.1, and 33.9 percent, respectively, in 1945, 1946, and 1947.[14]

Because of the real dislocations surrounding the economies during each of the stabilization episodes, the employment and output results may only be circumstantial evidence bearing on rational behavior. For that reason, a study of the movements of real balances is of interest.

---

[11] The reference for Sargent's conclusion on Germany is F. D. Graham (1930, p. 287). However, Graham reports (p. 317) that among trade union members, those wholly unemployed rose from 6.3 percent in August 1923 to 28.2 percent in December (when the series ends) while those partially unemployed rose from 26.0 percent in August to 42.0 percent in December 1923. Thus, while unemployment initially rose dramatically, it was short-lived and did not persist into 1924.

[12] This survey was undertaken by the Allied Mission to Observe the Greek Elections (1946) and is analyzed in Jessen and others (1947).

[13] See Bank of Greece (1948, p. 72).

[14] National income data for 1945-1947 are reported in High Board of Reconstruction (1950); for 1944, see Delivanis and Cleveland (1949, p. 22).

B. Real Balance Holdings

If one starts from the premise that economic agents in Greece realized that the hyperinflation of 1943-44 was caused by a chronically unbalanced budget covered by recourse to advances from the Bank of Greece, one must then ask whether the set of events on November 11, 1944, convinced them that the fiscal money supply regime had changed such that they could expect future stability in the price level.

For economic agents to believe that the November 11 reform was a regime change they had to believe that 1) convertibility of the drachma into BMA pounds, 2) the government's 2 billion drachma overdraft at the Bank of Greece, and 3) the promise of substantial foreign aid would be sufficient to limit new money issues to noninflationary proportions. Does the movement in real money balances show us they were convinced?

In Figure 2, real money balances are plotted for the 25 months following this first effort at reform. While three different prices indices are used to deflate the note series, all tell a similar story. The analysis will, however, use the series deflated by the market price of the gold sovereign for, as noted earlier, it is the least encumbered by prices that were either frozen or subject to state control.

In examining these data, one notices immediately that they do not exhibit the more or less uniform increase over time that characterizes similar data in the other studies. Rather, for 1945, the level of real balances shows large fluctuations—a rapid rise followed by an equally spectacular decline. Is this pattern, so much at variance with the other studies, consistent with rational expectations?

To answer this question, two somewhat different models of rational behavior should be distinguished. One implies that the economy is inhabited by a sort of omniscient agent who, when presented with a new set of information, is able to assess its significance quickly and act accordingly. The agent is able to do so even in those instances in which there could be a good deal of uncertainty about important pieces of information; an uncertainty that can only be reduced by observing the government's actual performance. This model is a kind of ultrarational expectations view of the world. The other behavior model implies that agents are less omniscient. In many instances they can be expected to

93

consume more time in gathering and processing the significance of new information. The additional time may be due to the uncertainty of the information. This should not be taken to mean that expectations are formed adaptively. Agents are still assumed to be forming expectations based on information concerning the monetary and fiscal policies to be pursued by the government.

If the omniscient behavior model is applicable, one might have expected the Greeks to have rejected the November 11 reform as being without substance, as it did not contain the crucial elements identified by past studies as being important in stabilizing economies—particularly, the overhaul of the fiscal system and the creation of an independent monetary authority. Nevertheless, the five-fold increase in real note balances from December through March 1945 far exceeds similar behavior in the other stabilization efforts.[15] Obviously, the Greeks reacted positively to this reform. How might this behavior be explained? The explanation makes use of the less than omniscient behavior model in a world in which policy announcements are clouded with uncertainty.

Using this model, the explanation holds that agents had some notion that the November 11 reform indicated that the government was serious in trying to deal with the economic crisis. However, one major uncertainty in their evaluation of the reform's substance was the likely value of foreign aid to the Greek budget, this being the crucial element in the Greek effort to achieve a balanced budget. While the dollar value of this aid was known to be substantial, its value to the Greek budget was highly uncertain. To reduce this uncertainty required information on how much aid was to be delivered, when it was to be delivered, the prices at which it was to be sold, and the costs to distribute it. Only the passage of time in which the government's performance could be observed would yield information to reduce the uncertainty on these crucial elements and enable the Greeks to see whether the reform had substance. The evidence presented suggests that it did not take long for information to become available that the

---

[15] Comparable increases were two-fold for Austria (September-December 1922), 1.7-fold for Hungary (March-June 1924), and 2.4-fold (August-October 1946), 1.5-fold for Germany (December-March 1924) and 1.8-fold for Poland (January-April 1924).

net revenue from this aid would be small. Since this outcome was obvious, the Greeks must then have entertained little hope for a balanced budget and noninflationary issues of money, that is, the reform was seen to be without substance. As a consequence, real balances declined in April and May of 1945.

This decline was interrupted by the appointment of Varvaressos as economic czar with his startlingly new rent tax, whose potential to raise revenue was great. Since the elements of his reform program were contradictory, time was again required to assess their substance. Once he resigned and the potency of the rent tax was reduced, economic agents became convinced that this reform was also without substance. The entire preceding nine months were then viewed as having consisted of two temporary changes in policy in the context of a regime remarkably like the one that had generated the hyperinflation. As a result, real money balances declined precipitously, and, in December 1945, they were barely above their level one year earlier. Whether they would have continued to decline cannot be known for Greece and Great Britain signed the Convention in January 1946.

Once the Anglo-Hellenic Convention was signed and the institutional changes put in place, the actual money supply process did in fact change. While it remained true that the budget deficit would still require borrowing from the Bank of Greece, the resultant note issue would be held to noninflationary proportions through open market operations in gold sovereigns. Under these circumstances, did individuals perceive that this reform had substance (i.e., that a regime change had taken place)? The evidence suggests that they did and did so quickly.

We observe behavior much like that noted in the other studies. The four-fold rise in real note balances during 1946 closely approximates in magnitude similar behavior one year after the German and second Hungarian efforts were undertaken. In addition, this rise in real balances is more or less continuous, which is also similar to all of the other European stabilization experiences.[16]

---

[16] One year after stabilization, real note balances had increased in Austria 2.6-fold; in Hungary 2.6-fold (first hyperinflation) and 4.4-fold (second hyperinflation); in Germany 3.8-fold; and in Poland 1.8-fold.

III. Conclusion

Economic behavior in Greece ultimately paralleled that observed in the other stabilization episodes. It took three reforms and success was not achieved until the Greeks put in place those changes the other studies identified as crucial to a regime change. The Greek experience, however, somewhat weakens the case for ultrarational expectations. The behavior of real balances during the first two reforms suggests that the public could not fully evaluate the possibility that these reforms constituted genuine regime changes without additional time to evaluate the government's actual performance—even when the nature of the reform might have suggested that a genuine regime change had not taken place.

One can conclude that, while the adaptive expectations-unit cost-core inflation view of the world is deficient as an explanation of Greek behavior during stabilization, the highly idealized version of rational expectations may not be entirely consistent with the evidence either. Rather, it may take time for individuals to evaluate and process new information.

6

Some Further Thoughts on the
Hungarian Hyperinflation of 1945-46

(with William A. Bomberger)

We were tempted to begin this note with a phrase commonly used by those who wish to comment on an earlier paper, namely, "In a recently published article in this journal…" Upon reflection this seemed a little inappropriate as the article which prompted our attention appeared in 1947 (Winkle, 1947). Notwithstanding its age, it has both interest and relevance to contemporary problems in public finance. In particular, it is applicable to governments who attempt to raise revenue from the inflation tax.

It is now widely acknowledged that cases of hyperinflation[1] arose because the governments in question were forced for one reason or another to raise most of their revenue from the inflation tax. Hungary in 1945-46 is no different from the others (including its own 1923-24 hyperinflation). Indeed, Dr. Winkle (1947, Table 3, p. 185) documents this point. In no month did the Hungarian government cover more than 14.3 percent of its expenditures from explicit taxes. The remaining revenue was obtained from the inflation tax.

A question crucial to the point we wish to make concerns why the Hungarian hyperinflation of 1945-46 was so severe. In fact, why was it the worst on record?[2] This question is not addressed by Winkle nor by

---

[1] Based on the arbitrary definition of Cagan (1956), eight cases have been identified: Austria (1921-22), Germany (1922-23), Greece (1943-44), Hungary (1923-24) (1945-46), Poland (1923-24), Russia (1921-24), and China (1945-49).
[2] To give some relative magnitude to the Hungarian episode, when the old currency was exchanged for the new at the time of stabilization, the conversion rate was 400 octillion to one. This contrasts with the one-trillion-to-one conversion rate in the famous German hyperinflation.

others who have written on this topic.[3]

Winkle attributes the inflation mainly to the use of the inflation tax and only partially to the massive wartime destruction and dislocation of the Hungarian capital stock. While we agree with his diagnosis, we find nothing in it to explain the severity of this episode. We believe that it is to be accounted for by the unique Hungarian experience with indexed money. This is at variance with Winkle's conclusion: "...the Indexed Money System had actually little effect on the inflation" (op. cit., p. 180).

We do not wish to be too critical of Winkle's conclusion, for subsequent developments in inflation theory, especially the pioneering work of Cagan (1956) and Bailey (1956) have refined the way we think about the inflation process. However, Keynes (1923) had substantially developed the approach prior to Winkle's article. In this early work, Keynes discussed inflation as a tax, identified the money stock as the base against which the tax is levied, and addressed the question of the optimum rate at which the tax should be levied, i.e. the optimum rate at which new money should be issued.

It is in this inflation-taxation context that one can readily explain how the indexed money of Hungary contributed to the severity of the hyperinflation.

The Hungarian government indexed its money stock in four stages. On January 1, 1946, whilst the inflation was yet mild, it instituted a unit of account in terms of which taxes were to be paid. Its purpose was to preserve the purchasing power of its revenue. On January 10, the government forced the large banks in Budapest to supply indexed deposits primarily to safeguard government revenues from further depreciation once the taxes had been collected. Their additional purpose was to reduce the velocity of money by providing money holders with an attractive option relative to commodities, gold, and foreign currencies in which to hold their wealth.

Later, on July 9, 1946, three weeks before stabilization, all remaining deposits were indexed, principally those in the Postal Savings

---

[3] The standard accounts of this era are Nogaro (1948), Varga (1949), Cagan (1956), Ausch (1958), and Falush (1976).

Bank.[4] In the interim, in late May 1946, the Hungarian government was having great difficulty getting the public to accept the notes of the central bank which it obtained against the discounting of treasury bills. To finance its operations, the government decided that the Hungarian treasury should issue its own notes and that they should be denominated in the indexed unit of account—thus was born the world's first indexed currency.[5]

The successive stages of indexing, undertaken for worthy objectives, had one negative but crucial consequence—they substantially reduced the tax base against which the inflation tax could be levied. Once indexing occurred, the government was theoretically returning a portion of the inflation tax revenue to the public. The portion it kept was determined by (1) the proportion of nonindexed money to the total money stock, and (2) its practice of not allowing the full rise in the price index to be reflected in the scaled-up value of the indexed money (see Nogaro 1948, pp. 530-531 and Winkle 1947, p. 180).

Since the effect of indexing was the same as though the tax base had been reduced in the absence of indexing, to obtain the same real revenue as before indexing, the Hungarian government was forced to accelerate the rate of increase of its notes. The consequence was an acceleration in the rate of inflation.

It is hard to avoid the conclusion that these indexed deposits and, ultimately, notes, were anything other than a major contributing factor to the severity of the hyperinflation. They clearly hold the lesson that when governments attempt to raise their revenues from inflation taxes, they should be wary of instituting indexed money.

---

[4] It is interesting to observe human behavior in response to indexing. On January 31, 1946, deposits in the Postal Savings Bank made up 48 per cent of total banking deposits. As they were not indexed, they declined in importance, reaching a low of 16 per cent at the end of May. After they were indexed, they again grew in importance, reaching a high of 54 per cent on July 31, 1946, the eve of stabilization. See the National Bank of Hungary's *Hungary in Statistical Tables* (1947, p. 28).

[5] Hungary had experimented with indexed money during its 1923-24 hyperinflation. This experiment occurred at the very end of the episode and was unimportant. For a discussion of this early experiment, see Ecker-Racz (1933).

7

The Greek Hyperinflation
and Stabilization of 1943-1946[*]

The Greek hyperinflation started during the Axis occupation and was the result of an excessive reliance by the puppet government on the inflation tax. The inflation reached a peak in November 1944 after liberation. The Greek government undertook three stabilization efforts spread over eighteen months before price level stability was achieved. The final effort involved fiscal reform and the creation of an independent supracentral bank. Controversy surrounds the origin and nature of the transition costs involved in stabilizing an economy. The Greek stabilization cannot resolve all the issues raised.

Seven episodes of inflation severe enough to be called hyperinflation have occurred during the twentieth century.[1] Among them is the Greek experience of 1943-1944. In terms of average and maximum monthly rises in prices, it would rank below Hungary II but above Germany, though in terms of duration and total rise in prices it would rank behind both. When its initial stabilization occurred the Greek government converted its unit of account, the old drachma, for the new drachma at a rate of 50 billion to one, compared with conversions of one trillion to one for Germany and 400 octillion to one for Hungary II.

Unlike the initial efforts made by Germany, Austria, and Hungary I and II to end their hyperinflations, Greece's first attempt did not result

---

[*] I am indebted to Phillip Cagan, Gardner Patterson, Thomas Woodward, Robert Anderson, William Bomberger, and two anonymous referees for their numerous comments.

[1] The definition of a hyperinflation belongs to Phillip Cagan (1956). According to his definition, Austria, Germany, Poland, Russia, Greece, China, and Hungary (after both World Wars) had hyperinflation. China's experience is analyzed in Babcock and Makinen (1975) (chapter 2 in this book).

in price level stability. Inflation continued for an additional 15 months, albeit at a much reduced rate. Price level stability was finally achieved when, in a third reform, certain legal and institutional changes deemed essential to the successful stabilizations were put into place. The Greek effort is similar in many respects to that of the Poles, whose success at stabilization required two reforms spread over three years.

Whether stabilizations are costly to enact is controversial. Some contend that the experience in Germany, Austria, Poland, and Hungary I and II demonstrates that a convincing change in monetary and fiscal regime can minimize the transition costs in unemployment and lost output. Others dispute this contention, citing the absence of staggered long-term nominal contracts during hyperinflations as the reason the transitions appear to be easy. Still others contend that costs related to the adjustment of expectations are too narrow a concept of transition costs. They cite the longer-term costs of rationalization—as distorted relative prices are adjusted to the new steady state following stabilization.

I. The Hyperinflation

The Greek hyperinflation was set in motion by World War II. At its outbreak Greece was neutral, but not immune to war. Most notably its foreign trade and tariff receipts, a major revenue source, declined. The scarcity of imported raw materials led to a further decline in industrial production (averaging 30 percent lower in 1940 than in 1939). War, especially the Italian conquest of Albania, necessitated unplanned military expenditures. While the budget showed a surplus for fiscal 1939 (September 1, 1938-August 31, 1939) of 271 million drachmas, the decline in revenues and the extraordinary expenditures produced a deficit of 790 million drachmas for fiscal 1940. Notes advanced by the Bank of Greece covered the deficit. The Greek tax system depended on specific rather than ad valorem taxes, a shortcoming characteristic of other countries with experience of hyperinflation. The system made it difficult for tax revenue to keep pace with inflation.[2]

---

[2] For the role played by limitations on the ability to tax and specific taxes in the German hyperinflation see Witt (1983).

The Italians invaded Greece on October 28, 1940; the Axis conquest began and was completed by May 1941. During the period of resistance the Greek budget deteriorated further. Tax revenue declined and expenditures for military purposes rose 10-fold. Advances from the Bank of Greece continued to fund the deficit. Prices rose during the period 4.6-fold while the money supply increased from 1.8- to 2.2-fold.[3] With the installation of a puppet government in Greece, one might have expected the deficit to decline. This did not happen. Two new costs replaced military outlays: an indemnity, and support of the occupation army of about 400,000 men. These varied from one-third to three-fifths of all expenditures during the occupation, and notes advanced from the Bank of Greece again paid the bills.

Indemnities have played a prominent role in hyperinflations in Germany, Austria, Hungary I and II. Sargent, Galbraith, and Teichova believe they played an important role in the German and Austrian episodes because they caused uncertainty about fiscal and monetary policy.[4] Schuker, indeed, suggests that Germany purposefully engineered its hyperinflation to reduce its indemnity.[5] No evidence exists that the Greek puppet government purposefully resorted to inflationary finance to persuade the Axis to reduce its indemnity. And an indemnity is not always present. Poland, China, and Russia had a hyperinflation without an indemnity; and Bulgaria (after World War I), Vichy France, and Finland (after World War II) paid an indemnity without a hyperinflation.

The Greek puppet government, by choice or necessity, did not tax to cover its expenditures. Revenue declined, covering less than 6 percent of expenditures in the final year of occupation. The decline was the result of a disastrous fall in national income. In 1938 the national income was approximately 67.4 billion drachmas, declining in real terms to 23 billion in 1941 and 20 billion in 1942. There it remained for the next two years.[6] Unlike inflation in Germany, Austria, and Hungary

---

[3] No continuous price series exists for the whole of the inflation period except for quotations of the gold sovereign.

[4] See Sargent (1982), Galbraith (1975), and Teichova (1983).

[5] See Schuker (1978).

[6] The German economic exploitation of Greece was systematic and many Greeks starved. Large quantities of wheat, other foodstuffs, and drugs to ease

I, then, the initial stage of the Greek inflation did not produce an economic boom, because of the Axis policy of economic exploitation and the absence of credit. As in Hungary II credit was not an important source of the rise in note circulation.[7]

Prices measured in terms of the gold sovereign rose 155-fold during 1941-1943 (and the money supply rose 72-fold), but their behavior during late 1942 and early 1943 is unusual. The price of the sovereign reached a peak in October 1942, then declined dramatically. By December it had fallen to 43 percent of its October value. It fell again slightly in both January and February 1943, when it stood at approximately 38 percent of its October value. Observers linked the fall in prices to the expectation that liberation was at hand, following the successful Allied military operations in North Africa. Others linked the fall to the arrival and distribution of aid goods by the Red Cross. Table 1 records the progressive acceleration in prices and money supply and the level of real money balances.

By Cagan's definition, hyperinflation began in October 1943 while Greece was still occupied by the Axis. There was a rapid rise in the velocity of money, motivated by expectations of future inflation. In the initial stage the occupation authority pursued a policy that aggravated the tendency of velocity to rise. Finding some Greeks hesitant to accept notes, the authority began to pay with gold sovereigns and gold 20-franc coins. Over 1,300,000 sovereigns entered Greece in this way. While the practice undoubtedly decreased the rate of issue of paper money, it raised the velocity of money, for two reasons. It reduced public confidence in the future worth of the drachma, encouraging the public to hold its wealth in other forms. And by creating a closer substitute for money than, say, commodities, the practice increased the elasticity of, and reduced the demand for, domestic money (that is, it raised velocity). As a consequence, the tax base against which the inflation tax could be levied was reduced, and the rate of note issue and

---

the deprivation began to arrive in September 1942. They were furnished by the United States and Canada and distributed by the Red Cross.

[7] Sargent's data show that in Germany, Austria, Poland, and Hungary I a substantial portion of the notes were issued on discount of private commercial paper at negative real interest rates. For the Hungary II experience see Bomberger and Makinen (1983) (chapter 4 in this book).

Table 1. Monthly Percentage Rate of Inflation and Note Issue and Index of Real Note Balances in Greece, 1940-1946-a

	Inflation -b	Note issue	Real note index	Inflation -b	Note issue	Real note index
	1940			1941		
January			1.00		5.2	1.86
February			1.00		4.9	1.95
March		1.1	1.01		14.1	2.22
April		10.8	1.11		c	
May	1.1	10.3	1.25	364.0	c	
June	-1.1	4.5	1.32	50.2	24.3-d	0.40
July		-0.8	1.22	8.2		0.37
August		4.7	1.27	40.3	20.7	0.32
September		1.8	1.30	8.1	16.1	0.34
October		11.5	1.45	71.4	15.7	0.23
November		12.7	1.63	37.7	11.2	0.19
December		8.5	1.76	-26.2	12.2	0.28
	1942			1943		
January	1.7	8.5	0.30	-4.8	9.8	0.31
February		10.4	0.33	-6.7	9.2	0.36
March	73.5	16.1	0.22	19.8	15.9	0.35
April	35.4	16.5	0.19	5.7	20.2	0.40
May	16.8	16.5	0.19	40.5	11.2	0.32
June	-0.3	19.1	0.23	28.2	14.5	0.28
July	122	20.5	0.12	4.9	22.0	0.33
August	50.4	17.2	0.10	10.3	22.1	0.36
September	10.9	19.7	0.10	18.0	22.6	0.38
October	62.3	28.3	0.08	81.9	33.3	0.28
November	-22.6	21.5	0.13	64.4	32.8	0.22
December	-44.4	15.7	0.27	24.8	38.9	0.25

Source: Delivanis and Cleveland (1949, Statistical Appendix).

	1944			1945		
January	99.2	24.7	0.16	35.5	270.0	0.15
February	77.4	29.6	0.12	7.1	78.0	0.24
March	166.7	49.5	0.06	20.0	42.0	0.29
April	142.5	118.0	0.06	122.2	65.0	0.21
May	188.4	85.5	0.04	58.3	22.0	0.16
June	22.6	95.8	0.06	-36.8	17.4	0.30
July	188.5	114.6	0.04	33.3	9.2	0.25
August	556.0	321.6	0.03	12.5	22.4	0.27
September	675.1	1,220	0.05	66.7	15.9	0.19
October	13,800	9,400	0.03	46.6	31.3	0.17
November	160-e	800-e	0.02	59.1	25.1	0.13
December	f	f	0.05	160.0	31.3	0.07
	1946					
January	-17.6	33.6	0.11			
February	-4.5	61.6	0.19			
March	-4.1	27.5	0.25			
April		30.4	0.33			
May	-0.9	7.1	0.35			
June	1.7	5.8	0.37			
July	1.7	7.8	0.40			
August		11.6	0.44			
September	0.5	3.2	0.46			
October		-1.2	0.45			
November	0.4	-7.4	0.42			
December		14.8	0.48			

a-Percentages computed as the first differences of natural logs.

b-Rate of inflation measured by the rise in the price of the gold sovereign.

c-No data exist on the note issue for April and May.

d-Percentage change from March.

e-Percentage change calculated to November 10.

f-Percentage change for December cannot be computed as no observation is available for the end of November.

inflation required to yield a constant stream of real resources for the government was raised.[8]

On October 18, 1944, the Greek government-in-exile returned to Athens to confront hyperinflation and wartime destruction. Inflation continued, though indemnity and occupation costs were no longer present; they were replaced by expenditures for unemployment benefits and the care of large numbers of refugees.[9] Moreover, because the government exercised a delicate authority only in the Athens area (the Communists controlled the remainder of the country), it had a limited ability to raise and collect taxes. The daily expenditures and receipts of the government for the month preceding the first attempt at stabilization show that revenues covered about 0.4 percent of expenditures, with the remainder covered by advances from the Bank of Greece.

The rise in velocity and fall in real money balances forced the government to enact a stabilization program. The government was living off the inflation tax. As the tax base declined toward zero, the government's ability to use it ended. The rise in velocity was dramatically illustrated by the fall in real money balances. On the eve of stabilization the real balances were only about .4 percent of their 1938 average. The Greeks typically held a drachma note for 40 days in 1938 before spending it; by November 10, they typically held the note for about four hours.

II. The Stabilization

There is seldom an opportune time to effect a stabilization. The Greeks and their British advisers prepared the initial program in haste. A number of conditions militated against its success. The Greek economy collapsed just 23 days after the government returned to Athens. Because the stabilization occurred during the war, it was impossible to restore Greece's export trade. The country's principal prewar trading partners were members of the Axis, and it was difficult to obtain

---

[8] See Nichols (1974).

[9] An explanation of the role of unemployment and other social costs in the German and Austrian hyperinflations is given in Holtfrerich (1983) and in Teichova (1983).

critical raw materials to revive domestic industry and commerce.

The November 11 stabilization program had two essential features. The government was limited to an overdraft of 2 billion drachmas and the old drachmas were converted for new at a rate of 50 billion to one. The new drachma converted into British Military Authority pounds at a rate of 600 to 1, but only in lots larger than 12,000 drachmas. Beside the old and new drachma, the military pound remained legal tender in Greece until May 31, 1945. It was not legal tender in Great Britain nor convertible into ordinary pounds. Moreover, convertibility placed no constraints on the fiscal and monetary policies of the government. The British furnished as many pounds as the Greeks desired (up to a limit of £3.0 million, at which time convertibility would cease—the ceiling was never reached).[10] The government neither changed the tax system nor announced expenditure cuts, assuming that the sale of aid goods would provide some 75 percent of its expected revenue.[11] The civil war of December 1945-January 1946 spoiled the scheme and turned the printing press on again.

Prices rose in the first seven months after stabilization, but at a much reduced rate. The cost of living index rose 140 percent (measured as May over November). Because the index contains commodities and services (principally rent) whose prices were officially fixed or controlled, it understates the price rise. When the price of the sovereign is used the rise is shown to be over 800 percent. The government budget deficit declined as revenues rose from 6.5 percent of expenditures in February to more than half in May. Almost half of the revenue came from the sale of aid goods. The net revenue from these sales was small because distribution costs were high. Distribution costs exceeded sales revenue in 1945 largely because the government decided to use the aid program to redistribute income. All materials of war including food and clothing were provided without cost by the British.

---

[10] This limit was part of a secret treaty concluded between Britain and Greece on November 10, 1944. See Patterson (1948).

[11] The British furnished substantial military and economic aid from the time of liberation. On April 1, 1945, the United Nations took over civilian relief aid. The purpose of the aid was also to raise significantly the daily caloric intake of the population.

The behavior of real money balances indicates the public's acceptance of the reform. The government was successful in remonetizing the economy. Through May 1945, real balances rose three-fold (using the sovereign price as a deflator), which is comparable to the Hungary II experience (for the other episodes, the increase was: Austria and Hungary I, 2.1-fold; Poland, 1.8-fold; and Germany, 1.3-fold).

During April and May 1945, Greek officials became increasingly concerned, for the economy failed to revive, exports remained a minute fraction of imports, and inflation started to accelerate again. The price of the gold sovereign rose from 6,000 drachmas on April 2 to 11,000 on May 1 and to 19,500 on May 31. On June 3, Kyriakos Varvaressos, a prominent economist, was named economic czar. Varvaressos thought Greece's failure to recover was caused by inadequate assistance from abroad and a lack of effective state control. He set in motion an ambitious but somewhat inconsistent recovery program to increase foreign assistance, revive domestic production, and impose controls on wages and prices. The net result seems to have been to redistribute income in favor of the working and poorer classes.

Increased assistance from abroad took the form of an acceleration in foreign aid deliveries ($300 million for 1945) and a $25 million credit from the United States Export-Import Bank. To revive domestic production, the government sought to reduce the amount of savings going into gold hoards by monopolizing the sale and purchase of sovereigns, and to spur work incentives by raising the wages of lower-paid workers (including the civil service) and reducing prices on a large number of items. Controls were then placed on prices at the retail level and on all wages and salaries. A special market police force was created for enforcement. These provisions merely worsened the budget deficit, by reducing revenue and increasing expenditures. Varvaressos responded with a special tax on rents. Because rents had been frozen in Greece since 1940, they were insignificant. To capture this huge subsidy for the state the government classified all commercial, industrial, and professional establishments into three broad categories and imposed monthly assessments equal to 15, 10, and 6 times monthly rents on the occupants. So that the occupants would bear the assessments the market police were to rigidly enforce price controls.

The government expected the tax to yield 2.5 billion to 3.0 billion drachmas per month, a sum sufficient to balance the budget.

The Greek civil service, unsurprisingly, was unable to enforce the program. Moreover, the special rent tax antagonized merchants, shopkeepers, factory owners, and doctors, who began closing businesses in massive protests. By mid-August Greek citizens were openly evading the ceiling prices and the market police proved ineffectual. Varvaressos resigned on September 1.

Prices fell in June 1945, rose sharply in July, and again in August. State receipts for the three months covered 47, 75, and 58 percent of expenditures, respectively. The controls imposed by Varvaressos were dismantled and exemptions and exclusions granted from the rent tax. To compensate, the government imposed additional taxes, but the deficit worsened. For the final four months of 1945 receipts covered 52, 51, 56, and 39 percent of expenditures. Despite assistance from the United Nations and Britain the Greeks were unable to deal with their mounting budget deficit. Public confidence declined, as measured by the fall in real money balances which reached a peak in June 1945, six times their December 1944 level. They then fell rapidly and were only 40 percent larger by the end of 1945.

The British offered a plan to restore the financial and economic health of Greece, the Anglo-Hellenic Convention. Concluded on January 24, 1946, it gave top priority to arresting inflation through budget reforms that adjusted the specific tax rates, improved tax collection methods, and increased revenue from the sale of aid goods. To make it difficult for the government to obtain advances from the Bank of Greece, the Convention specified the establishment "of a Currency Committee which will have statutory management of the note issue" and that "new issues of currency will only be made with the unanimous approval of the Committee." The Committee consisted of three Greek cabinet ministers, one Briton, and one American. It met in April 1946 and remained a feature of the Greek economy into the early 1950s. Through its control of the note issue this supracentral bank exercised a pervasive influence on government expenditures, foreign exchange, and credit.

To enforce fiscal and monetary discipline, Greece consented to stabilize the drachma in terms of the pound and dollar through open-market operations in gold sovereigns (the drachma was devalued and parity set at rates prevailing in the black market). This restored internal gold convertibility. The position of the gold reserve became an indicator of the degree of inflationary pressure and the need for action by the Currency Committee.

The Bank of Greece began open-market sales of gold sovereigns. Prices began to fall. Fiscal deterioration continued into early 1946 (in January and February receipts covered only 45 and 36.5 percent of expenditures, but rose to over 50 percent in March), but then the situation improved. For February and March the government borrowed 204 billion drachmas from the Bank of Greece but only 196 billion for the final nine months of 1946. The rise in national income aided stabilization; it increased 62 percent in 1946 and 34 percent in 1947 (in 1946 it was still only about one-half its 1938 level). Public confidence was restored as demonstrated by the four-fold rise in real balances, comparable to their rise in Germany and Hungary II one year after their successful stabilizations (in Austria and Hungary I the rise was 2.6-fold and in Poland 2.5-fold). By January 31, 1947, the public was, however, holding real money balances only about 40 percent as large as it held, on average, during the final five months of 1939. Hyperinflation may have had a long-lasting influence on asset choices and transaction arrangements.

III. The Transition Costs

Historical studies and simulations of Phillips curves for modern industrial countries show that the transition from high inflation to price level stability can be protracted and costly.[12] Critics discount the results, arguing that the behavior of economic agents will not remain invariant when monetary and fiscal regimes change. Rather, they will modify their expectations and compensation demands, permitting brief transition periods and small production and employment losses.[13] Because the stabilization of hyperinflationary economies involves drastic changes in regimes, stabilizations have become a testing ground for the critics. Sargent claims that his evidence supports the rational

---

[12] See Gordon (1978) and Okun (1978).
[13] See Sargent and Lucas (1978).

expectations view because unemployment either fell (Germany), got no worse (Hungary I and Poland), or while it rose (Austria), the rise started before stabilization. Bomberger and I have claimed that in Hungary II the rise in unemployment was less than expected and might have been due to other factors.[14] There are reasons for questioning the relevance of the findings for other episodes. In each country stabilization occurred during major real dislocations, making it difficult to identify its specific cost. For example, Austria and Hungary I were greatly reduced in size and Austria forced to absorb great numbers of civil servants from the old empire. Germany lost substantial territory and Hungary II was a major battlefield. And hyperinflation economies are unlikely to have staggered long-term nominal contracts and economic agents with adaptive expectations. Rapid reductions in inflation can occur without severe costs. Such a finding cannot discriminate between the rationalist and conventional views.

The Greek experience provides no further insight. While real national income and industrial production rose substantially in 1946 and 1947 and unemployment declined from 197,000 in the summer of 1946 to 122,000 on December 31, 1947, few staggered nominal contracts were likely to have been in force when stabilization occurred.[15]

Garber claims that Sargent's concept of the transition costs is too narrow.[16] He argues that even if economic agents correctly predict and respond to new policy regimes, large unemployment and output costs might still emerge because in severe inflations relative prices are likely to change: wages relative to profits, skilled wages relative to unskilled,

---

[14] Sargent's conclusion for Germany comes from Graham (1930, p. 287). Graham also shows (p. 317) that the wholly unemployed among trade union members rose from 3.5 percent in August 1923 to 28.2 percent in December while the partially unemployed rose from 26 percent to 42 percent. For the Hungarian experience, see Bomberger and Makinen (1983) (chapter 4 in this book).

[15] The index of industrial production (1939 = 100) rose from 38.3 in January 1946 to 59.7 in March 1947. Unemployment data were not gathered systematically. The observations for 1946 and 1947 were taken, respectively, from a survey made by the Allied Mission to Observe the Greek Elections (1946) and Bank of Greece (1948, p. 72).

[16] Garber (1982).

consumer goods relative to producer goods, and so forth. The changes create incentives to alter the capital intensity of production, the technical nature of capital, the quantity of capital, and the allocation of resources. The alterations are often made possible by loans at subsidized interest rates and by government using the proceeds of the inflation tax to expand the size of state-owned enterprises such as railroads and public utilities. In addition, the desire to economize on the use of money encourages vertical integration. Once stabilization occurs and relative prices adjust to the new steady state, new incentives changing the industrial structure can cause lost output and unemployment. Garber provides evidence that the costs were considerable for Germany and not incurred until 1925-1926.

Data are not available to quantify the rationalization costs for the other hyperinflations.[17] They may be small in the Greek case as Greece did not experience an industrial boom, its national income was chronically depressed, credit was insignificant, and the proceeds of the inflation tax were not used to expand state-owned enterprises.

IV. Conclusions

The origin of the Greek hyperinflation is similar to that of other episodes during which governments relied too heavily on the inflation tax. Those governments were forced to enact a stabilization program when the tax base disappeared. The Greek program was also similar to those enacted by the other countries. Unlike the other experiences, price level stability did not follow immediately after the initial effort. It occurred 18 months later when, in a third reform embodied in the Anglo-Hellenic Convention, the fiscal system was strengthened and an independent monetary authority (the Currency Control Committee) which was committed to maintaining stable prices was created.

The total cost of the stabilization cannot be accurately measured, but the evidence suggests that it may have been small. Because of severe wartime dislocations and the absence of numerous staggered long-term nominal contracts, the cost incurred in Greece may not be

---

[17] For a qualitative discussion of the change in production technique and resource reallocations during the Austrian hyperinflation, see Walré de Bordes (1924).

indicative of the cost other high-inflation countries contemplating stabilization can expect to incur.

8

The Demand for Money, the "Reform Effect," and the Money Supply Process in Hyperinflations: The Evidence from Greece and Hungary II Re-examined

(with Robert B. Anderson and William A. Bomberger)[*]

"The Monetary Dynamics of Hyperinflation" by Philip Cagan (1956) is rightly regarded as a classic contribution to monetary economics. It is the origin of at least two fruitful branches of ongoing research. The primary branch has been the search for a stable money demand function in hyperinflation episodes. Cagan also discussed the money supply process, but this second branch of the literature has as its modern point of departure another classic paper by Sargent and Wallace (1973).

Of the seven hyperinflations Cagan studied, four have received more attention than the others: Germany, Poland, Greece, and

[*] This paper is part of a larger study we have completed in various configurations of authorship on the 1945-46 hyperinflation in Hungary and the 1943-44 hyperinflation in Greece. Our research on Hungary has benefitted from the generous assistance of Dr. L. László Ecker-Racz, the economic counselor at the U.S. Legation in Budapest during 1945-46. We are sad to note that on August 5, 1987, Dr. Ecker-Racz died. We have also discussed the Hungarian episode with Dr. Arthur Karasz, president of the Hungarian central bank from August 1945 through December 1945 and a member of its board of directors until June 1946. Our research on Greece was helped by Dr. Gardner Patterson, economic adviser to the Allied Commander-in-Chief in Greece during 1944-45 and the American member of the first Currency Committee, a supra central bank put in place to stabilize the Greek economy. We thank them together with Raj Jain for their assistance which enabled us to complete this project. We also gratefully acknowledge the helpful comments of two referees.

Hungary's second episode following World War II (hereafter Hungary II). In order to fit a money demand schedule for these four episodes, Cagan had to exclude several observations occurring at the end of each hyperinflation.[1] The level of real money holdings observed at these times was quite high compared to the values predicted by equations estimated from earlier observations. Cagan suggested that one reason for the breaks in his estimated money demand functions might have been the expectation of imminent monetary reform on the part of money holders.[2]

Following Cagan, a significant number of subsequent estimates have also been based on the shortened data sets for these episodes (Khan 1977 is a good example). Excluding late observations has a high cost, however, since these data sets are quite short to begin with.

Attempts to examine Cagan's "reform" hypothesis also continue to appear in the literature. For example, Flood and Garber (1980, 1983) and LaHaye (1985) have employed innovative econometric techniques in an attempt to determine whether money holders, during the relevant hyperinflations, came to anticipate a monetary reform.[3]

Sargent and Wallace also found three of these four episodes to be troublesome. In testing to determine the type of monetary regime that

---

[1] The excluded observations were: Poland (2), Greece (3), Germany (4), and Hungary II (5). In addition, an eighth hyperinflation occurred in China during its civil war of 1945-48. Babcock and Makinen (1975; chapter 2 of this book) analyzed this episode in the manner of Cagan and report several outliers that appear to be similar to those reported by Cagan.

[2] Cagan's adaptive expectations mechanism would overestimate actual expectations of future inflation if a monetary reform and the resulting decrease in inflation were considered probable. Cagan suggests this interpretation for the outliers on his pages 55-57. He also mentions the possibility that the outliers resulted from a misspecification of the functional form of the money demand equation. Cagan does not prefer this explanation and subsequent work has not emphasized this point. He also mentions and evaluates (pp. 58-64) a second possible failure of the adaptive expectations mechanism: a rising coefficient of expectation during the high inflation of the latter months of hyperinflation. He finds some evidence of this effect, but suggests that it is responsible for some of the serial correlation in the estimates, not the outliers. This point is brought out most clearly in footnote 19, page 63.

[3] Flood and Garber addressed the "reform effect" only in their 1980 paper and then only for Germany.

generated the hyperinflations, they obtained results for Greece that were inconsistent with the type of regime that Cagan envisioned, and they were unable to ascertain the nature of the regime in Poland or Hungary II.

The purpose of this paper is to re-examine two of these episodes, Greece and Hungary II. We have uncovered new data for the money stock and prices during the Greek hyperinflation. We have also found new data and have a new interpretation of the data used by Cagan for Hungary II. Using these new data, we have re-estimated Cagan's original money demand specification and have repeated the influential Sargent-Wallace causality tests. We find that the outlier problems disappear when the Cagan technique is applied to the new data for these two episodes. The original reason for shortening these data sets, therefore, disappears. In addition, the new Greek and Hungarian data yield evidence in favor of the Sargent-Wallace conjecture regarding the direction of causation between money and prices. This latter result is at variance with their original findings for Greece and Hungary II, but consistent with their results for the majority of the hyperinflation episodes.[4]

Our paper is divided into four parts. The first part reviews the data problems. The second examines the money demand outliers for the Greek and Hungary II hyperinflations. The third examines the money-price causation for these two hyperinflations. The final section presents our conclusions.

I. The Data Problems

One of the great contributions of Cagan's study was that he assembled from diverse sources a time series on money and prices for each European hyperinflation. In doing so he often had to make interpretations and assumptions. It is no reflection on Cagan's careful and exhaustive efforts that subsequent work has occasionally uncovered other time series or questioned some of his assumptions. Indeed, considering the empirical thrust of Cagan's original article, it is

---

[4] Tang and Hu (1983) in a recent paper show that a similar monetary regime characterized the Chinese hyperinflation.

puzzling to us that scholars inspired by his work have spent so little time trying to expand and refine his data set. Much more attention has been devoted to econometric technique than has been applied to improving the data used to test those techniques. In our view, many of the puzzles in these hyperinflation episodes can only be resolved by a further examination of the data.

The data on the Hungarian money stock are a case in point. Cagan was aware that Hungary had experimented extensively with both indexed deposits and currency. Yet, the data sources he used were remarkably silent on the degree to which indexed and nonindexed components were commingled, so he simply assumed that the data contained only nonindexed components. Bomberger and Makinen (1980, 1983) explain why this is incorrect. The data Cagan used commingle the nonindexed notes of the central bank and all deposits (both indexed and nonindexed) of the principal commercial banks. The importance of the indexed components increased as the hyperinflation intensified, and they ultimately came to dominate the money stock. We believe that the failure to account for the commingled data is responsible for the outliers Cagan found in this episode and also the absence of the price-level-to-money causation that Sargent and Wallace found.[5] In addition to being able to separate indexed from nonindexed deposits at commercial banks, our research has uncovered a complete monthly time series of deposits at the Postal Savings Bank and more frequent (weekly) observations on the outstanding note issue of the central bank (for 1946).[6]

---

[5] A potentially serious error should be noted in the United Nations (1947) source from which Cagan drew his data on commercial bank deposits. For July 1946, the source lists total bank deposits as 24×10^{34}. In the underlying source (see the National Bank of Hungary's *Hungary in Statistical Tables,* 1947) the correct figure is 24×10^{28}. Both Sargent and Wallace (1973) and Flood and Garber (1983) used the incorrect observation. We have not assessed the implications of this error for the Flood and Garber work, but think it may be important for Sargent and Wallace's findings. It did not affect Cagan's results because the July observation was excised from his work.

[6] Our sample period for Hungary runs through May 1946. During this period only the deposits of the commercial banks were indexed (subsequent to January 10, 1946). The deposits of the Postal Savings Bank (which varied from 16 percent to 54 percent of total deposits over the sample period) were not

In the Greek case, our research has uncovered an alternative series on the money stock and two additional price series, one of which may be preferable for estimating the expected rate of inflation. Cagan's money stock data were drawn from a time series on the note issue of the Bank of Greece published in the appendix to Delivanis and Cleveland (1949). An alternative time series for this same note issue is available in Agapitides (1945). The two series are identical until August 1942. From that point through October 1944 the monthly observations given in Agapitides report a smaller money stock than the corresponding observations in Delivanis and Cleveland. For the final two months of 1944, after which it ends, the Agapitides series reports a larger money stock than the Delivanis and Cleveland series.[7] [8] Interestingly, both studies cite the Bank of Greece as the source for their money data. Which series is correct?

We have no conclusive answer, but we prefer Agapitides data for two reasons. First, Patterson (1948) explains that the Bank of Greece followed the practice of listing as "notes in circulation" all notes issued from its Athens office including those sent to its various branches and held in their vaults. If, as is likely, the central bank, in anticipation of future inflation, "stockpiled" an ever larger quantity of notes in order to meet future commitments (and if these were in part held at its branches), the recorded stock of issue would run ahead of the amount actually in circulation. It is our supposition that the Agapitides data may record notes in circulation whereas the Delivanis and Cleveland data

---

indexed during this period. Our measure of currency includes only the note issue of the central bank. The indexed currency issued by the Hungarian treasury functioned only at the end of the hyperinflation during June and July 1946, a brief period excised from our sample for reasons given below.

[7] The average per month by which the money series in Delivanis and Cleveland exceeds that given in Agapitides is, for September-December 1942, 11 percent; for all of 1943, 10 percent; for January-July 1944, 26 percent; and for August-October 1944, 900 percent.

[8] Delivanis and Cleveland report an observation for November 11, 1944, the day of stabilization (supposedly 1/50 billionth of the outstanding note issue measured in old drachmas). Agapitides reports observations for the end of November and December measured in old drachmas, but no observation for November 11, 1944.

include all notes issued, including those not yet in circulation.[9]

Second, the Agapitides data are easier to reconcile with what happened in the post-reform period. The money stock reported in Delivanis and Cleveland on the date of the reform, November 11, 1944, is listed as 121 million new drachmas. Yet, when the conversion of the old drachma for new was finally completed, 222 million new drachmas had been converted, almost twice the Delivanis and Cleveland figure. Patterson (1948, p. 66) speculates that a huge sum of old drachmas were in fact issued subsequent to the November 11 reform. While the issue of money in the post-reform period has no bearing on the estimates of the demand for money during the hyperinflation, it is relevant in trying to determine which series is more accurate overall. For this purpose, it is significant that Agapitides' series was larger in November and December 1944 than the Delivanis and Cleveland series.[10]

Both Delivanis and Cleveland and Agapitides report a price index for goods and services. While they differ in composition (Agapitides is for a lower-calorie diet) and geographic coverage (the Delivanis and Cleveland index measures inflation in Athens alone while Agapitides covers both Athens and Piraeus), they may be less desirable for estimating the expected rate of inflation than an alternative we have also uncovered: the black-market price of the British gold sovereign.

It is usually believed that the inflation rate in the money demand function measures the opportunity cost of holding money. On this interpretation what is sought is the rate of increase of the price or prices of the major alternatives to money as a store of value. A lack of knowledge concerning other possible alternatives has led investigators to assume that nonperishable commodities are the major alternative for the majority of hyperinflations. Finding a suitable index to measure the rate at which they rise in price has proven difficult, however.

---

[9] We know little about Professor Agapitides other than that he was Secretary-General of the Superior Economic Council for Greece.

[10] We note that the Greek data on the reciprocal of real balances reported in Cagan's article contains three printing errors. The observations for July, August, and September 1944 should be 2.3513, 2.3789, and 2.5609. The errors have probably had little influence on subsequent work because most authors have used the excised sample for Greece which runs through August 1944.

Frequently, an index either of wholesale or consumer prices has been used as a proxy, even though it may contain services such as housing and utilities which cannot be stored and whose prices may rise much more slowly than the prices of nonperishable commodities.

The two major indices available for Greece are for consumer prices. Agapitides provides a detailed description of the components of his index. Important weights are given to tramway tickets, water, electricity, and rent. Not only are these items nonstorable, but their prices were subject to substantial state regulation. They only rose significantly in the final months of the episode. Moreover, even the prices of commodities that might have served as an alternative store of value were subject to measurement problems.[11] For these reasons we believe that the available consumer price indices may not accurately reflect the rate at which money holders expected the prices of the alternatives to money to rise. Thus, we experimented by using both the two consumer price indices and the black-market price of the gold sovereign, a known alternative to currency as a store of value.[12] The sovereign price is also subject to criticism, however, in that the price of gold may be influenced by specific conditions of supply and demand that make it inappropriate as a proxy for the opportunity cost of holding money. (All of the new data can be found in the Appendix.)

---

[11] So systematic was the Axis exploitation of Greece during the occupation, that the Greeks faced massive starvation. To deal with this prospect, the Axis powers permitted the United States and Canada to send supplies through the International Red Cross. These goods were priced in the Agapitides index in the following way: the official price for the actual quantity supplied to a family of four was used, and when this quantity was less than that specified in the budget underlying the index, the black market price was used to value the deficiency, to the extent it could be obtained. There is reason to believe the Delivanis and Cleveland price index was similarly constructed. We wonder about the extent to which the receipt of foreign aid, which was both uncertain and temporary, altered the expectations of inflation. While the aid goods held down the actual rate of inflation, they may not have altered inflationary expectations.

[12] For a discussion of the important role played by the gold sovereign in the Greek hyperinflation, see Makinen (1986) (chapter 5 in this book).

120

II. The Outliers

Cagan's (1956) preferred explanation for the money demand outliers was the anticipation by money holders of an imminent monetary reform. We consider the relevance of the "reform effect" for these episodes in Part A. In Part B we consider the necessity of invoking the reform effect for the alternative data sets.

A. The Reform Effect

Could the prospect of a monetary reform have led economic agents in Greece and Hungary to hold larger money balances than they would have held if they had expected the hyperinflations to continue? We are particularly interested in what can be learned about these prospects by looking at the historical record, and whether a reasonable person knowing what the Greeks and Hungarians knew in the later months of their hyperinflations would have behaved as Cagan supposed.

In a way, the term "reform effect" is ambiguous. What Cagan had in mind was the belief by economic agents that a change in the monetary and fiscal regime was about to occur that would lead to a much lower rate of inflation, if not a stable price level, in the near future. As Gurley (1953) clearly demonstrates, this is not the only kind of "reform" that has occurred in response to hyperinflation. He describes many "monetary reforms" that merely deleted the zeros from the unit of account without otherwise altering the monetary and fiscal regime. If this type of "reform" was anticipated in Greece and Hungary, there would have been no reason for anyone to have held a larger money balance. If expected monetary reforms explain the outliers, then it should be possible to show that economic agents in Greece and Hungary knew the nature of the monetary and fiscal changes that the reforms would bring about. If they did not, then even if they expected a genuine regime change, this could scarcely be called a rational expectation.[13]

---

[13] Gurley discusses why some of these reforms may have caused the demand for money to decline. It should be noted that in each of the hyperinflations the unit of account was ultimately changed either at the time of stabilization or

Consider Greece. If the "reform effect" hypothesis is correct, the Greeks came to expect a regime change in late August 1944, six weeks prior to the end of the German occupation, during a period when it could be said, "...there was, in effect, no recognized government for a large section of the community" (Capie 1986).[14] The "reform effect" would require that the ungoverned Greeks anticipated correctly when the war would end in their beleaguered country and also what the plans of the new government would be. In fact, when the Greek government-in-exile entered Athens on October 18, 1944, it came without a stabilization program. Patterson presents a detailed account of the next 23 days, at the end of which the Greek government was forced to embark on the first of its three attempts at stabilization (spread over 18 months). Patterson explains that the government returned without a budget and without any plan for financing its activities much beyond resort to the printing press. Only after the merchants in Athens closed their doors rather than accept the drachma did the government try to reverse the deteriorating economic situation. In short, the first stabilization effort was probably not much less of a surprise to the government than it was to the Greeks. Moreover, when it did occur on November 11, it was little more than a cosmetic change of the type described by Gurley (in fact, Gurley classifies it among his "Type I" reforms that did not lead to stabilization).[15]

It might, however, be argued that the mere return of the government-in-exile was a confidence-building step. Although this might be true, it could have had the opposite effect as well. When the government-in-exile returned, it did so only to Athens. It did not control the rest of Greece. There, control was exercised by a communist-led partisan front. A civil war between the returning royalist government and the communists was imminent and actually broke out

---

shortly thereafter. In both Greece and Hungary II the change occurred at the time of stabilization.

[14] During the final weeks of occupation, the German army was systematically destroying or rendering inoperative the roads, railways, canals, and port facilities; and rival partisan bands were in open conflict, an environment that may not have been conducive to expectations of a successful stabilization.

[15] For the particulars of the reform, see Makinen (1986; chapter 5 in this book).

within weeks as the government attempted to extend its writ beyond Athens.[16]

On the basis of this evidence we question whether it would have been reasonable for the Greeks to have predicted a regime change leading them to increase their desired money balances in August 1944. They may have done so, but it seems to us that it would not have been as a result of rational economic calculation.

In the case of Hungary, Cagan was forced to exclude all observations after February 1946. If the "reform effect" was responsible for this shift in his estimated equation, it implies that the Hungarians anticipated a regime change a full five months (stabilization occurred on August 1, 1946) before it happened during a time when Hungary was experiencing the most intense inflation ever recorded. Although the Hungarians knew the date of the scheduled monetary reform all of our evidence suggests that they did not know the particulars of the program. If that is correct, they could not have known in advance whether a genuine regime change was impending or merely one of Gurley's cosmetic reforms that would leave the rate of inflation unaffected.[17]

Moreover, they did not learn the date of the reform until late May or early June 1946, not February. In early May, the communist party which ultimately formulated the monetary reform, began to speak of stabilization by August (see Ecker-Racz 1946).[18] [19] In late May, the Hungarian Treasury began to issue what became indexed currency.

---

[16] Even if the confidence building argument were correct, it would influence only the October 1944 observation. It would leave unexplained the August and September buildup of real money balances.

[17] Hungary had already had one cosmetic reform. In December 1945, shortly after the hyperinflation got underway, the government imposed a tax on notes such that three out of every four had to be surrendered to the authorities. The exchange did not apply to bank deposits. While this "reform" did slow the inflation, it did so for only a very short time.

[18] At this time Hungary, though occupied by the Soviet army, was governed by a coalition in which the communist party was a distinct minority.

[19] In an oblique reference, Winkle (1947) states, "stabilization and the new currency were decided upon about April, 1946." Without further elaboration, we are unable to determine exactly what was known by the public in April 1946. Winkle also fails to give the date of the agreed-upon stabilization.

These notes bore the legend that after July 31, 1946, they would no longer be legal tender and could not be used to pay taxes or purchase any state supplied service. We were told (Karasz 1981) that this legend was added to inform the public that August 1st would be the date of the stabilization.

We do not question that an expected regime change could have led to larger holdings of real balances than would have been held if hyperinflation had been expected to continue unchecked, but we do question whether such regime changes actually were expected in the case of Greece or Hungary II. We believe the evidence just presented strongly implies that they were not.

B. The Cagan Money Demand Function, One More Time

As is well known, Cagan's demand for money function is a test of the joint hypothesis that in hyperinflations the demand for money depends on the expected rate of inflation, p^e, and that expectations are formed "adaptively" from past observations of actual inflation, p, or

$$(1) \quad p_t^e = p_{t-1}^e + b_1 e_t$$

where e_t is the most recent forecast error:

$$(2) \quad e_t = p_t - p_{t-1}^e$$

The procedure used by Cagan involves constructing alternative p^e series from a given p series by using alternative values of b_1, the so-called coefficient of expectation. One then selects the appropriate p^e series by successively regressing the logarithm of real money balances, m, on the alternative p^e series and a constant term, or

$$(3) \quad m_t = a_0 + a_1 p^e + \text{error term}$$

The appropriate p^e series (and the underlying coefficient of expectation, b_1) is the one that provides the best fit.

Table 1. Demand for Money in Greece
$$m_t = a_0 + a_1 p^e + \text{error term}$$

Sample period and data base	a_0	a_1	b_1	$\hat{r}$	MSE	R^2
January 1943–August 1944						
D-C money and prices	1.89 (15.20)	-3.43 (12.19)	0.18	0.64	0.02	0.97
Agapitides money and prices	1.91 (8.42)	-3.96 (11.62)	0.22	0.89	0.01	0.99
D-C money and sovereign price	-5.61 (44.52)	-3.42 (12.72)	0.19	0.71	0.02	0.98
Agapitides money and sovereign price	-5.50 (48.65)	-4.63 (20.96)	0.17	0.82	0.01	1.00
January 1943–October 1944						
D-C money and prices	0.90 (1.32)	-0.37 (2.43)	0.99*	0.94	0.05	0.95
Agapitides money and prices	2.03 (17.77)	-5.20 (21.86)	0.10	0.63	0.02	0.99
D-C money and sovereign price	-6.47 (12.2)	-0.37 (2.88)	0.99*	0.91	0.07	0.92
Agapitides money and sovereign price	-5.78 (35.94)	-3.49 (17.78)	0.17	0.75	0.03	0.99

Notes: $\hat{r}$ is the estimated autoregressive parameter. We have adjusted for first-order autocorrelation using an AR1 process. Numbers in parentheses are t statistics.

* This is the upper value at which the search was ended.

Sources: The Greek data are taken from Delivanis and Cleveland (1949) ("D-C") and Agapitides (1945).

Our purpose in re-estimating Cagan's demand for money function is to deal with the outlier problem empirically. As Sargent and Wallace (1973) explain, the type of monetary regime that Cagan believed caused the hyperinflation episodes is one in which the money supply is endogenous. Thus, the parameter estimates of Cagan's demand function are likely to be inconsistent. We did not deal with this problem.[20] We did, however, make some changes to the Cagan equation to reflect the suggestions of Cagan's econometric critics and to exploit our data more effectively. In particular, since the Durbin-Watson statistic for both Greece and Hungary indicate the presence of serial correlation in the disturbances, each was re-estimated with a correction for first-order autocorrelation.

Our results for Greece, reported in Table 1, show that when equation (3) is estimated over the Cagan period (January 1943-August 1944), both money series yield similar estimates of the relevant parameters regardless of which of the three price series is used to measure inflationary expectations.[21] When the period is extended to cover the final two months of this hyperinflation, however, the parameter estimates in the equations using the Delivanis and Cleveland money series exhibit instability regardless of which price series is used to measure inflationary expectations. This is not true when the Agapitides money series is used with either consumer or sovereign prices as measures of inflationary expectations.

We have also investigated the implications of the new data for another of Cagan's hypotheses: the conjecture that the coefficient of expectation rises as inflation intensifies. Using the Delivanis and Cleveland money and price series we find that the estimated coefficient of expectations rises from .18 to .26 as the (Cagan period) sample is reduced by excluding the first six observations (those from January through June 1943). This finding is consistent with Cagan's comment on the Greek results (p. 59). Alternatively, using the Agapitides money and sovereign price series, the coefficient of expectation remains

---

[20] For a broad-based criticism of demand for money studies and their implied inconsistent estimates, see Cooley and LeRoy (1981).

[21] Note that these results and those for Hungary II are similar to those reported by Cagan (1956, p. 43). Thus, the parameter values are fairly stable when corrected for serial correlation.

unchanged at 0.17 as the sample is first extended to include the late outliers and then reduced by excluding the first six observations.[22]

Use of the gold sovereign price raises several further issues. Frenkel (1977, 1979) discovered that during the German hyperinflation a forward market in foreign exchange functioned, and used the data it provided to extract measures of inflationary expectations. He found these measures significant in explaining German money demand. Abel and others (1979) extended Frenkel's work by supposing that both commodities and foreign monies were competing substitutes for domestic currency. This was possible because purchasing power parity did not hold on a monthly basis during the German hyperinflation. They show (Figure 1, p. 99) that there was substantial variation in the ratio of the consumer price index to the spot rate of exchange, and they estimate that the demand for money responded negatively both to the actual rate of consumer price inflation and the expected rate of inflation extracted from the relationship between the spot and forward exchange rate.[23]

Unfortunately, for the other hyperinflation episodes, forward exchange markets do not appear to have functioned as they did in Germany. This is true for both Greece and Hungary II. It should be remembered that the Greek episode occurred during the Axis occupation and the Hungarian during the Soviet occupation. There were no foreign exchange markets, no forward contracts, and no opportunities to speculate on the possibility that the drachma and the pengö might be returned to their prewar exchange values.

Nevertheless, for Greece the intensity of the inflation does vary depending on whether the consumer or sovereign price index is used, as shown in Figure 1.[24] We have attempted to explore the question of

---

[22] At various places in this study, we report only the results of alternative tests. The estimated equations from which these results are drawn are available on request from the authors.

[23] Holtfrerich (1977) also uses the relationship between spot and forward rates to account for the foreign component of the overall demand for German marks during the hyperinflation.

[24] Our research has failed to uncover data for Hungary comparable to the sovereign for Greece.

**Figure 1. Relative Prices in the Greek Hyperinflation,
January 1942 (= 100) to October 1944**

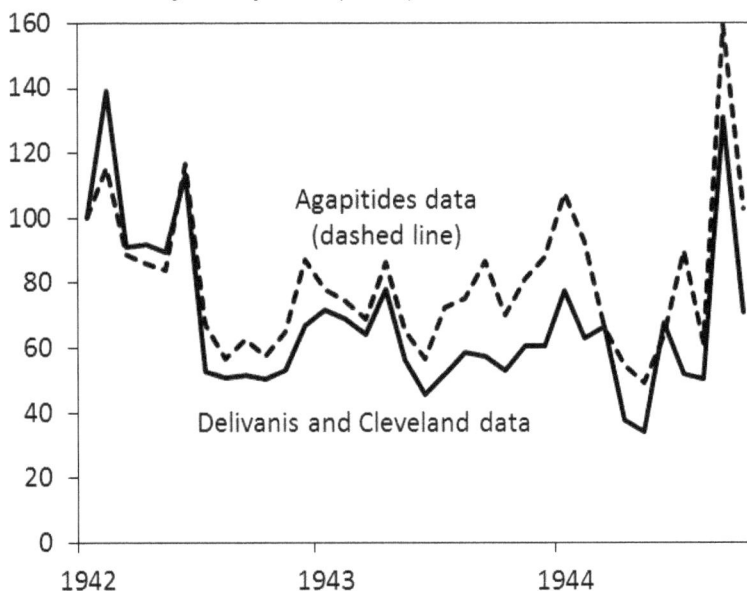

the appropriate deflator for the money supply and the appropriate inflation rate in two different contexts. We first used a technique employed by Abel and others (1979) to estimate the money demand in Greece with alternative deflators and alternative (pairs of) expected inflation variables. Three results are worthy of mention: (i) the Delivanis and Cleveland money supply combined with any measure of prices does not yield results with significant explanatory power for the expected inflation variables, (ii) with the Agapitides money supply, use of the sovereign price as the deflator produces a degree of explanatory power modestly superior to the other alternatives, and (iii) with real money balances based on the Agapitides money supply and sovereign prices, measuring expected inflation using the Agapitides price series does not add explanatory power to the equation which already has the expected sovereign price inflation as a regressor.[25]

---

[25] The estimates are based on Fair's (1970) two-stage technique. The instruments are as follows: time, time squared, lagged inflation, and lagged (log

Our second approach is based on an interesting discussion by Webb (1983) about the appropriate deflator for real money balances when more than one option is available for measuring inflationary expectations. He argues persuasively that the deflator should reflect the transactions needs of those holding money balances whereas the inflationary expectations term should reflect the opportunity cost of holding cash. We implemented Webb's notion by estimating the simple Cagan equation deflating the Delivanis and Cleveland and Agapitides money series by their respective consumer price series while using the sovereign price to measure inflationary expectations. For the Cagan period (January 1943-August 1944) the results are virtually indistinguishable from those in Table 1. When the period is extended to October 1944, the Delivanis and Cleveland equation does not exhibit functional instability, but the coefficients a_0 and a_1 are barely significant at the 5 percent level. This is not true with the Agapitides data. The results for both data sets and time periods, however, show a lower coefficient of expectation than those in Table 1 indicating a slower adjustment of expected to actual inflation.

We take these results as a modest confirmation of our choice of the Agapitides money supply and sovereign prices for a useful money demand specification.

The Hungarian results are shown in Tables 2 and 3. In obtaining them, we departed from Cagan in several ways. First, our data are different. As noted above, we have a complete time series of deposits at the Postal Savings Bank on a monthly interval. We have also separated indexed from nonindexed deposits at commercial banks, and,

---

of) real money balances. The estimates referred to in result (iii) in the text are as follows:

Using the log of Agapitides money deflated by the sovereign price as m, and the inflation rates of sovereign prices and Agapitides prices as p1 and p2, respectively, the estimates are

(1) $m_t = -6.77 - .79\hat{p}_{1t} + u_t - .68u_{t-1};$ MSE $= .147,$ $R^2 = .929$
     (8.90) (4.90)   (6.81)

(2) $m_t = -6.60 - .68\hat{p}_{1t} - .23\hat{p}_{2t} + u_t - .85u_{t-1};$ MSE $= .147, R^2 = .930$
     (11.11) (2.32) (0.60)   (5.42)

t values in parentheses.

Table 2. Demand for Money in Hungary, August 1945-May 1946

$$m_t = a_0 + a_1 p^e + \text{error term}$$

	a_0	a_1	b_1	$\hat{r}$	MSE	R^2
Aug. 1945-Feb. 1946						
Notes	3.06	-3.43	0.16	0.38	0.041	0.982
	(33.10)	(24.30)				
Notes and unindexed	3.34	-3.34	0.18	-0.57	0.003	0.999
deposits	(122.71)	(74.12)				
Aug. 1945-May 1946						
Notes	2.38	-1.85	0.16	0.77	0.009	0.729
	(9.13)	(7.94)				
Notes and unindexed	2.49	-1.65	0.14	-0.59	0.174	0.678
deposits	(6.27)	(4.18)				

Notes: $\hat{r}$ is the estimated autoregressive parameter. We have adjusted for first-order autocorrelation using an AR1 process. Numbers in parentheses are t statistics.

Sources: The Hungarian data are taken from the National Bank of Hungary's *Hungary in Statistical Tables* (1947b) and the *Annual* and *Monthly Reports* of the National Bank of Hungary (the central bank). The portion of indexed to nonindexed deposits is from Ausch (1958). Both price and money stock data were converted to natural logs. The estimates using notes makes use of the mixed weekly-monthly data.

for 1946, have uncovered weekly observations on the outstanding note issue of the central bank. For deflating these more frequent note issue observations and generating measures of expected inflation, a synchronous price series has been constructed by interpolating price index observations available on a similar, but not identical basis.[26] In

---

[26] Our method for doing this can be described as follows. Since Cagan used monthly data, the units for b_1, the adjustment parameter in (1), are in terms of (months)$^{-1}$. Presumably Cagan used this formulation because more frequent data were not available, not because he assumed that individuals revised their expectations of inflation only once a month. A consistent method for exploiting data from a period n days long would be to (a) convert the change in the logarithm of prices over the period to a monthly rate and (b) construct

**Table 3. Demand for Money in Hungary with Shift Variables,
August 1945-May 1946**

$$m_t = a_0 + a_1 D_t + a_2 p_t^e + a_3 \widehat{p}_t^e + \text{error term}$$

Money measure	a_0	a_1	a_2	a_3
Notes	3.07	-1.73	-3.46	2.45
	(20.21)	(7.93)	(12.31)	(7.62)
Notes and all deposits	3.34	-2.56	-3.21	3.11
	(33.01)	(12.72)	(16.61)	(13.51)
Notes and unindexed deposits	3.33	-2.37	-2.91	2.54
	(38.32)	(13.93)	(19.24)	(14.03)

Money measure	b_1	$\widehat{r}$	*MSE*	R^2
Notes	0.16	0.40	0.025	0.946
Notes and all deposits	0.19	-0.45	0.028	0.99
Notes and unindexed deposits	0.22	-0.50	0.022	0.993

Notes: See notes to Table 2.

Tables 2 and 3 we indicate which measures of the money stock have been used.

Second, to exploit the data, we introduced shift variables as regressors to capture the effect of the introduction of indexed deposits in Hungarian banks on January 10, 1946. These shift variables are of two types. The first is a traditional (constant term) shift dummy variable of the form:

$D_t = 0$ before January 10, 1946,
1 after January 10, 1946.

---

an expected inflation observation for time t according to (1a) $p_t^e = p_{t-1}^e + k e_t$ where $(b - k) = (1 - b)^{n/30}$. The reader may verify that if the inflation rate is constant for four successive periods which total one 30-day month ending at time t, use of (1a) will result in the same value for p_t^e as equation (1) above produces for one end-of-month observation. Using this procedure we have constructed a mixed monthly and weekly sample for p^e from August 1945.

The second allows for the possibility of a slope shift subsequent to the institution of indexed deposits and can be expressed as

$$(4) \quad \hat{p}_t^e = D_t p_t^e.$$

When the two additional regressors are combined with the basic Cagan formulation, the resulting estimating equation is

$$(5) \quad m_t = a_0 + a_1 D_t + a_2 p_t^e + a_3 \hat{p}_t^e.$$

When the simple Cagan equation is estimated, as shown in Table 2, the quality of fit undergoes a marked deterioration as the period is extended through May 1946.[27] Allowing for shifts in the demand schedule provides an estimate of money demand, as shown in Table 3, that does not deteriorate as the time interval is extended.[28]

Thus, for both Greece and Hungary, the use of new data permits a stable demand function to be estimated for the entire hyperinflation episode. It is no longer necessary to invoke the "reform effect."

III. The Monetary Regime and the Hyperinflation Process

Sargent and Wallace (1973) drew attention to the nature of the monetary regime or money supply process underlying Cagan's description of the hyperinflation episodes. Cagan had assumed that the governments in question resorted to creating money as the principal means for financing a more or less constant flow of real resources.

---

[27] Had we not accounted for the indexation of bank deposits in January 1946, but used only total deposits, the R^2 would have fallen to .541.

[28] In addition, these estimates are consistent with a shift in relative asset demands caused by the appearance of a new indexed form of money. If a substantial amount of transactions can be financed by using the new indexed deposits, one should expect a pronounced shift to them by those holding notes and unindexed deposits. Those who continue to use notes and unindexed deposits are likely to be individuals or businesses who are forced to do so by the nature of their transactions or who are inattentive. In either case, the remaining demand for unindexed money may be less sensitive to further increases in the rate of inflation. Our calculations bear out these observations.

Sargent and Wallace showed that such behavior can give rise to a stochastic money supply process in which inflation "Granger-causes" money growth. If, in addition, money growth does not "Granger-cause" inflation, Cagan's forecasting scheme in which only past inflation is used to forecast future inflation may be "rational." Using Cagan's data, they found that for Germany, Austria, and Hungary I, the hypothesis that inflation does not cause money growth can be rejected and the hypothesis that money growth does not cause inflation cannot be rejected. This supports the assumption of one-way causation which could make Cagan's forecasting procedure "rational." Sargent and Wallace found that the Greek data provide evidence of the opposite type of one-way causation, while the data from Poland, Russia, and Hungary II cannot reject the hypothesis that neither variable causes the other.[29]

The Sargent and Wallace results for Germany have recently been challenged by Protopapadakis (1983) who demonstrates that they are specific to the time period of the sample. By dropping the final observations from the sample he is able to obtain evidence consistent with one-way causality from money to prices. He suggests that the Sargent and Wallace causality result follows from a tendency in the final months of hyperinflation for the ordinary tax revenue of government to fall considerably, necessitating a greater reliance on the inflation tax and money issue.

In explaining his causality findings, Protopapadakis quotes two standard works on the German hyperinflation which state that the German central bank discounted large amounts of commercial paper, a tendency which Webb (1985) clarifies and which was also noted by Bomberger and Makinen (1975) for Germany as well as several other hyperinflation episodes. If a central bank has other objectives besides financing budget deficits, the government's revenue from money creation will diverge from the rate of money issue by the central bank. As a result, the feedback from prices to money may be altered in intensity and dependability.

Small sample sizes make it impossible for us to duplicate the tests

---

[29] Frenkel (1977, 1979), using his alternative measures of inflationary expectations, derives causality results for Germany that support Sargent and Wallace.

employed by Protopapadakis, but there are also reasons for believing that his findings may not generalize to the cases of Greece and Hungary. First, our causality tests are already run over periods that are slightly different from the hyperinflation periods suggested by a rigid application of Cagan's definition. For reasons given below, in the case of Greece we have excluded the first ten days of November 1944, the final climactic days of this episode. For Hungary, the final two months of maximum inflation are excluded.

Second, unlike Germany, the central banks in both Greece and Hungary were little more than appendages of the state treasury. Data given in Delivanis and Cleveland suggest that the note issue of the central bank is exactly equal to the budget deficit.[30] Bomberger and Makinen (1983) explain that over 90 percent of the notes and deposits supplied by the Hungarian central bank were for the government.[31] In both countries there was little or no credit granted to the private sector.

Because the samples from Greece and Hungary II have few observations, Sargent and Wallace (1973) did not use the type of lead-lag estimation common in making Granger tests. Rather, using an economizing technique suggested by Klein (1958), they estimated equations such as (6) and (7) that embody the alternative regimes:

$$(6)\ X_t = a_0 + a_1 \sum_{i=0}^{t-1} h^i m_{t-1} + a_2 h^t + a_3 m_{t+1} + a_4 m_{t+2} + a_5 t + e_t$$

---

[30] Delivanis and Cleveland (1949, p. 94) show the fraction of state revenue that took the form of notes advanced by the Bank of Greece. From their data on note issue it can be shown that all the notes were advanced to the credit of the state. The absence of credit to the private sector is consistent both with the massive fall in Greek national income and the collapse of commercial banking during the Axis occupation.

[31] While a detailed monthly breakout is not available, it is known that the central bank did issue some notes and deposits by discounting private sector bills. This was confined to the early months of the episode (July-December 1945) and amounted to less than 10 percent of the total discounts. During 1946, the central bank discounted only treasury bills. On May 31, 1946, out of a portfolio of 93.7 quintillion pengö of bills, 93.6 quintillion were treasury issues.

$$(7)\ m_t = b_0 + b_1 \sum_{i=0}^{t-1} n^i X_{t-1} + b_2 n^t + b_3 X_{t+1} + b_4 X_{t+2} + b_5 t + u_t$$

where m is the rate of growth of the money supply; X is the rate of inflation; t is a time trend; and h and n are constants which can take on values between -.99 and +.99, the correct value of which is determined by a best fit criterion; and e and u are disturbance terms. Like Sargent and Wallace, our search over h and n was carried out over the above interval in increments of 0.01. The equations were corrected for serial correlation using the method of Cochrane and Orcutt.

For Greece we used observations through October 31, 1944, rather than November 10 (the date of stabilization), because neither the Agapitides money nor price series had an observation for this date. Our estimates for Hungary necessitated several changes. First, we added a dummy variable to equations (6) and (7) to account for any shift in note demand that might have occurred with the introduction of indexation in January 1946. Second, because the sample is so small, we used three additional observations that occurred before the hyperinflation got underway. Third, our money stock variable consisted only of central bank notes. This seemed to us the relevant monetary variable given the type of money supply process Cagan had in mind. Fourth, we used observations only through May 1946. We did not use the final two months of this episode because the introduction of indexed Treasury currency in June and the indexation of Postal Savings bank deposits in July would have required additional dummy variables making an effective estimate impossible, given a degrees of freedom constraint.

Table 4 displays the F-statistics for the tests of the rival hypotheses underlying the alternative monetary regimes. In Table 5 we show the parameter estimates of (6) and (7).

For Greece we have used sovereign prices and both money series. The hypothesis that money growth does not cause inflation cannot be rejected at the 95 percent level for either money series. The hypothesis that inflation does not cause money growth can be rejected at the 95 percent level for the Delivanis and Cleveland money series and at the

Table 4. *F*-Statistics for Greece and Hungary (*X* versus *M*)

Country	*m* regressed on *X*	*X* regressed on *m*	Degrees of freedom	Critical values of *F* 0.05	0.01
Greece —Delivanis and Cleveland	2.53	6.58	11	3.98	7.20
—Agapitides	0.24	8.21	11	3.98	7.20
Hungary	3.89	967.49	2	19.00	99.00

99 percent level for the Agapitides series.[32] A similar result is found for Hungary II: one-way causation from inflation to money growth is indicated. The results are consistent with the Sargent and Wallace conjecture about causation and the rationality of Cagan's expectation-generating mechanism.

IV. Conclusions

The results presented in this paper reinforce those of Phillip Cagan. By using new sources of data, we believe we have been able to resolve one of the puzzles originating in his work: why there were outliers in Greece and Hungary II. It is not necessary to assume that economic agents in these two countries were able to anticipate an end to hyperinflation while still lacking an objective basis for such a forecast. Moreover, causation evidence based on these data are consistent with the monetary regime and the expectation-generating mechanism assumed by Cagan. When this result is added to those obtained by Sargent and Wallace and Tang and Hu, it means that only two of the eight hyperinflations (based on data for the full sample) have not been

---

[32] When the Delivanis and Cleveland money and price series are used, we obtain results similar to those of Sargent and Wallace, i.e., we cannot reject the hypothesis that the regime was one in which money growth causes prices and we can reject the alternative that prices cause money growth. When the Agapitides money and price series are used, however, we cannot reject the hypothesis that money growth does not cause prices (at the 95 percent level) and, while the alternative that prices do not cause money growth can be rejected at the 95 percent level, it cannot be rejected at the 99 percent level.

found to fit the pattern of one-way causation from inflation to money growth.

We recommend that the new data we have uncovered should be used in addition to or as a substitute for the traditional data sets. It may be useful to repeat some of the tests from this large literature using these data.

**Table 5. Greece, February 1943-August 1944;
Hungary, April 1945-March 1946**

A. Inflation Regressed on Money Creation

	a_0	a_1	a_2	H	a_3
Greece	-69.37	-0.327	68.6	0.99	1.592
—D-C	(0.519)	(0.849)	(0.517)		(3.171)
Greece	-107.4	-0.430	106.3	0.99	1.474
—Agapitides	(1.01)	(1.476)	(1.008)		(3.588)
Hungary	-0.434	1.124	-0.288	-0.89	0.668
	(29.866)	(19.055)	(9.402)		(16.362)

	a_4	a_5	a_6	R^2	$\hat{r}$
Greece	-0.424	0.737		0.851	-0.17
—D-C	(1.401)	(0.559)			
Greece	-0.243	1.109		0.86	-0.51
—Agapitides	(0.957)	(1.06)			
Hungary	-0.684	0.181	-0.947	0.999	-0.54
	(56.048)	(43.3)	(34.431)		

B. Money Creation Regressed on Inflation

	b_0	b_1	b_2	n	b_3
Greece	59.04	0.259	-58.299	0.99	0.024
—D-C	(0.694)	(2.221)	(0.692)		(0.209)
Greece	92.8	0.238	-91.799	0.99	0.051
—Agapitides	(1.525)	(2.852)	(1.522)		(0.623)
Hungary	174.66	0.212	-172.82	0.99	0.265
	(0.455)	(1.107)	(0.455)		(3.342)

	b_4	b_5	b_6	R^2	$\hat{r}$
Greece	-0.268	-0.599		0.935	0.01
—D-C	(2.346)	(0.725)			
Greece	-0.025	-0.918		0.942	0.01
—Agapitides	(0.309)	(1.552)			
Hungary	-0.05	-1.733	-0.691	0.984	-0.95
	(0.380)	(0.450)	(2.192)		

Notes: The numbers in parentheses are t values. The coefficients of

a_6 and b_6 apply only to the Hungarian estimates. These coefficients are for the dummy variables designed to capture the effects of instituting indexed bank deposits. The dummy variable takes a value of 1 for January 1946 and zero for all other months (experimentation placing the dummy in other months failed to yield a significant coefficient). The monthly series for Hungary consists only of monthly observations (i.e., the mixed monthly-weekly series is not used). All data are converted to natural logs. The estimates were corrected for serial correlation using the Cochrane-Orcutt procedure. $\hat{r}$ is the estimate of the autoregressive parameter. "D-C" is Delivanis and Cleveland (1945).

Appendix

Table A1. Data for Post-World War II Hungarian Hyperinflation

Date	Price index (July 1945 = 1)	Notes (bn)	Total deposits (bn)	Indexed deposits (bn)	Nonindexed deposits (bn)
1945					
July 31	1.2	16.3	5.4		
Aug. 31	1.9	24.4	6.7		
Sept. 30	4.2	41.9	8.8		
Oct. 31	27.1	106.9	14.7		
Nov. 30	146.9	355.5	37.3		
Dec. 31	468.7	765.4	98.5		
1946					
Jan. 7	518.0	778.2			
Jan. 15	595.9	942.9			
Jan. 23	645.5	1,113.2			
Jan. 31	820.6	1,646.4	281.5	29.6	251.9
Feb. 7	992.3	1,921.8			
Feb. 15	1,422.3	2,721.7			
Feb. 23	3197. 1	3,975.9			
Feb. 28	4,914.8	5,237.8	1,579.7	562.3	1,013.3
Mar. 7	6,310.7	9,339.4			
Mar. 15	7,942.6	15,568.4			
Mar. 23	11,968.1	22,292.4			
Mar. 31	21,163.0	34,001.5	16,831.4	8,673.3	8,160.0
Apr. 7	36,315.5	59,397.1			
Apr. 15	73,865.4	110,304.5			
Apr. 23	169,396.9	181,316.6			
Apr. 30	404,339.4	434,304.0	443,742.6	193,881.0	247,954.4
May 7	946,002.0	1,083,817.4			
May 15	3,506,047.9	2,913,891.4			
May 23	18,624,714.6	14,118,548.7			
May 31	127.04mn	65.6mn	125.9mn	70.491mn	55.784mn
July 7	575.07mn	501.44mn			
June 15	8.3874bn	4.6914bn			
June 23	319.49bn	78.393bn			
June 30	10.794trn	6.2775trn	23.594trn	16.593trn	
July 7	73.056qdrn	3.5616qdrn			
July 15	3.8708qntn	76.037qdrn			
July 23	1.131sxtn	41.232qdrn			

Date	Money supply (billions)		Price indices		
	Agapitides	Delevanis-Cleveland	Agapitides (1940 = 1)	Delevanis-Cleveland (1940 = 1)	Gold sovereign (1,000 drachmas)
1941					
Jan.	16.2	16.2	1.06	1.13	1.06
Feb.	17.0	17.0	1.06	1.13	1.06
Mar.	19.3	19.3	1.10	1.16	1.06
Apr.	21.3	21.3	1.13	1.16	1.06
May	22.7	21.3	1.57	1.45	4.93
June	24.1	24.1	2.00	2.00	7.40
July	24.0	24.0	3.19	3.01	8.00
Aug.	29.1	29.1	4.05	3.80	11.22
Sept.	33.8	33.8	5.67	5.01	12.13
Oct.	39.1	39.1	7.57	7.19	20.80
Nov.	43.5	43.5	12.45	10.09	28.65
Dec.	48.8	48.8	16.13	14.91	21.13
1942					
Jan.	53.0	53.0	18.82	16.08	21.50
Feb.	58.5	58.5	26.20	18.59	21.50
Mar.	67.9	67.9	29.69	24.70	37.25
Apr.	79.1	79.1	40.56	32.50	50.50
May	92.2	92.2	46.28	37.10	59.03
June	109.8	109.8	58.44	51.30	58.83
July	132.2	132.3	60.21	65.60	130.50
Aug.	155.1	155.1	87.22	83.20	196.21
Sept.	168.8	185.6	97.82	102.0	217.53
Oct.	211.6	238.3	155.9	151.9	352.87
Nov.	264.2	289.7	127.1	132.6	273.00
Dec.	307.6	335.1	89.1	99.0	151.72
1943					
Jan.	353.0	367.8	90.7	84.2	144.35
Feb.	390.2	401.9	81.3	74.8	134.71
Mar.	442.1	465.7	90.8	82.9	161.32
Apr.	510.5	560.2	116.5	109.9	170.50
May	593.7	622.8	117.8	116.9	239.63
June	670.6	712.7	122.1	130.1	307.18

Table A2. Data for Greek Hyperinflation

Date	Money supply (billions)		Price indices		
	Agapitides	Delevanis-Cleveland	Agapitides (1940 = 1)	Delevanis-Cleveland (1940 = 1)	Gold sovereign (1,000 drachmas)
1943					
July	804.2	869.3	146.3	174.6	322.24
Aug.	973.7	1,062.1	182.7	200.0	355.23
Sept.	1,154.1	1,301.7	211.4	271.7	419.12
Oct.	1,475.8	1,734.7	354.6	400.7	762.40
Nov.	2,047.1	2,303.9	663.2	761.7	1,253.08
Dec.	2,666.3	3,199.2	828.5	1,026.1	1,562.89
1944					
Jan.	3,444.5	3,989.6	2,114.7	2,509.0	3,112.00
Feb.	4,565.0	5,167.8	3,052.0	3,826.0	5,520.00
Mar.	6,401.0	7,722.2	8,594.3	7,290.0	14,720.00
Apr.	13,157	16,839.0	11,814.6	14,620.0	35,700.00
May	26,381	31,237.7	30,713.0	37,750.0	102,964.00
June	45,630	61,133.1	74,922.0	60,390.0	126,260.87
July	89,048	131,192.9	165,954	244,740	364,230.77
Aug.	238,101	552,851.9	1,052,280	1,099,070	2,390,846.15
Sept.	1,696,691	7,305,500	21,223,000	22,082,000	18,528,000
Oct.	30.483mn	694.57mn	1.6041bn	1.9863bn	2.5831bn

Table caption: **Table A2. Data for Greek Hyperinflation (continued)**

9

The Transition from Hyperinflation to Stability: Some Evidence

(with G. Thomas Woodward)[*]

I. Introduction

The nature, characteristics, and functioning of monetary regimes is central to monetary economics. Special interest has often focused on the type of regime that produced the world's episodes of hyperinflation and on changes to bring about successful stabilization of prices (Sargent 1982, Bomberger and Makinen 1983, and Makinen 1984).

This paper attempts to adduce some evidence of these regime changes from data on money and prices. Specifically, it demonstrates on the basis of changes in the Granger causal ordering of the data that the monetary regimes existing before stabilization did indeed come to an end. In this way, the paper follows up on the work of Sargent and Wallace (1973) in which causation tests on hyperinflation data provide statistical undergirding for the qualitative descriptions provided in the historical accounts of the stabilizations.

In this century, hyperinflation has occurred in European countries seven times: in Germany, Austria, Hungary, Poland, and Russia following the First World War, and in Greece and Hungary at the end of World War II. All of the episodes have been the subject of research. In the most famous of studies of hyperinflations, Cagan (1956) hypothesized that each was the result of a regime in which governments attempted to extract by means of money creation

[*] The authors wish to thank Phillip Cagan, Thomas Dernburg, William Bomberger, and Robert Anderson for their comments on an earlier draft of this paper. They also gratefully acknowledge the helpful comments of the two referees.

amounts of real resources that could only be obtained through accelerating inflation.

In a paper whose primary purpose was to explore circumstances under which adaptive expectations are rational, Sargent and Wallace demonstrated that such a regime will be one in which causation in the sense of Granger (1969) runs from inflation to money. Since the creation of money to pay for resources generates inflation, each subsequent effort by the government to secure resources by means of note issue will require still larger quantities of notes—and hence, greater inflation. As a consequence, note issue comes to depend on previous price increases; that is, inflation "causes" money growth. If expectations are rational, prices will be raised in anticipation of future note issue. Since the note issue is determined by the inflation rate, the past history of prices provides market participants the information required to set new prices. Money drops out of the chain of causation so that money ceases to "cause" inflation.

This hypothesis is well suited to a Granger-Sims style causation test. If the Sargent and Wallace hypothesis is correct, then the past history of prices should predict money. On the other hand, the past history of money should be expected to add little or nothing to the ability of past values of prices to predict current prices. Granger-causation is precisely this. If lagged values of prices and money explain current values of money better than past values of money alone, prices are said to Granger-cause money. If lagged values of money and prices fail to explain current prices better than lagged prices alone, then money does not Granger-cause prices. These two results would indicate unidirectional influence of prices on money; no feedback from money on prices would occur.

Testing for causation along the lines suggested by Sims (1972), Sargent and Wallace find support for their reasoning in the results for Germany, Austria, and Hungary I (see their Tables 1 through 5). Results for Greece suggest that causality is two-way—both from inflation to money and money to inflation.[1] For the remaining three cases, Poland, Russia, and Hungary II, their evidence suggests that

---

[1] The Greek evidence is mixed. At a 5 percent level, two-way causality is present. However, at the 1 percent level the evidence is consistent only with the hypothesis that causality runs from money to inflation.

there is neither causality from inflation to money nor from money to inflation. However, Bomberger and Makinen (1983) have recently furnished evidence that the Cagan data set for money compiled for Hungary II, used by Sargent and Wallace, commingles indexed and nonindexed deposits. Given Sargent and Wallace's explanation for their causality findings, one would expect them to want to use only nonindexed money for the purposes of their test. When only non-indexed money is used, Anderson, Bomberger, and Makinen (1988) show that the results for Hungary II are consistent with Sargent and Wallace's principal findings: causality runs from inflation to money. Using an alternative money series for Greece, they reached the same conclusion.

These econometric results, and the behavioral model which predicts them, are consistent not only with a regime in which a fixed quantity of resources is being extracted by means of money creation, but also a monetary authority following a real bills doctrine (Sargent 1977). In the real bills case, an effort to discount private paper at a below equilibrium interest rate leads to overissue of currency. The resulting inflation will increase the nominal quantity of money that the private sector wishes to borrow at a given real interest rate. If this demand is satisfied by the central bank, an even larger note issue is generated. Again, the rate of inflation "causes" money growth.

Whether a real bills regime or a regime in which the government is attempting to secure resources for its own use by means of inflation, we know that in terms of our conventional notion of causality, it is money growth that is causing inflation. We can say this because controlling money growth is a prerequisite for controlling inflation. In Sargent's words this conventional definition of causation is "invariance with respect to intervention," that is, money causes inflation because, regardless of the institutional rules determining money growth, "the stochastic process for inflation is an invariant function of the stochastic process governing money creation."

Granger causality is merely defined by whether money is of any use in predicting inflation. Where money growth is endogenous, and dependent on past inflation, it does not predict or "cause" inflation in the Granger sense, even though halting the money growth would halt the inflation. This is why Granger causality is so well suited to determining the existence of a certain institutional setting or regime, and why changes in the Granger causal ordering can tell us if that regime has changed.

The institutional reforms that successfully stabilized these hyperinflations were (1) the recreation of an independent central bank with sufficient autonomy to refuse the government's request for notes on the basis of unsecured credit, i.e., the central bank was no longer obliged to provide the monetary wherewithal to allow the government to command a more or less constant fraction of real resources, and (2) reform of government's fiscal practices to sufficiently increase tax revenue and reduce expenditures to bring the budget to near balance and reduce the need for money financing.[2] Where these reforms were implemented, they should have severed the linkage between past inflation and new money issue and, therefore, changed the Granger causal ordering of the data. Although tests of Granger causality were conducted by Sargent and Wallace on the hyperinflation data, none have been undertaken for the post-stabilization periods. Such follow-up tests, however, would provide statistical support for the hypothesis that it was indeed the endogenous money supply regime that generated the hyperinflations and that it was the termination of these regimes that brought stability.

II. Methodology

In many studies of Granger causality (including the Sargent and Wallace study), the researchers have chosen to use the Sims version of the test. Sims shows that the Granger formulation is equivalent to estimating the following two equations:

$$(1) \quad x_t = \sum_{i=-n}^{n} z_i m_{t-i} + e'_t$$

---

[2] These studies have concentrated on the lessons relevant for stabilization in market-oriented economies and thus have not included the stabilization in Soviet Russia.

$$(2) \quad m_t = \sum_{i=-n}^{n} h_i x_{t-i} + e_t''$$

where m and x are the growth rates of money and prices respectively. These are the equations estimated by Sargent and Wallace for the German episode.

If money Granger-causes prices, then future prices will significantly add to past prices in explaining current money. Similarly, if prices Granger-cause money, then future money will add to the ability of past money to explain current prices. By subjecting the leads to joint tests of significance in each equation, the null hypothesis of no causation can be rejected. Sargent and Wallace, whose study supported the hypothesis of unidirectional causation of money by prices, used 4 leads and 6 lags in each equation.

For our study we have chosen the same lead-lag specification as Sargent and Wallace in order to maximize the comparability of the results.[3] Thus, we follow their example by estimating equations (1) and (2). Rates of growth of prices and notes are used. The equations are estimated ordinary least squares and corrected for serial correlation using "quasi differenced" values (i.e., they are first estimated by least squares and then the data are multiplied by $(1 - \rho)$, where ρ (rho) is the least squares estimate of the first order autoregressive parameter— again, the same technique used by Sargent and Wallace). F statistics are computed for the leads in each equation.

The time series used covering the post-stabilization periods are: Austria, September 1922-December 1925; Germany, December 1923-October 1926; Greece, January 1946-March 1948; Hungary I, January 1924-December 1926, Hungary II, August 1946-December 1948; and Poland, January 1924-December 1926.[4] We aimed for three years of data for each country where possible.

Our most significant departure from Sargent and Wallace is in the

---

[3] Limited experimentation with other lead-lag patterns failed to alter our conclusions.

[4] While these time intervals comprise the periods from which our observations are taken, the actual regressions are run over somewhat shorter periods because the regression equations use leads and lags.

use of note issue for our money variable. Sargent and Wallace included deposits in their measure (making it akin to M2). We view the use of notes as more appropriate to the Cagan hypothesis. If the government is trying to claim a fixed amount of resources by means of inflation, it can do so only through the creation of base money. Money created within the banking system will not add to the government's claim on resources.[5] While the government may issue bonds to claim more resources, and while these bonds might be purchased by banks as part of the deposit expansion process, they would only have been so in lieu of lending to the private sector, and would not increase the size of the money supply. Hence, only note issue can truly represent the claim placed on the real resources by the government through an inflation tax.

While an end to the causal nexus from prices to money can be expected as a consequence of stabilization, it should not be expected that a money-to-price causal link will reappear. Successful stabilizations are accompanied by rapid remonetizations of the economy. This permits a large increase in the money supply without a resulting price increase as agents increase their holdings of real balances.[6] This fact suggests another limitation of Granger-Sims style testing. Relationships between variables such as money and prices can too easily be overwhelmed by third factors—in this case by the effect of revised inflation expectations on money demand.

Yet, limitations imposed by data availability prevent the use of more complete tests, such as the development of money demand functions that could accommodate the rapid change in desired real balances and reveal the relationship between money and prices. Similarly, series on real interest rates, which would provide further statistical evidence on

---

[5] For the most part, very little deposit money existed by the end of the hyperinflations. Considerable time passed before the revival of deposit banking occurred after stabilization. Only in Germany were deposits a significant fraction of the money supply.

[6] Our data show the following relationship between the percentage rise in high-powered money and the percentage rise in the price level for each country, respectively, 36 months after stabilization: Germany (141.7, 2.9), Austria (290.7, 5.9), Hungary I (309.2, 77.3), Poland (485.8, 65.4), Greece (556.8, 54.1), and Hungary II (692.22, 22.5).

Table 1. F-Statistics (X versus M) for European Hyperinflations

Country	X regressed on M	M regressed on X	Degrees of freedom	Critical values of F	
				.05	.01
Germany	0.25	0.77	4/10	3.48	5.99
Austria	1.78	1.03	4/15	3.06	4.89
Hungary I	0.83	4.12	4/11	3.36	5.67
Poland	0.36	1.80	4/11	3.36	5.67
Hungary II	14.66	0.125	4/4	6.39	15.98
Greece	0.96	0.165	4/2	19.25	99.25

the nature of the monetary regimes before and after stabilization, are impossible to construct. Lacking these, Granger causality tests are the best econometric approach we can think of to use to investigate the nature of these regimes, in spite of their limitations.

III. Results

Our overall results are summarized in Table 1.[7] In five of the six cases we cannot reject either the hypothesis that inflation does not cause money or that money does not cause inflation. In other words, our results indicate an absence of an influence running from inflation to money or from money to inflation. In the single exception, the case of Hungary II, we are left with a somewhat ambiguous result analogous to that obtained by Sargent and Wallace for Greece. At the 5 percent level of significance, the critical value of the F statistic is such that the results would suggest that causality runs from inflation to money. However; at the more demanding 1 percent level, the Hungary II results conform to the others.

The near uniformity of our results is in accord with salient characteristics of the various stabilizations noted in the descriptive studies of these episodes. A central conclusion of these studies is that the stabilizations were successful because they were accompanied by or produced by a regime change that altered the behavioral rules of

---

[7] Detailed results for individual countries are available on request.

conduct of central banks. When our results are compared with Sargent and Wallace's (see their Tables 1 through 5) we can confirm that the behavior of the central bank did change in Germany, Austria, Hungary I, and Greece. No longer were these central banks the handmaidens of the respective fiscal authorities supplying high-powered money on demand.

Each stabilization had as a central tenet the reconstruction of an independent and autonomous central bank. As such, the reform legislation enjoined the central bank from advancing notes to the fiscal authorities (government) on an unsecured basis, i.e., on the basis of treasury bills. In all cases, the respective central banks lived within this legal restraint for at least the period of our study.[8]

The one anomalous result—that for Hungary II—tempts us to find an explanation. Admittedly, any such explanation, *ex post*, amounts to a rationalization. But it is hard to pass up the opportunity to discuss the Hungary II experience in more detail, since certain unique aspects of its stabilization program can explain this result.

The econometric evidence would suggest no change in regime. Yet the descriptive evidence presented by Bomberger and Makinen (1983) indicate a regime change. Except for an initial overdraft, the government was forbidden to borrow from the central bank. An inspection of the weekly balance sheets of the National Bank of Hungary (the central bank) for the post-stabilization period confirms that the government lived within this legal prohibition. This suggests an inconsistency between the econometric results and descriptive treatment of the stabilization.

The answer may lie in the operation of monetary policy following stabilization. In any regime, some mechanism must exist to help authorities determine how much money to create. In a regime in which stability of the price level is the primary goal, but in which the economy must be remonetized, the central bank faces a dilemma about the rate of note issue. Money creation must be restricted to hold prices steady, yet the reduction in inflationary expectations resulting from

---

[8] To be more precise, in the case of Germany, Poland, and Hungary II, the governments were allowed an initial overdraft at the central bank of a fixed amount in order to finance expenditures until the new taxes imposed as a part of the fiscal reforms yielded sufficient revenue.

stabilization requires a rapid expansion of the monetary base. A constant money growth rate is not very useful at such an early stage in the stabilization program; it would likely be disastrous.

Insofar as the post World War I stabilizations were concerned, exchange rates provided a target for policy. Those episodes took place concurrently with the reconstruction of the international gold (or gold exchange) standard. Indeed, these programs were an integral part of the establishment and maintenance of fixed exchange rates.[9] In Greece, the third and successful effort at stabilization in January 1946 involved the central bank setting a fixed exchange rate for the drachma in terms of dollars and pound sterling, and using open market operations in gold sovereigns to prevent any divergence between the market and the official rate. Such central bank behavior was identical to that of the central banks in the four World War I stabilizations discussed by Sargent (1982).

It was really only in Hungary II that this was not an option. The August 1, 1946 stabilization was accompanied by the introduction of a new unit of account, the forint. The forint was given a gold content but was not itself convertible into gold or foreign currencies. Indeed, in the economic chaos in Europe following World War II, during which Hungary was not yet a Soviet satellite, little foreign trade was carried on outside carefully arranged official agreements. In this environment, maintaining a fixed exchange rate had no meaning since a free market in foreign exchange did not function. However, the Hungarian central bank was intent on stabilizing the internal price level. While it continued to maintain real interest rates at low levels, it allocated credit carefully, and adhered to ceilings set on the monthly issue of notes. If the Bank used the behavior of the price level as a guide to setting these ceilings, it could explain the anomalous econometric results of causality in Hungary II.

---

[9] We do not mean to suggest that a gold standard or fixed exchange rate system will always produce price level stability. Our interpretation of our results is made in the context of a particular historical setting. In some other setting, the gold standard could be compatible with inflation or even deflation. Moreover, one could envision other monetary regimes that would be conducive to price level stability and an absence of findings of causality from money to inflation or from inflation to money.

In all the other episodes, the targeting procedures used would have made note issuance dependent on variables other than the price level, and based on movements (in foreign exchange rates or sovereign prices) that could be monitored on a weekly and even daily basis. But if the price level was the criterion for setting money growth targets, causality from monthly observations of prices to money would result. It merely would shift from a direct to an inverse relation.

Inspection of the coefficient signs (not shown) in the Hungary II causation tests indicates that this may, indeed, be what happened. In the equation with money as the dependent variable, all of the lagged inflation rate coefficients are negative. This is also the case for the first and largest of the lead note coefficients in the equation with inflation as the dependent variable.

While the descriptive accounts of the other stabilizations explicitly address the means by which monetary policy was conducted, and confirm that the exchange rates and the sovereign price did function as targets, we cannot find any information on how policy was conducted in Hungary II. We know that monthly ceilings on note issuance were set with an aim to controlling inflation. We also know that the initial issuance of money was calculated to yield a particular price level in accordance with what was known about the Hungarian economy. But we do not know how the monthly ceilings were determined in the absence of any market indicators such as were available in the other episodes.

This suggests a line of further research on the conduct of the second Hungarian stabilization. But it also raises the possibility that the anomalous Hungary II result is the exception that proves the rule. Given the alternative targets available to the Hungarian authorities for determining money growth, it is quite possible that prices were used, so that the regime change was uniquely one from a positive inflation-to-money-growth connection to a negative one.

IV. Conclusion

Overall, the econometric evidence presented in this paper is in close conformity with three descriptive treatments of the end to some of the most turbulent episodes in monetary history.

The Cagan hypothesis that the great hyperinflations were generated by governments' attempt to garner revenue through money creation has specific implications for causality between money and inflation. Sargent and Wallace adduce evidence that is largely consistent with this hypothesis. Our research further confirms this hypothesis by showing that the implied causality disappeared after the monetary regime changed. In addition, the comparative results for Hungary II versus the other episodes provide hints concerning the methods used by the monetary authorities for gauging the proper rate of monetary expansion during the stabilization.

Appendix

Data Sources

The money supply series selected is confined to the notes of the central bank for several reasons. Some countries used only currency, as deposit banking was in its infancy. In others, the hyperinflation led to the almost exclusive use of currency (for an explanation of this phenomenon see Bomberger and Makinen 1980 [chapter 3 in this book]) and, in the post-stabilization period, deposit banking was slow to revive. In one instance, deposit data are present, but not for a long enough period (we desired a minimum of 36 observations).

Austria

Notes for 1922 and 1923 were taken from Sargent (1982); for 1924, 1925, and 1926 from issues of *Regelmathige Jahressitzung der Generalversammlung der Österreichischen Nationalbank* (Vienna: Österreichische Nationalbank). Wholesale prices were taken from *Statistische Nachrichten*, v. 4 (Vienna: Österreichisches Statistisches Zentralamt, 1926), and *Memorandum sur les monnaies et les banques centrales, 1913-1925*, v. 2 (Geneva: League of Nations, 1926).

Germany

For the post-stabilization period in Germany various note issues are

available; in particular, those of the Rentenbank, an intermediate step in
the reconstruction of an autonomous central bank. Thus, the money
series is a combination of Reichbank and Rentenbank notes, coin, and
other energency note issues (generally by state-owned enterprises).
Notes and wholesale prices were gathered from the Report of the
Reichbank; Statistishes Reichsamt (Wirtschaft und Statistik),
*Vierteljahrshefte zur Konjunkturforschung, Herausgegeben vom Institut für
Konjunkturforschung* (Berlin: Verlag von Reimar Hobbing, 1926); *and
Memorandum on Currency and Central Banks, 1913-1924,* v. 1 (Geneva:
League of Nations, 1925).

Greece

The note issue and price data were taken from Delivanis and Cleveland
(1949). Private deposits, while present, were unimportant until 1949.
Alternative price indices are available. Because they contained
commodities and services whose prices were either frozen or subject to
state control, we chose the market price of the gold sovereign, the
principal alternative to commodities as an inflation hedge, as our price
index.

Hungary I

Notes were taken from the annual reports of the National Bank of
Hungary for 1926 and 1927 and wholesale prices for these years were
gathered from *Annuaire statistique hongrois* (Budapest: Office central de
statistique du Royaume de Hongrie).

Hungary II

Notes and wholesale prices were taken from the monthly bulletins of
the National Bank of Hungary for 1946, 1947, and 1948. Deposit data
are available for only a part of this period—1946 through mid-1948.
They lack complete coverage (deposits ranged in size relative to notes
from 23 percent in August 1946 to 76 percent in June 1948).

Poland

The money series consists both of the note issues of the Bank of Poland and the Polish Treasury (both were legal tender). Money and wholesale prices were compiled from *Rocznik statystyki Rzeczypospolitej Polskiej* (Warsaw: Bank Polski); *Compte rendu des opérations de la Banque de Pologne* 1924, 1925, and 1926 (Warsaw: Bank Polski); *Memorandum sur les monnaies et les banques centrales, 1923-1925* (Geneva: League of Nations, 1926); and *La Banque de Pologne et la monnaie polonaise* (Paris: Jan Dziewanowski, 1933).

10

The Taiwanese Hyperinflation and Stabilization of 1945-1952

(with G. Thomas Woodward)[*]

On the list of recognized hyperinflations one will not find Taiwan.[1] Its hyperinflation of 1945-49 has either gone unrecognized or is assumed to be part of the hyperinflation then occurring on the mainland of China during its civil war. Yet, the Chinese Nationalist government attempted to isolate Taiwan from the mainland inflation by creating it as an independent currency area. And during the later stages of the civil war it was able to end the hyperinflation on Taiwan, something it was unable to do on the mainland despite two attempts.

The experience on Taiwan is worth recounting. Hitherto our knowledge of stabilizing hyperinflation economies has been confined to European episodes. On Taiwan we can examine how an economy in a different institutional setting reacted to the traditional tools of monetary and fiscal policy.[2] In addition, a unique aspect of this stabilization was the creation of bank deposits offering high real interest rates. These deposits appear to have played a role in the stabilization, and help explain the unusual behavior of real money balances during the stabilization period. Finally, unlike most of the European episodes, the stabilization program on Taiwan was undertaken with little prospect of balancing the budget or bringing money creation under control, with two and a half years passing before

[*] The authors wish to thank Robert Worden and Donald DeGlopper for assistance in translating and two referees for their numerous helpful comments.
[1] The Taiwanese episode accords with the definition originated by Cagan (1956).
[2] The relevance of the mainland stabilization is limited since it occurred after the Communist takeover in 1949-50.

price stability was achieved. It, therefore, provides insight into the public's perception of and reaction to stabilization policies. The events cast doubt on some of Sargent's (1982) conclusions about the nature and perception of regime changes and the rationality of expectations.

I. Hyperinflation

In November 1945, Taiwan reverted to Chinese sovereignty. A hyperinflation was then in progress on the mainland, the legacy of war with Japan financed mainly by currency issues, a method of finance continued during the ensuing civil war. On Taiwan, however, the notes of the Bank of Taiwan (which was basically a commercial bank) remained the principal medium of exchange for five more months. The inflation there was under way as a consequence of the release of pent-up demand suppressed during the war by price controls and rationing.

To isolate the major areas of the country previously ruled by Japan (Manchuria and Taiwan) from the ongoing inflation, the Nationalist government created each as a separate currency area tied to the rest of China by adjustable exchange rates. The provincial government of Taiwan was authorized to adjust the rate according to purchasing power parity as measured by the price level prevailing in Shanghai and in Taipei, Taiwan's capital. Despite frequent adjustments, the Taiwanese currency was usually undervalued.

In May 1946, the Bank of Taiwan was authorized by the Nationalist government to issue a new local currency, the "taipi," in an amount of 5.3 billion yuan (the unit of account on the mainland). There were no reserves for the taipi and the amount that could be issued was subject to approval of the mainland government. Thereafter, the public finance practices of the Taiwanese government paralleled those on the mainland in that a major source of revenue was derived from the inflation tax. While detailed budget data are not available for Taiwan during this period, an inference can be drawn from the balance sheet of the Bank of Taiwan and those of other leading banking institutions. In June 1948, 78.2 percent of all outstanding loans made by lending institutions were made by the Bank of Taiwan, of which 70.3 percent were made to the government of Taiwan or its enterprises. By May 1949, the eve of stabilization, almost 90 percent of all loans had their origin in the Bank of Taiwan, with nearly 82 percent destined for the public sector. The clear implication is that the budget was seriously out of balance.

As hyperinflations intensify, the flight from money reduces the base against which the inflation tax can be levied. To obtain the same level of real resources then requires a higher tax rate, and inflation races ahead of the accelerating rate of money creation. This was true in Taiwan. The average monthly rise in the Taipei wholesale price index during 1946, 1947, and 1948 was, respectively, 11.3, 18.5, and 22.5 percent. For the first five months of 1949, prior to the June 15 stabilization, the average rise was 53 percent (during May, prices rose 102 percent). The corresponding average monthly rise in the money supply was, respectively, 9.8, 9.8, 23.8, and 23.5 percent (39.5 percent for May).[3]

The literature on hyperinflation episodes often attributes the rise in prices to a decline in real income. Where the data are available, however, the decline cannot account for the rise in prices. Even though data on real output are not available for 1945 and 1946, similar conclusions can be drawn concerning the role of real output in Taiwan's hyperinflation. While real output declined during World War II as a result of Allied bombing (falling in 1944 to less than half its 1942 level), it underwent substantial revival from 1947 on. Industrial production declined into 1946, but more than doubled between 1946 and the time of stabilization. The growth in economic activity, then, mitigated the rise in prices.

The magnitude of Taiwan's hyperinflation was much lower than on the mainland. The average monthly increases in prices and money supply were about one-third and one-fourth as great, respectively. Because its inflation continued for almost four years, the ultimate rise in the price index would make its hyperinflation more severe than those experienced in Austria, Hungary I, and Poland and slightly less severe than the Russian episode. In terms of the monthly average rise in prices, it is the mildest of the hyperinflations.

---

[3] These data are taken from Liu (1970, Appendix Tables A-11, P-1, and P-11, pp. 2, 18, and 19).

II. Stabilization

By the end of May 1949 real money balances had fallen to between 1.5 percent and 6.2 percent of their pre-hyperinflation levels (depending on the date used as the beginning of the episode). Because the fortunes of the Nationalists on the mainland were bleak, a complete repudiation of the currency was a genuine likelihood. Thus, a major reason for undertaking a stabilization program was the belief that it was necessary for the survival of the government. On June 15, 1949, the Nationalists unveiled their program. Its major provisions were:

(1) A unit of account known as the New Taiwan dollar (hereafter NT$) was to replace the taipi yuan.

(2) One NT$ was to be exchanged for 40,000 taipi yuan.

(3) The government repaid its advances from the Bank of Taiwan with gold, silver, and commodities, and the Bank then assumed many central banking functions.[4]

(4) A ceiling of NT$200 million was placed on the issuance of new notes with the reserves of the Bank of Taiwan sufficient to ensure a 100 percent gold, silver, and commodity cover.

(5) The NT$ was made partially convertible in that foreign exchange was available for a variety of external payments at the rate of NT$5 for US$1. Export earnings had to be surrendered at the same rate (although 80 percent was paid in the form of an exchange certificate that could be sold or used for importing goods).

(6) A Gold Savings Deposit Program was created allowing individuals to deposit NT$ in accounts paying gold at maturity.

Absent from the program was any major effort to reduce the budget deficit. With the task of fighting a civil war and rebuilding a war-damaged economy, the Nationalist government was not in the position to cut its outlays. Moreover, the bulk of any new taxes would have to be borne by the island's indigenous population. In this environment the Nationalists were cautious in imposing heavy new taxes on their hosts. There were efforts to streamline the bureaucracy and some minor tinkering with the tax system, but no overhaul of the fiscal system

---

[4] While the offices of the Bank of China were moved to Taiwan late in 1949, the central bank was not activated until 1961.

occurred as had accompanied the successful European stabilizations. As a percent of GNP, the Nationalists in 1950-52 raised only 70 percent of the revenue raised by the Japanese.[5] Indeed, the island's task of balancing the budget was made more difficult by the need to support the entire apparatus of national government.

Inflation did not come to an immediate end. It did slow dramatically. From the middle of June through December 1949, the wholesale price index rose by 82 percent in contrast with a 729 percent increase for the first five months (see Figure 1). The government during this period lived within the NT$200 million ceiling, ensuring a 100 percent metallic or commodity cover. Nevertheless, the money supply measured as currency rose 243 percent and as M1, 290 percent. The Bank of Taiwan's balance sheet indicates that the majority of new notes continued to be advanced to the public sector. Because foreign exchange was unavailable for all purposes, and the pressures for external transfers great, a black market developed in foreign exchange. By December, the rate was NT$8 per US$1, as opposed to an official rate of 5 to 1. (The market price of foreign exchange certificates also exceeded the official rate.)[6]

During 1950, currency grew 90 percent while M1 grew 99 percent. By June 1950, the NT$200 million ceiling on new notes was exceeded. An "extra-limit issue" of NT$50 million was authorized (to be covered 100 percent by a commodity reserve). At the year's end, the outstanding note issue still had a gold reserve of 80 percent.

During 1950 the Taipei wholesale price index rose by 89 percent, but the rise was quite variable. For January and February, prices rose 20 percent and 11 percent, respectively. The price level was stable from March through June. For August through October, the rise in prices

---

[5] For a complete description of the fiscal reform, see Riegg (1978).

[6] Although the government was liberal in granting foreign exchange (approved purposes included all goods and services "harmless to health" (Liu, p.7), all requests had to be supported by documentation assuring its use for approved purposes. The government's ability to process these applications was overwhelmed. Thus, even legitimate demands for foreign exchange found their way to the black market along with demands related to unapproved goods and capital exports.

Figure 1. Prices and Money Supply in Taiwan, 1945-1953

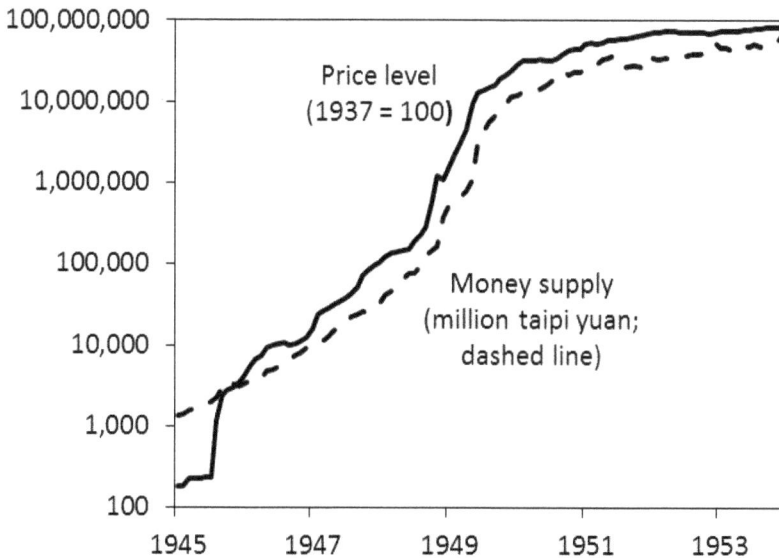

was 34 percent. Prices then rose only 1.8 percent in November and 2.4 percent in December. The government continued its policy to make foreign exchange available, but brought its selling rate of the NT$ more into line with the black market rate.

In March 1950, the stabilization effort was augmented by the Preferential Interest Rate Deposit (or PIR) program, a system of time deposits at the Bank of Taiwan and other commercial banks paying positive real rates of interest.[7] Initially offered with a maturity of one month (three-month, six-month, and one-year accounts were eventually made available as well), the accounts paid interest at the rate of 7 percent per month.

Since the commercial banks were obliged to pay high real rates for these funds, they were forced to charge high real rates on the loans they made. The program provided that all the funds from these deposits that banks were unable to lend out could be redeposited with the Bank of Taiwan at an interest rate at least equal to the rate the banks paid to

---

[7] These were high real rates *ex post*. We have no measure of expected inflation and, hence, no measure of the *ex ante* real rate. The acceptance of these deposits by the public suggests that the *ex ante* rate was at least positive.

their depositors.[8]

The deposits rose from NT$2 million early in 1950 to over NT$37 million in August (equal to about 13 percent of high-powered money). As the inflation rate slowed, the government apparently believed that the rate payable on the accounts could be reduced. In July, the rate on the one-month account was reduced by one-half to 3.5 percent per month and in October it was reduced further to 3.0 percent. The decrease led to a withdrawal of these deposits, and by December 1950 they had fallen to only NT$26 million (or about 7 percent of high-powered money).

The outbreak of the Korean War in late June 1950 ensured the ultimate success of Taiwan's stabilization effort. This prompted the United States to commence a large aid program. While the Nationalists had previously received substantial U.S. aid, it was terminated with the mainland's fall in late 1949. Thus, when the stabilization got underway, it was not benefiting from U.S. support.

Although only a small amount of aid would reach Taiwan in 1950, by the end of 1951 it was 10 percent of GNP. Besides military assistance, a large fraction of the aid consisted of consumer commodities and industrial raw materials that the government could sell to generate revenue.

In February 1951, another "extra-limit" currency issue of NT$95 million was authorized. Thereafter, the limit on currency issue placed no effective restraint on money growth. In April, the exchange stabilization fund became depleted and individuals could no longer convert the NT$ for external payments. Severe restrictions were then imposed on all foreign payments, imports were limited, and the NT$ was devalued. At the same time, the interest rate on PIR deposits was raised by over one-third. The deposits then grew over five-fold (by the end of 1951, they were equal to about 30 percent of high-powered money). Moreover, the value of U.S. commodity aid imports grew almost three-fold in 1951 over 1950 (in U.S. dollars commodity aid

---

[8] There is some dispute on this point. Irvine and Emery (1966) and Liu report that only the excess of deposits over loans were deposited. Mao (1967) and Kuo (1983) assert that all the preferential deposits had to be redeposited with the Bank of Taiwan. Examination of primary sources supports Irvine and Emery and Liu. Riegg (1978) also supports this view.

increased from $20.5 million to $56.6 million).[9]

With the introduction of the PIR deposits, the definition of money becomes arbitrary. During 1951, the money stock measured by currency grew 53 percent (34 percent during the second half of the year), as M1, 61 percent (it actually declined by 1 percent during the second half of the year as the PIR deposits were substituted for demand deposits), and as M1 plus the PIR deposits, 83 percent (7.4 percent during the second half). According to all measures, money growth decelerated during the year, as did prices (the Taipei wholesale price index rose 53 percent for the year, but only 18.5 percent during the second half).

In 1952, price level stability was achieved. For the year as a whole the Taipei wholesale price index rose only 3.4 percent (during the final six months it actually declined 1.3 percent). The money supply measured as currency rose 36 percent; as M1, 42 percent; and as M1 plus PIR deposits, 62 percent (the PIR deposits alone increased by 179 percent and at the end of the year were equal to almost half of high-powered money). Lasting stability was still several years away. Until 1961, prices tended to rise at high single digit and occasionally double-digit annual rates. Yet, the threat of renewed hyperinflation was over.

III. Interpretation

Successful stabilizations undertaken in Europe required both fiscal and monetary measures. Producing balanced budgets (or surpluses) reduced the pressure on the monetary authorities to provide the wherewithal to finance the deficit. In addition, the monetary authorities were given considerable independence to refuse the government's request for credit. Specifically, laws were passed that prohibited the central bank from discounting treasury bills or that imposed gold reserve requirements on all notes.

Unfortunately for Taiwan, neither a major increase in taxes nor an independent central bank was possible. Hence, the reform consisted mostly of trying to restore public confidence in a new currency by

---

[9] There is some conflict in the various studies about how much aid reached Taiwan each year. These data are from *Taiwan Statistical Data Book* (1966, p. 139).

making it partly convertible into gold and foreign exchange. It thus resembled the two failed stabilization attempts on the mainland more than it did either the European programs or recent stabilizations in Latin America.[10] Apparently, the Nationalists continued to believe that if zeroes were lopped off the currency unit, and the money associated with precious metals, inflation would end.

Selling gold and foreign exchange to bolster confidence in the new currency was a help, but it could not persist in the face of a chronically unbalanced budget. The government was addressing its fiscal imbalance by selling assets (hard currency) abroad and earning seigniorage on its newly created notes. Providing foreign exchange to the public to import goods was no different from using the exchange to cover its purchases. For the foreign exchange and gold, the government received currency it had previously disbursed through spending. Hence, monetary expansion was reduced in the same way as if the government had spent the gold and foreign exchange directly. This could work only as long as hard currency and assets were available.

Similarly, to the extent that quasi-convertibility or the promise of stability restored confidence in the currency and increased the public's willingness to hold money, the government could money-finance some of its expenditures with minimal inflationary impact. Yet, without budgetary changes, confidence could not last, for as its gold stock diminished, currency was not retired from circulation. In addition, the government's initial allocation of NT$56 million at the 40,000-to-1 conversion rate amounted to a four-fold increase in the amount of circulating currency over the end of May 1949, and it could be expanded further before reaching the issue limit. Combined with budgetary pressure to produce more notes, further increases in prices were inevitable.[11] Seigniorage could be earned for only so long under

---

[10] The stabilization program on Taiwan may appear to be an example of a "heterodox" approach due to the variety of elements contained in it. In fact, most of these elements either amounted to the same thing (i.e., convertibility) or were not part of the original plan (such as the PIR accounts). Price controls, for example, did not appear to be part of the stabilization plan. They existed in part to affect other goals such as land reform and were otherwise ineffective. Rationing was also used, but mostly to pay public sector employees in kind.

[11] An additional, apparently minor, source of money growth was the conversion of mainland currency held by refugees into New Taiwan dollars.

such circumstances.

The Gold Saving Deposit Program was used by the public as a means of acquiring gold by withdrawing deposits as early as possible. It became a significant drain on gold supplies and the program was terminated in June 1950. The loss of hard currency indicates the degree to which the government covered its deficits through asset sales. By 1951, 1.45 million ounces of gold and US$6.6 million were sold to the public. The hard currency assets of the Bank of Taiwan were exhausted in the spring of 1951 (indeed, the Bank owed more than US$10 million).

One element of the government's finances that helped reduce the need for money creation was an aggressive effort to borrow from the public to cover the deficit. In 1950, the sale of bonds raised receipts equal to more than a quarter of the deficit. In 1951, this ratio was further increased to almost two-thirds. Unfortunately, these figures overstate the success of this switch in financing since the central bank bought some fraction of these issues and thereby increased the monetary base. By the end of 1952, government bonds constituted roughly 25 percent of the total amount lent by the Bank of Taiwan to the public sector.

A much larger contribution to the stabilization effort was made by the PIR accounts since they also enabled the government to borrow from the public instead of from the central bank. Because the mandated interest rate on the deposits exceeded the level that would have equilibrated the supply of deposits with loan demand, an excess supply of funds that could not be lent to private borrowers was created. The redeposit feature guaranteed that this excess supply of funds would find its way to the Bank of Taiwan. The deposits (and redeposits) then provided the Bank with a means of advancing credit to the public sector without issuing new notes. This reduced the rate of growth in the monetary base. In terms of the consolidated central bank-central government balance sheet, the Chinese government had, through recourse to redeposited PIR deposits, a means to finance more of its deficit by borrowing from the public. Consequently, the real effect of these deposits was to shift a large fraction of deficit financing from note issue to what amounted to bond sales, reducing the rate of money growth.

This description of the role of the PIR accounts contrasts with that of Irvine and Emery (1966) and Liu (1970), who emphasize the role of the deposits in "immobilizing" and "absorbing excess liquidity." It is unclear whether they mean that the accounts reduced velocity or the money multiplier; indeed, they seem to argue that the accounts diverted funds into savings that would have been spent.

The accounts could not have reduced velocity because they did not offer an incentive to hold additional money balances. Rather, by offering an alternative to money, they should have reduced money demand. Nor could they have absorbed "excess liquidity" in the form of reserves, for they also would have tended to raise the deposit-to-currency ratio, so that the net effect of the deposits, except under implausible configurations of the reserve, currency, and deposit ratios, would have been to swell the supply of money—not shrink it. If anything, they would have increased inflationary pressure by substituting for money and reviving deposit banking. Any effect they may have had on saving, by itself, would have done little or nothing to improve the inflation situation. While an autonomous increase in saving is deflationary, any effect of the PIR accounts on saving would have been due to the high real interest rate they bore—a phenomenon that decreases money demand and increases velocity and prices.

Tsiang (1985) argues that the PIR deposits helped reduce inflation by drawing more savings into the banking system from "underground" or "curb" money markets and that this reintermediation of the economy reduced the need for the Bank of Taiwan to create money to satisfy private loan demand.[12] Central bank discounting of private paper, however, appears to have been a relatively minor source of money creation during the hyperinflation. Therefore, reducing lending to the private sector—even if it had been prompted by interest rates too low to equilibrate supply and demand—would have had little effect on the inflation rate. The crucial characteristic of the deposits appears to be how they provided a substitute source of public finance.

And as a borrowing program the PIR deposits were significant. For 1951, for example, funds redeposited at the Bank of Taiwan increased

---

[12] McKinnon (1973) also mentions reintermediation, but as a source of improvement in economic efficiency.

NT$125 million (this does not include deposits placed initially with the Bank of Taiwan that could not be profitably lent to private borrowers). This was more than three times the 1951 amount of counterpart aid and equal to 40 percent of the budget deficit. Presumably this NT$125 million otherwise would have been created as high-powered money to finance the public sector.

Sargent and Wallace (1981) note that under certain assumptions, a shift from money to bond financing may not result in a reduction in inflation. Their "unpleasant monetarist arithmetic" shows that if real interest rates exceed the economy's growth rate, additional borrowing by the government will imply a future deficit that can only be money financed. The expectation of future inflation that this engenders can prevent even a temporary respite from inflation resulting from the interim reduction in money growth.

This analysis assumes no future changes in taxes or primary (i.e., noninterest) expenditures. The rates of real interest and growth, along with the maximum tolerable level of taxation, define a point of no return, after which no plausible fiscal reform can bring the budget into balance short of debt repudiation. If the point of no return is near, and agents' assessment of the prospects of fiscal reform poor, then no shift from money finance to debt finance can improve inflation, if only because interest rates high enough to compensate lenders for the risk of repudiation (by inflation or other means) would be so high as to make repudiation (and more inflation) more likely.

Yet, with a high real growth rate and the point of no return far in the future, the chances for fiscal reform in the more distant future may be enough to permit a shift from money to bond financing to influence inflation. Moreover, in Taiwan's case it is not clear that agents realized that the spread of PIR accounts would make future budget balance more difficult. The circuitous nature of the financing made it less likely that the public understood that the accounts were a means for debt financing of the government. Indeed, to our knowledge, no one has pointed out this role for the PIR accounts.

This is suggested by the PIR program itself. One wonders why the government did not directly borrow at high interest rates. There are some possible explanations, but none are as persuasive as the

Table 1. Revenues and Expenditures for All Levels of Government in Taiwan, 1950-1953 (mn New Taiwan dollars)

	1950	1951	1952	1953
Expenditures	1,954	2,430	3,576	3,745
Receipts	1,587	2,121	3,521	3,846
Current revenue	1,527	1,964	3,467	3,791
Income from property	60	156	55	55
Counterpart fund aid	0	40	470	313
Balance	-367	-309	-55	102
Percent of expenditures	19	13	2	n.a.
Revenue from bond sales	96	195	105	29
Not covered by bond sales	-271	-114	50	131

Source: Taiwan, *Statistical Yearbook of the Republic of China* (1975, p. 237).

possibility that the government never understood the monetary implications of the PIR program, and that the program never was part of any coherent stabilization plan. In all likelihood, its monetary consequences were just a fortuitous outcome of an effort to do something else. We note that in two contemporary experiences, analogous efforts were made to employ alternative financial instruments insulated from ongoing inflation. In the case of post-World War II Hungary, deposits (and eventually currency) were indexed for inflation (Bomberger and Makinen 1983). In the formative stages of the Greek hyperinflation, the occupying German authorities used gold sovereigns to purchase commodities (Makinen 1986). In these cases, the innovation worsened the inflation. It may only be luck that the Chinese (impelled perhaps by the same motivations as the Germans and Hungarians) hit upon a mechanism that actually helped slow the inflation rate.

Of course, it is a fiscal overhaul that is required for the permanent success of a stabilization program. It was the fiscal regime change on Taiwan, as in the European episodes, that finally brought price stability. It was the aid program that brought the budget to near balance, and when the aid program reached its full proportions in 1952, prices stabilized.

Data are not available for a comparison of the budget just before and immediately after the initiation of the stabilization plan. Inferences on the transition must be drawn from central bank advances. These indicate no sudden improvement. The data for the following years indicate budgetary improvement only after aid became available (see Table 1). Deficit reduction from 1950 to 1951 is accounted for entirely by counterpart aid and the sale of property (another temporary source of receipts). In 1952, counterpart aid accounted for all the reduction in the deficit. Moreover, the budget numbers betray only part of aid's deficit reduction role because they show only the counterpart aid. Taiwan also received direct assistance in noncounterpart form. These goods were important in reducing expenditures that otherwise might have been undertaken, especially for defense, which was reduced in real terms between 1950 and 1951 while the armed forces were reequipped. Regardless of the form aid took, it reduced inflation by reducing the amount of government spending financed by the creation of high-powered money.

Besides the aid program and the PIR deposits, the deceleration of the inflation rate during 1951 and the stability of prices in late 1952 was assisted by a substantial increase in real output. This was aided by the enormous amount of human capital brought to Taiwan by the nearly half-million civilian refugees from the mainland (equal to almost 10 percent of the native population) who arrived in late 1949.

IV. Implications

It is interesting that the aid program, which was decisive in bringing price stability to Taiwan, was announced 13 months after the stabilization. The PIR deposits came after nine months had passed. No one could have known in advance how rapid economic development and the resulting growth in tax revenue might be. In short, the stabilization was embarked upon with neither an actual nor a promise of change in the fiscal or monetary regime.[13]

Nevertheless, the hyperinflation ended. While inflation continued at a high rate, it did slow dramatically. Agents in the economy were

---

[13] Alternatively, one might say a regime change occurred, but that it was not of the type identified by Sargent as necessary for ending hyperinflation.

**Figure 2. Real Balances in Taiwan, 1945-1953
(million taipi yuan divided by price level index)**

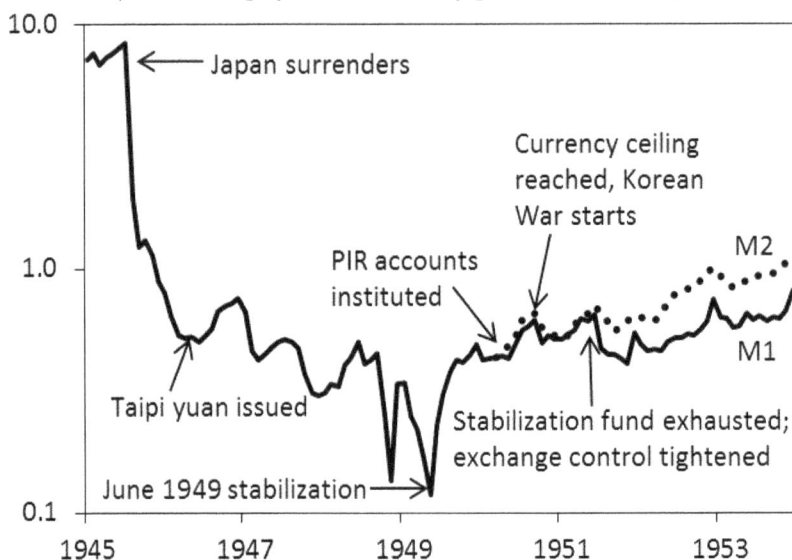

apparently willing to put some confidence in the currency solely on the promise of a convertibility that obviously could not be maintained. The behavior of real balances shows this. For the hyperinflation and immediately thereafter, their behavior mirrors other episodes: at the time of stabilization they were only a fraction of their value at the beginning (see Figure 2). Their rebound immediately following the stabilization is significant; by July, they had recovered from the depths achieved in the final, worst months of the hyperinflation.

Following some further increases in early 1950, however, real balances flatten and even drop somewhat, so that by the beginning of 1952, they are lower than at the end of 1950, having reached only 40 percent of their 1937 level, the last "normal" year available for comparison. This behavior is explained by the prevalence of the PIR deposits. These deposits substituted for money as a temporary abode of purchasing power. When they are included in the money measure (M2), the data reveal the continued climb of real balances (to 54 percent of the 1937 level). The continuation of this general upward trend in the 3½ years after stabilization is consistent with the behavior one would expect if the public believed that a regime change had taken place.

In other words, even though no regime change occurred at the time of the program's implementation, the public appears to have behaved as if one did. This conclusion is buttressed by the change in the causal relationship between money and inflation which also occurred at the time the program began.

Sargent and Wallace (1973) explain that under appropriate assumptions, the existence of a regime that attempts to extract a fixed proportion of resources from an economy by means of money creation implies a specific causality relation between money growth and inflation. Since the creation of money to pay for resources generates inflation, subsequent note issue by the government has to be increased in response to inflation's effects on the nominal cost of resources to be extracted in later periods. As a consequence, note issue comes to depend on price increases; that is, inflation "causes" money growth. If expectations are rational, agents should set prices based on money growth. And since the rate of note issue depends on past inflation, they should be able to predict the rate of money creation from the past history of prices. Inflation comes to depend on past inflation; money creation drops out of the chain of causation.

This implies a unidirectional causal ordering from prices to money. That is, Granger-Sims style causation tests should show that the lagged values of prices and money explain current values of money better than past values of money alone, while at the same time lagged values of money and prices fail to explain current prices any better than past prices by themselves. A successful stabilization should break this causal nexus from prices to money. A regime change designed to end hyperinflation requires the monetary authorities to reassert control over money creation. With monetary policy no longer subservient to financing the fiscal shortfall, past inflation should cease to be a predictor of note issue.[14]

---

[14] Makinen and Woodward (1988) show that the transition to stabilization and beyond does not necessarily imply a reversal of the Granger causal ordering of inflation and money creation. This results because the stabilization implies a remonetization of the economy as the costs of holding money balances

However, the causal nexus can also be broken by a change in the public's expectations. If agents no longer believe that past prices determine the monetary requirements of the government, then they should no longer be setting new prices based on past inflation. Their resulting willingness to absorb increases in the money supply without corresponding increases in prices should mean that prices no longer Granger-cause money.

Sims tests run on data from the periods before and after June 1949 are summarized in Table 2.[15] The F-values for the equation predicting prices test the contribution of future rates of money growth to the prediction of current observations of inflation, thus indicating whether or not inflation "causes" money growth. For the hyperinflation period we are unable to reject the null hypothesis of no causation from money growth to inflation. However, within a 95 percent confidence interval, the null hypothesis of no causation from prices to money is rejected, implying a regime in which inflation leads to money issue. During the stabilization period the null hypothesis of no causation in either direction cannot be rejected. A Chow test was performed to be sure that the split sample really reflects two different underlying

---

decrease and velocity falls. Any linkage from money to prices during such a period is weak.

[15] The Sims version of testing for Granger causality involves leading and lagging observations of the independent variables. The estimating equations are:

$$(1)\ P = a + bT + \sum_{t=4}^{-6} k_t M_t + e$$

$$(2)\ M = c + dT + \sum_{t=4}^{-6} z_t P_t + e$$

where P is inflation and M money growth, T is a trend and e an error term. F-tests are performed on the lead variables. In our tests of the subperiods, all observations are confined to the subperiods in question. For example, for the stabilization period, the lagged observations do not involve using any values from the hyperinflation period and similarly for the leading observations used during the hyperinflation period.

Table 2. Prices versus Money in Taiwan, 1945-1953

	1945-1949	1949-1953	1945-1953
Money regressed on prices F-statistic	2.47	0.98	1.41
R^2	0.74	0.25	0.32
Prices regressed on money F-statistic	3.02	1.17	11.12
R^2	0.72	0.23	0.53
Degrees of freedom	21/4	30/4	76/4
Critical value of F: .05	2.84	2.69	2.49
Critical value of F: .01	4.37	4.02	3.58

distributions. F-statistics of 22.55 and 4.46 (money growth and inflation as dependent variables, respectively) were both significant at the 1 percent level, rejecting the hypothesis that the pre- and post-stabilization regressions are the same. Regressions using notes instead of money yielded the same result.

This could be evidence of a regime change. But since we know that no regime change occurred, it must be taken as evidence that agents perceived a change, and, thus, that the June 1949 reform meant to them that the government would end the practices it had engaged in to cause hyperinflationary money growth.

Data on real balances are frequently supplemented by data on unemployment. Presumably, the expectations that influence individuals to hold larger real balances will lead them to moderate their demands for money wage increase. Since this moderation prevents nominal wage increases from becoming excessive *ex post* real increases when the inflation slows, the economy can make the transition from hyperinflation to price level stability without the necessity of experiencing a prolonged period of high unemployment. Examining the Taiwanese data would tend to lead to a similar conclusion.

The stabilization was accompanied by positive growth in national income, but at a rate substantially less than the 1947-1949 pace. That earlier pace, however, could have been artificially high because of the recovery from the large-scale destruction of World War II, and the use of inflation tax proceeds either to expand state enterprises or distributed as subsidized loans to the private sector. Evidence from several other hyperinflations suggests that they were also characterized by a booming economy. To the extent that the inflation tax revenue was used for state and private enterprise expansion, resource misallocation could have resulted and been responsible for some of the slower growth after stabilization.[16]

While the time series on unemployment only begins in 1951, it reveals that for that year and for 1952, the ratio of unemployed to the active labor force was 7.8 percent. It then rose slightly and remained above 8.0 percent for the next four years. This rate is remarkable when it is recalled that Taiwan was forced to absorb nearly a half million mainlanders early in the stabilization.

Thus, if one examines the Taiwanese experience as Sargent did for four European experiences, one might be led to the same conclusion: that a regime change was perceived, price-setting behavior was immediately affected, and the transition costs of bringing inflation down were significantly moderated.

The problem with this conclusion is that the stabilization program lacked the presence and promise of a regime change. The central bank could not refuse the government's request for credit and the budget deficit made convertibility impossible to maintain. When the regime changed later, it did so as a result of serendipity (the PIR program that raised the amount the government would borrow from the public) and an unforeseen windfall (the aid program prompted by the Korean War).[17]

Sargent's proposition that the perception of a regime change can ease the transition costs to price stability requires first that people perceive regime changes. He takes the experience that behavior changed in the European cases as evidence that indeed such changes

---

[16] Garber (1982) has identified and measured a number of resource misallocation costs due to a distortion of relative prices that occurred during the German hyperinflation. Because some central bank lending was to government enterprises, there is reason to believe that such costs may have occurred in Taiwan during the stabilization.

[17] If one does accept the applicability of "unpleasant monetarist arithmetic," our conclusion is merely reinforced: rational agents would have to have realized that the PIR accounts were making no contribution to the stabilization.

can be discerned. But it must not only be true that when a regime change takes place people perceive it, it must also be true that when no regime change occurs people do not erroneously perceive one nonetheless. This is implicit in his analysis elsewhere (Sargent 1983), where he argues that the failure to have the elements necessary for successful stabilization will add to its transition costs.

In Taiwan the public appears to have believed in a nonexistent regime change—based on the kind of evidence used by Sargent. And Taiwan is not an isolated instance. Makinen (1984) has shown that in Greece the public reacted favorably to two reforms that failed to contain elements necessary to stabilize prices. Thus, the public may have difficulty in distinguishing regime changes from superficial changes in economic policy. This suggests that the public (at least in some circumstances) may be willing to believe in a stabilization solely on the basis of its announcement, with little evidence that it can succeed, and raises the issue of what achieves credibility and what fails to achieve it. If the public finds the mere promise of stabilization partly credible, might they find a genuine regime change less than totally so? If hyperinflations provide us with economic experiments to test public reactions to changes which are large and events that are highly visible, these questions become more troublesome in the case of less rapid inflations and less dramatic stabilization programs.

V. Conclusion

During the period 1945-49 Taiwan experienced a hyperinflation separated from the ongoing hyperinflation on the mainland by adjustable exchange rates between the currencies in use in the two regions. An attempt to stabilize prices was implemented in June 1949, but for a variety of reasons it did not contain the two elements essential for bringing about stable prices: a balanced budget and an independent central bank capable of refusing the government's request for credit.

The government's policy at first consisted of using its reserves of hard assets to cover much of its deficit, reducing money creation as a consequence. As these reserves were being exhausted, it embarked on a program of borrowing from the public through high-yielding bank accounts. Finally, massive U.S. aid helped bring the budget close to balance. Along with the revival of tax revenue that came with economic growth, this ended rapid inflation by mid-1952—three years after the stabilization program began.

The behavior of real balances, along with apparent lack of significant transition costs, and the results of Granger-Sims style causation tests point to a significant adjustment of public behavior in response to the initial stabilization program. In other countries, these kinds of observations have been taken as evidence that a regime change has been perceived and acted upon. In Taiwan, however, a regime change did not occur immediately, even though it did occur ultimately. This raises questions about the public's ability to distinguish genuine from superficial changes in fiscal and monetary policies.

11

Inflation Uncertainty and the Demand
for Money in Hyperinflation

(with William A. Bomberger)

Macroeconomic analysis is devoting increased attention to the effects
of various kinds of uncertainty on such traditional constructions as the
investment schedule and the Phillips curve.[1] One area in which such
analysis has proven empirically fruitful is the investigation of the
suggestion by Klein (1977, pp. 692-697) that the demand for money is
affected by uncertainty regarding future inflation. Although the
theoretical basis of this suggestion provides no unambiguous prediction
about the direction of the effect, empirical work has forced researchers
to search for measurable proxies for inflation uncertainty.[2] The search
is complicated by the facts that: (a) a consistent measure of uncertainty
requires a modeling of an expected inflation series over the period to
be examined[3] and, (b) a strong test requires data collected from a

---

[1] The theory by Lucas (1973), that the slope of the Phillips curve depends
upon the magnitude of the inflation uncertainty or aggregate demand
uncertainty, is the best known and most important example.

[2] In addition to Klein (1977), Allen (1979), Blejer (1979), Eden (1975), Frenkel
(1977), Pautler (1981), Pou (1976), and Smirlock (1982) have estimated
demand for money functions with uncertainty variables as proxies.

[3] As discussed more fully in the next section, an economic agent's uncertainty
with respect to his forecasts of inflation should be based on observations of
his past forecast errors. These errors cannot be measured without modeling
his forecasts as a first step.

Measures of uncertainty which are simply variances of previous inflation
about some mean require no such modeling. Klein's original estimates (1977,
p. 701) use a five-term moving standard deviation about a moving mean
centered on the observation in question. This is, however, actually a measure
of the variability of inflation rather than the uncertainty or unpredictability of
inflation. Allen (1979), Blejer (1979), Pou (1976), and Khan (1977) (in a very

period during which the effects of changes in uncertainty are not swamped by other influences on money demand.

Because of these factors it is useful to examine the role of inflation uncertainty within the context of Cagan's model of the demand for money during hyperinflation and to estimate the effect of such uncertainty with Cagan's data. The advantages of this approach are: (a) an operational model of expected inflation already exists within this framework against which additional results can be compared and their significance appraised, (b) during hyperinflation the relevant portfolio choice is between money and inventories of goods (or barter), therefore uncertainty with regard to the relative rate of return (the inflation rate) may be important, (c) because these data presumably encompass an experience during which uncertainty with respect to future inflation varied a great deal, they should bear traces of the effect on money demand more visibly than data gathered from less turbulent times.[4]

In Section I the method of estimating the effect of inflation uncertainty on money demand is explained and briefly compared with previous work. Empirical results are presented in Section II. Conclusions are presented in the final section.

---

different context) construct variables along this line. Klein and Blejer acknowledge the conceptual deficiency of this kind of proxy.

[4] Only Khan (1977) uses both the Cagan model and the Cagan data (with an inflation variability proxy). His work is, however, not closely related to the issues raised in this or the other studies listed above. Rather, he investigates the conjecture that forecasts of future inflation are more quickly revised when inflation has been more variable.

Klein (1975 and 1977) and Smirlock (1982) have used U.S. data for their analyses. Blejer (1979) and Pou (1976) have used data from Latin America. Only the studies by Allen (1979), Eden (1975), Frenkel (1977), and Pautler (1981) are directly related to our efforts in that they draw upon the European hyperinflation episodes examined by Cagan. Frenkel's work has limited applicability because the data used are only available for Germany. Allen also restricted his study to the German data while Eden, for unexplained reasons, restricted himself to the German, Austrian, Polish and first Hungarian data. Pautler, also for unexplained reasons, used only the German, Polish and first Hungarian data.

I. The Uncertainty Variable

The theoretical basis for suspecting that uncertainty with regard to future inflation affects the demand for money is uncomplicated. Increased uncertainty about future inflation implies that the real rate of return from holding money balances is more uncertain and the "quality" of the bundle of services provided by money is diminished.[5]

Depending on the way in which money services enter into the money holder's utility function, this decrease in services per dollar may lead to a flight from money or an increase in money holdings to replace part of the lost flow of money services.

The task of constructing a variable which represents inflation uncertainty and varies systematically over time presents some difficulties for a formal analysis. Presumably, a representative money holder possesses a subjective probability distribution of possible inflation outcomes over a specified horizon. The mean of this distribution represents his point estimate of future inflation or "the expected inflation rate." Inflation uncertainty is presumably measured by the variance or standard deviation of this subjective distribution.

If one alleges that inflation uncertainty varies over time, one must picture a forecaster who revises not only the mean but also the variance of his subjective distribution each period. Efforts to model the mechanism which describes the revision of the mean almost universally focus on the past inflation observations as the primary data processed by the forecaster. Presumably past forecast errors are the most relevant data for estimating and revising the variance.

Most previous efforts at constructing an uncertainty proxy are consistent with this concept of uncertainty. They construct an equation which generates inflation forecasts ("expected inflation") and use the observed forecast errors of the recent past to construct a measure for uncertainty.

For example, Smirlock fits an ARIMA (0, 2, 1) process to the inflation data from the forty quarters ending in the quarter in question

---

[5] Boonekamp (1978), Eden (1975 and 1976) and Klein have developed three somewhat different models which predict that uncertainty with respect to future inflation may be an explanatory variable in a traditional demand for money equation. The argument of this paragraph paraphrases Klein's theory.

and uses the estimated variance as the uncertainty proxy for that quarter. Klein (1977) uses annual data to fit an AR(1) process to the inflation data from the 12 years ending in the year in question and uses the estimated variance as the uncertainty proxy for that year. In a rather unorthodox mixture of methods, Pautler (1981) takes the ARIMA process he fits for the entire sample period to generate an "expected inflation" series but uses only the forecast errors for the five months ending in the month in question to construct the uncertainty proxy for that month. A crucial aspect of each of these methods is the use of a fixed number of past forecast errors to construct the current uncertainty value. The forecaster presumably only uses forecast errors within a fixed past horizon. As each period passes, a new forecast error is observed and another past forecast error is discarded in estimating the reliability of the current forecast.

Although none of the authors above explain the theoretical basis for the fixed horizons (or even the reason for their choice of the horizon length), the practical reason is clear. Unless one requires that agents discard observations moderately distant in the past, the resulting uncertainty proxy will exhibit very little variation over the sample.

This procedure largely vitiates any claim to "rationality" on the part of the forecaster, at least with regard to his estimate of the uncertainty. A "rational" forecaster in a stable environment would not discard information. It is conceivable that some environment in which the evolution of mean inflation is described by a stable mechanism but the variance of inflation is changing in a systematic way would render this behavior rational. No formal description of such a process is given in any of these papers.

The method employed in this paper, as explained in detail below, is no more "rational" than its predecessors. It does, however, extend the concept which lies behind previous methods in a somewhat more consistent way and avoids the arbitrary choice of a fixed backward-looking horizon which is common to each of the studies mentioned above.

As a justification for discarding observations in the past, the idea of a changing inflation generating process (or the perception of a changing process on the part of economic agents) has some appeal. However, if one accepts this concept, the "fixed horizon" method seems arbitrary even if the "rationality" of the procedure is not an issue. Basically, this procedure assigns to each observation a weight which depends on how distant the observation is from the present. As one looks at observations farther in the past, the weights remain constant until one reaches a fixed horizon. After this horizon is reached the weights are equal to zero. Hence the forecasters in Smirlock's study seem to regard data from 39 quarters in the past to be as relevant for purposes of forecasting as data from one quarter in the past, but regard data 40 quarters in the past as useless.

It seems more reasonable to assume that the relevance of past observations to current forecasting declines steadily as one looks farther into the past unless there has been a known regime change at some date. Indeed, Frenkel (1977, p. 662) has implicitly assumed such behavior by constructing an uncertainty proxy which consists of a weighted average of squared lagged errors where the weights decline geometrically as the lag increases. Although Frenkel provides no rationale for this procedure, it is clearly consistent with the argument expressed above. This procedure also allows a plausible way to avoid some of the arbitrary nature of the "fixed horizon" method by allowing the parameter of the geometric decay to be estimated rather than chosen beforehand.

Any such technique requires the construction of an expected inflation series as a preliminary step. Frenkel uses the forward exchange rate, a data set which requires no modeling of expectations formation but which exists only for the German hyperinflation. The procedure described below will use Cagan's adaptive expectations formulation to construct this series and combine it with a technique similar to Frenkel's for arriving at an uncertainty series. Indeed, the assumption of geometrically declining weights for past forecast errors to generate the variance of the subjective distribution of future inflation is quite in the spirit of Cagan's procedure which involves geometrically declining weights for past inflation rates in generating the mean of the same distribution. The specifics of the procedure are provided below.

The expected inflation rate, p^e, is formed adaptively from past observations of actual inflation, p:

$$(1) \quad p_t^e = p_{t-1}^e + b_1 e_t$$

where e_t is the most recent forecast error: [6]

$$(2) \quad e_t = p_t - p^e_{t-1}$$

Uncertainty with regard to future inflation is measured by s, a weighted sum of past squared forecast errors:

$$(3) \quad s_t = b_2 e^2_t + (1 - b)s_{t-1}$$

The procedure used by Cagan (1956, pp. 37-43) involves constructing alternative p^e series from a given p series by using alternative values of b_1. One then selects the appropriate p^e series by successively regressing the logarithm of real money balances, m_t, on the alternative p^e series and a constant term:

$$(4) \quad m_t = a_0 + a_1 p^e + \text{error term}$$

The appropriate p^e series (and the underlying b_1 value) is the one which provides the best fit. We estimate the following equation:

$$(5) \quad m_t = a_0 + a_1 p^e_t + a_2 s_t + \text{error term}$$

Alternative p^e series are constructed from the observed p series and alternative values for b_1 according to (1). Any given p^e series yields an observable series of forecast errors, e, when combined with the observed p series according to (2). Alternative values for b_2 are then used to construct alternative s series according to (3). The combination of b_1 and b_2 values which yield the best fit in (5) are then selected and

---

[6] Some timing definitions are in order. If the logarithm of the price level at data point t is P_t, then p_t is the inflation rate for the time period ending at the data point t, $P_t - P_{t-1}$. The expected inflation rate, p^e_t, is the forecast made at data point t for the period beginning at t and ending at $t + 1$. The forecast error, e_t, observable at data point t is $p_t - p^e_{t-1}$.

the results of that regression are reported.[7]

For comparison, a proxy for inflation variability, v, is defined as the variance about the average inflation rate for the five observations immediately preceding time t. This variable is included in an alternative money demand specification:

$$(6) \quad m_t = a_0 + a_1 p_t^e + a_2 v_t + \text{error term}$$

The appropriate value for b_1 is chosen according to the "best-fit" criterion for estimates of (6).

II. Empirical Results

Specifications (4), (5) and (6) were estimated using OLS for six of the data sets constructed by Cagan. Since nearly all of the resulting Durbin-Watson statistics indicate the presence of serial correlation in the disturbances, each equation is re-estimated with a correction for first-order autocorrelation (the values for b_1 and b_2 which provided the best OLS fit are retained in constructing the p^e and s variables). These results are reported in Tables 1, 2 and 3.[8] Before these results are interpreted, a few comments on the data are required.

Cagan reports data from outside the samples which he uses in estimating money demand. The extra data occur for two reasons: (1) Inflation data for some period before the beginning of each

---

[7] The resulting p series will depend upon the b_1 value only. The s series will depend upon the b_1 and the b_2 used. Klein uses an estimated standard error rather than an estimated variance. Blejer uses the average absolute deviation from mean inflation. An analogous statistic in this framework would be the square root of s or the square root of v (for variability, discussed below). Theory gives no guidance regarding this choice. It is simply a matter of functional form. Experiments were performed with the alternative "square root" variables. They provided similar results but uniformly poorer fits and less significant parameter estimates.

[8] The value of the intercept terms is not reported because they depend on such arbitrary factors as the choice of whether to measure currency units in thousands rather than millions or the choice of the base year for the price index.

hyperinflation are available. Cagan used these data to construct pre-sample observations for p^e which are helpful in constructing the within-sample p^e without the necessity of assuming an arbitrary value of p^e for the observation which immediately precedes the first within-sample observation. (2) Cagan excludes observations at the end of 4 of his samples because his regressions indicate a break in the demand for money function. That is, the levels of real money holding observed in these months are quite high when compared to the predicted values derived from the estimates of (4) for the earlier observations in the sample. Cagan (1956, pp. 55-7) interprets this phenomenon as evidence for the expectation of imminent monetary reform and excludes the observations on this basis.

The availability of pre-sample values of p is quite convenient for the construction of the s series. The p^e and s series are constructed entirely from observations on p combined with assumed values of b_1 and b_2. It seems reasonable that one would encounter rather low values for b_2. That is, observations of a few large (or small) errors in forecasts should not dramatically change one's estimate of the population variance.[9] However, low values for b_2 are rather inconvenient in a mechanical sense because they render the constructed s series sensitive to the unavoidably arbitrary choice for the initial value of s. The existence of substantial amounts of pre-sample observations for p alleviates this sensitivity considerably. The data for Germany, where 39 such observations are available, and for Russia, where 27 are available, are quite useful. For the other data sets (particularly Austria with four monthly pre-sample observations) one should have less confidence in the usefulness of the resulting s series.

The omission of end-of-sample observations seems unattractive. Therefore, two samples each have been used for Germany, Greece and

---

[9] There is no formal basis for this *a priori* belief, but it would seem to be a curious world in which it was reasonable to adjust one's estimates of the variance faster than one's estimate of the mean expected inflation rate. Constant variance models are the rule in currently used estimation techniques. At an extreme, if inflation followed a random walk generated by an error term with a known, constant variance, values of $b_1 = 1$ and $b_2 = 0$ would be appropriate.

Poland. One sample is identical to Cagan's shortened sample. The other includes all observations except the one in the month in which the currency reform occurred. The samples are thus increased by 3, 2 and 1 observations respectively.

The short sample from Hungary after World War II has been omitted. The addition of the s variable reduces the degrees of freedom of the regression results by 2 (a_2 and b_2). The sample Cagan estimated was so small that meaningful results could not be expected.[10] Finally, for simplicity and comparability of results across countries, the money variable is limited to the logarithm of real note holdings only.[11]

The results reported in Table 1 indicate why Cagan felt there was an anomaly in some late sample observations for Germany, Greece, and Poland. The addition of 3 and 2 observations to the German and Greek data sets, respectively, produces dramatic changes in the fit and the parameter estimates. Even the addition of a single observation to the Polish data set has a noticeable effect.

The results reported in Table 2 suggest that the inclusion of the s series is a plausible way of measuring the effect of inflation uncertainty on money demand. With the obvious exception of the Hungarian results, the pattern of estimated b_1 and b_2 values is plausible. The b_1 estimates are comparable to those reported in Table 1, although slightly lower (a mean value of .164 versus .204 for estimates of (4)). The b_2 estimates are substantially lower than the b_1 estimates (a mean value of .046).

---

[10] Cagan's sample yields only five degrees of freedom for his estimates. This method, which requires estimates of b_2 and a_2 would leave only two when a correction for autocorrelation is applied. This sample is accompanied by only three pre-sample observations for p, as well. The sample could be extended to include the explosive period Cagan excised from his sample, but a recent study, Bomberger and Makinen (1980), suggests that institutional changes during this period would add further volatility to the demand for notes.

[11] Bank deposits did not exist during the Russian hyperinflation. Data on deposits are unavailable for Greece and available only quarterly for the other episodes. Information on the behavior of the demand for broadly defined money would be of interest. However, cross-country comparisons, which are made below, would not be meaningful with the available data. In addition, the necessary use of interpolated data is unattractive, even if comparability across countries were not an issue.

Table 1. Estimates of Demand for Money, Corrected for First-Order Autocorrelation of Disturbances

$$m_t = a_0 + a_1 p_t^e$$

Country and period	a_1	b_1	R^2	ρ	MSE
Austria	-5.95	.09	.9859	.16	.00248
Jan. 1921-Aug. 1922	(34.5)			(0.7)	
Germany	-4.67	.23	.9511	.64	.00813
Sept. 1920-July 1923	(24.9)			(4.9)	
Germany	-1.59	.23	.6133	.77	.06652
Sept. 1920-Oct. 1923	(7.5)			(7.3)	
Greece	-4.00	.14	.9181	.47	.02409
Jan. 1943-Aug. 1944	(13.8)			(2.4)	
Greece	-1.91	.14	.6710	.59	.08800
Jan. 1943-Oct. 1944	(6.2)			(3.5)	
Hungary	-5.69	.14	.7305	.79	.01112
July 1922-Feb. 1924	(6.8)			(5.7)	
Poland	-2.92	.23	.9304	.46	.00751
Apr. 1922-Nov. 1923	(15.1)			(2.3)	
Poland	-2.68	.23	.9019	.49	.01018
Apr. 1922-Dec. 1923	(12.9)			(2.6)	
Russia	-3.15	.33	.9005	.56	.01018
Jan. 1922-Feb. 1924	(14.4)			(3.4)	

Notes: Numbers in parentheses are t-ratios. Rho (ρ) is the estimated parameter of the autocorrelation process in the disturbances.

With the exception, again, of the Hungarian results, the a_2 estimates are uniformly positive, consistent with the findings of Klein (1977, pp. 703-711). All of these a_2 values are significant at the 95 percent level except for the Austrian estimates.

The Hungarian results are clearly anomalous. The search for b_1 and b_2 values has been limited to the .01 - .99 range at .01 intervals. The Hungarian search ended in a corner result as indicated. It is impossible to interpret the estimated values for b_1 and b_2 adjust downward: (.01 and .99) as a plausible description of the way in which a forecaster would revise his mean forecast and estimated variance. Not surprisingly, the implausible s series resulting from these parameter values yields atypical a_1 and a_2 estimates (a_1 is nearly three times as large as any other estimate; a_2 is the only negative estimate encountered). There is no obvious explanation for this atypical behavior. Perhaps the phenomenon is related to the generally poor fit which the Hungarian data provide for any specification.

An interesting characteristic of the estimates using s is their relative insensitivity to the sample changes in the German, Greek and Polish data sets. As one switches from the shortened samples to the longer ones, the fit does not dramatically worsen, nor do the a_1 estimates dramatically change. Rather, the significance of a_2 increases greatly in the German and Greek cases. Perhaps, in these extreme cases, the effect of uncertainty is shown in sharper relief. Clearly, if the s specification is used, there is no reason to invoke the possibility of anticipated currency reform and exclude the extreme observations from the samples.

The variability measure, v, shown on Table 3 also tends to have a positive effect on money demand which becomes more significant when one lengthens the sample. However, the effect is neither so uniformly nor so significantly positive as that which the s variable provides.

An interesting possibility is suggested by comparing the a_1 and b_1 estimates in Table 1 with the analogous estimates reported in Table 2. As mentioned above, the mean value of b_1 across countries (exclusive of Hungary) declines as one switches from estimates of (4) to (5). The mean value of a_1 rises (in absolute value) from -3.056 to -5.538.[12] The variances of a_1 and b_1 across countries decline from 2.398 and .00686 to 1.967 and .00490, respectively, as one switches from estimates of (4) to (5).

One could interpret this pattern as an indication that the inclusion of the s variable not only increases the explanatory power of the

---

[12] The Hungarian estimates are excluded from both calculations of the mean. All calculations of the mean or variance of parameters across countries reported below are based on the same exclusion.

Table 2. Estimates of Demand for Money with Inflation Uncertainty, Corrected for First-Order Autocorrelation of Disturbances

$$m_t = a_0 + a_1 p_t^e + a_2 s_t$$

Country and period	a_1	a_2	b_1	b_2	R^2	ρ	MSE
Austria	-6.11	1.98	.10	.09	.9862	.15	.00259
Jan. 1921-Aug. 1922	(8.5)	(0.7)				(0.7)	
Germany	-7.21	6.63	.15	.09	.9655	.73	.00417
Sept. 1920-July 1923	(19.4)	(4.8)				(6.4)	
Germany	-7.03	4.16	.15	.09	.9638	.39	.02167
Sept. 1920-Oct. 1923	(22.3)	(14.4)				(2.6)	
Greece	-8.54	38.73	.08	.01	.9435	.37	.02276
Jan. 1943-Aug. 1944	(7.3)	(2.3)				(1.8)	
Greece	-6.82	15.02	.08	.01	.9410	.49	.02242
Jan. 1943-Oct. 1944	(13.7)	(8.1)				(2.7)	
Hungary	-24.38	-1.74	.01	.99	.8718	.78	.00568
July 1922-Feb. 1924	(5.1)	(5.8)				(5.6)	
Poland	-3.81	40.76	.25	.01	.9684	.17	.00570
Apr. 1922-Nov. 1923	(11.2)	(3.1)				(0.8)	
Poland	-3.72	45.33	.25	.01	.9558	.18	.00875
Apr. 1922-Dec. 1923	(8.8)	(2.8)				(0.8)	
Russia	-4.01	24.7	.24	.02	.9402	.34	.00966
Jan. 1922-Feb. 1924	(18.5)	(3.6)				(1.8)	

Notes: Numbers in parentheses are t-ratios. Rho (ρ) is the estimated parameter of the autocorrelation process in the disturbances.

estimating equation for each country, but also yields parameter estimates which are more similar across countries. To explore this possibility further, (4), (5), and (6) were estimated for a sample which pools the data from all countries. The results (not shown) produce a substantially higher R^2 for (5) than for (4) (.957 vs. 888). In addition, the parameter estimates for (5) from the pooled regressions are

**Table 3. Estimates of Demand for Money
with Inflation Variability, Corrected for
First-Order Autocorrelation of Disturbances**

$$m_t = a_0 + a_1 p_t^e + a_2 v_t$$

Country and period	a_1	a_2	b_1	R^2	ρ	MSE
Austria	-6.2	-0.9	.08	.9863	.16	.00252
Jan. 1921-Aug. 1922	(23.7)	(1.1)			(0.7)	
Germany	-5.2	1.1	.20	.9552	.69	.00647
Sept. 1920-July 1923	(20.8)	(1.8)			(5.6)	
Germany	-4.7	2.5	.20	.8422	.19	.15391
Sept. 1920-Oct. 1923	(8.5)	(4.3)			(1.2)	
Greece	-4.4	1.0	.13	.9178	.48	.02527
Jan. 1943-Aug. 1944	(10.0)	(0.6)			(2.4)	
Greece	-4.4	1.5	.13	.9322	.54	.02230
Jan. 1943-Oct. 1944	(13.4)	(7.9)			(3.1)	
Hungary	-5.7	-.07	.14	.7325	.78	.01185
July 1922-Feb. 1924	(5.9)	(0.0)			(5.6)	
Poland	-3.8	3.5	.22	.9675	.08	.00696
Apr. 1922-Nov. 1923	(11.2)	(2.6)			(0.4)	
Poland	-3.3	2.6	.22	.9390	.19	.01175
Apr. 1922-Dec. 1923	(7.4)	(1.4)			(0.9)	
Russia	-3.1	-1.8	.33	.9173	.52	.00947
Jan. 1922-Feb. 1924	(15.5)	(1.7)			(3.1)	

Notes: Numbers in parentheses are t- ratios. Rho (ρ) is the estimated
parameter of the autocorrelation process in the disturbances.

consistent with the parameter estimates for individual data sets. For (4)
the pooled estimates differ markedly from those shown in Table 1,
indicating heterogeneous specifications are being mixed.[13]

---

[13] It is by no means obvious that one expectations generating mechanism and
one demand for money schedule should be expected to describe all countries.
Rational expectations models imply, for instance, that different expectations
generating mechanisms should occur when forecasters confront different
environments. Nevertheless, empirical regularities which give order to a wide
variety of experiences are the goals which empirical researchers seek. If one

III. Conclusions

Data from six European hyperinflations have been used to adduce evidence in support of the hypothesis that uncertainty with respect to future inflation affects the demand for money when the alternative to money holding is holding inventories of commodities or engaging in barter.

The advantages of these results are: (1) they arise from a consistent use of the Cagan model in the sense that the expectations of economic agents with regard to inflation and uncertainty about future inflation are formed in analogous ways; (2) uncertainty about future inflation affects money demand in a uniformly positive way across five countries (Hungary is the exception) in which inflation was generated by similar fiscal regimes; (3) they reinforce Klein's (and Smirlock's) finding from U.S. data of a significant positive effect of uncertainty on money demand; (4) the addition of an uncertainty variable allows the inclusion of observations which Cagan was forced to exclude from his estimates; and (5) the addition of the uncertainty variable tends to make more uniform across countries the parameter which describes the formation of expected inflation (the adaptive expectations coefficient) and the elasticity of money demand with respect to expected inflation.

The results are, however, at variance with those produced by Allen, Frenkel and Pautler. Frenkel was unable to show that uncertainty with respect to future inflation had any effect on the demand for money in the German hyperinflation. The possible sources of the conflicting results are numerous: a different measure of the money supply (he includes deposits), a different measure of expected inflation, a different measure of uncertainty, and a different sample size (he excludes observations at the end of the sample). Unfortunately, one cannot investigate the generality of Frenkel's results because his measure of expected inflation, which is based on the forward exchange rate, is available only for the German hyperinflation.

Pautler's results are mixed. Generally, his uncertainty variable is not statistically significant. When it is, it enters with a negative sign. Allen's

---

can discover such a regularity, one may presume that if does not occur by accident.

results were also mixed with some significant negative coefficients. There is no obvious explanation as to why their mechanisms should generate an uncertainty variable which enters with a negative coefficient.

Finally, these results have at least one provocative implication. It is widely agreed that hyperinflation arises because governments attempt to raise abnormally large amounts of real revenue through the inflation tax. To the extent that erratic changes in the inflation rate generated by this process increase uncertainty about future inflation they also increase the tax base against which the inflation tax can be levied. That is, greater uncertainty increases the amount of real money balances held by the public for a given expected inflation rate. A monetary policy which generates greater uncertainty about future inflation will have the potential for increasing the inflation tax revenue of the government.

Epilogue: HyperFear

Hyperinflations are inherently fascinating. There is something fantastical about money that loses its value in an afternoon, denominations with so many zeros, and the extreme adaptations required for economic agents to cope with rapidly changing prices, making accounts of hyperinflations the nearest real-world equivalent of post-apocalyptic events. They capture our morbid interest in the same way that we find ourselves studying the details of disasters and gruesome accidents. As we see in this series of papers, however, they are also instructive for better understanding normal-world policies and principles. Effects that are too subtle to detect in more typical economic circumstances stand out in sharp relief at very high rates. Hyperinflations are worthy of serious study and will yield up useful lessons to those who take them seriously.

Yet there are individuals today who want to know if there is some direct, immediate, and literal lesson to be drawn. They ask if a serious inflation or hyperinflation can happen here or in the near future. In particular, they point to the huge federal deficits of the past several years (and those projected for the future), and to massive Federal Reserve purchases of assets that have been central to macroeconomic policy since the near collapse of the financial system in 2007-09. Surely, they observe, this is the very behavior we speak of in the analyses of hyperinflation contained in this volume. And if not here, then perhaps in Europe where some governments appear to regret their loss of the possibility of resort to the printing press. Shouldn't we be scared?

Although inflation is everywhere and always a *monetary* phenomenon, very rapid inflations, are, as far as we are aware, rooted in *fiscal* conditions. They appear not to have resulted from the pursuit of macroeconomic stabilization policy or even from policies aimed at rescuing financial systems. They have their roots in the failure of a government to cover its expenses with conventional revenue sources, and in the attempt to finance the shortfall with money creation—in an amount that exceeds the maximum that the inflation tax can collect in equilibrium. As a result, a dynamic process emerges in which the tax rate keeps rising in pursuit of revenue from an ever-shrinking tax base.

The upshot of this observation is that fears of a serious inflation or even hyperinflation in a major currency are almost entirely unfounded. In the European Union, those countries with central government deficits to finance are, as long as they part of the euro, unable to turn to money creation for revenue. The European Central Bank, on the other hand, while able to use the printing press, has no central government to speak of in need of financing.

In the United States, the Federal Reserve System has not expanded the money supply because of a failure of the government to otherwise sell its debt. Indeed, a substantial proportion of the expansion of the Fed's portfolio in the past few years has been in the form of private assets. The rapid growth in bank reserves in the U.S. has had nothing to do with the exigencies of public finance, and everything to do with the Fed's discretionary monetary policy. At the very foundation of that policy is an awareness of the costs of rapid inflation and a sensibility concerning an economy's need for a stable exchange medium. At the desired time, the Fed will be able and anxious to relieve itself of these assets and reabsorb the money that it has created.

In addition, the United States has a number of institutional constraints to prevent the resort to money-financed deficit spending. These include not just central bank independence that permits the Federal Reserve to refuse requests to buy Treasury debt, but also a complex system of Congressional authorization and appropriations, combined with legislatively imposed debt limits that serve as a circuit breaker to the kind of automatic spending decisions that can lead to continuing deficits in the face of financial reluctance to buy Treasury securities.

If there is any potential for a breakdown of our central bank commitment to low inflation, it lay in the limits of how much government debt markets will hold and the possibility that we could reach those limits, encountering difficulties in rolling over *existing* indebtedness. One reason that so many governments turn to the printing press is that the inflation tax is uniquely designed to be the slack variable in the government's revenue stream. For virtually all other forms of taxes, the legislature sets a tax *rate* that, interacting with the behavior of the tax *base*, produces an endogenous revenue *yield*. In the case of money finance, the government determines the yield, and then interacting with the base, the tax rate (i.e., inflation rate) is endogenously produced. In an environment with no or limited borrowing, therefore, the inflation tax is naturally the last tax to be determined, stretching or shrinking to fill a changing fiscal gap. Should circumstances suddenly swell the shortfall, it is the inflation tax that increases, precisely because it is automatic.

Consequently, in addition to the reasons outlined above, an important consideration that prevents that from happening here is that the U.S. government can borrow so easily. Treasury securities take up the slack. As long as U.S. securities are the world standard for the riskless asset, this can continue. However, one can imagine that the United States can reach the limit of how much debt it can sell. If it does, it would not only fail to be able to finance any current deficit, it would be unable to roll over previously incurred debt that matures.

Problems in rolling over debt have caused inflations in the past, although they do not have to.[1] If such a scenario were to arise, moreover, avoiding inflation would not be the only concern. Inability to sell debt has devastating consequences for the conduct of fiscal and even monetary policy. It would, for example, make financial rescues of the type undertaken four years ago impossible. Avoiding hyperinflation would be small consolation for the financial cost nonetheless incurred. The implications of funding problems, however, are not the focus of this volume, and must be taken up in another venue.

---

[1]See Makinen and Woodward (1989b, 1990).

Appendix: Select Publications by the Author and Coauthors

Select Publications by Gail E. Makinen

Books and Chapters

Monetary Policy and Price Stability, with Marc Labonte. Hauppague, New York: Nova Publishers, 2006.

The Economic Effects of 9/11: A Retrospective Assessment, with others. Honolulu: University Press of the Pacific, 2005.

"The National Debt: Who Bears Its Burdens," with Marc Labonte, and "The Retirement of the National Debt: Will it Increase the Size of the Federal Government," with Marc Labonte. In Jane Christensen, editor, *The National Debt: A Primer*. Hauppague, New York: Nova Publishers, 2004. "The National Debt: Who Bears Its Burdens" is also in James B. Lucas, editor, *National Debt and Deficits*, Hauppague, New York: Nova Publishers, 2005. It appears as well in Lawrence P. Neely and Patricia V. Lerner, editors, *Economic Policies: Issues and Developments*, Hauppague, New York: Nova Publishers, 2008.

"Seigniorage." In *Encyclopedia of Taxation and Tax Policy*, edited by Joseph J. Cordes, Robert D. Ebel, and Jane G. Gravelle. Washington, D.C.: Urban Institute Press, 1st edition 1999, 2nd edition 2004.

International Monetary Policy, with Marc Labonte. Hauppague, New York: Nova Publishers, 2003.

Saving in the United States: How Has It Changed and Why Is It Important?, with Brian Cashell. Hauppague, New York: Nova Publishers, 2003.

"The Federal Reserve: Should Its Mandated Goal Be Price Stability? The Issues and Technical Problems." In George B. Grey, editor, *Federal Reserve System: Background, Analysis, and Bibliography*. Hauppague, New York: Nova Publishers, 2002.

The Economic Expansion of the 1990s, with Marc Labonte. Hauppague, New York: Nova Publishers, 2002.

"Hyperinflation: Experience." In Peter Newman, Murray Milgate, and John Eatwell, editors, *The New Palgrave Dictionary of Money and Finance.* London: Macmillan, 1992.

"Funding Crises in the Aftermath of World War I," with G. Thomas Woodward. In Mario Draghi and Rudiger Dornbusch, editors, *Public Debt Management: Theory and Practice.* Cambridge: Cambridge University Press, 1990.

"The United States-Canadian Automotive Products Trade Act of 1965." In H. Peter Gray, William S. Milberg, and Phillip Bartholomew, editors, *Prospects for Canadian-United States Economic Relations Under Free Trade,* v. 8. Greenwich, Connecticut: JAI Press, 1990.

"Inflation and Stabilization in Bolivia: Comments." In Michael Bruno, Guido Di Tella, Rudiger Dornbusch, and Stanley Fischer, editors, *Inflation Stabilization: The Experience of Israel, Brazil, Bolivia, and Mexico.* Cambridge, Massachusetts: MIT Press, 1988.

Money, Banking, and Economic Activity. New York: Academic Press, 1981.

Money, the Price Level, and Interest Rates: An Introduction to Monetary Theory. Englewood Cliffs, New Jersey: Prentice-Hall, 1977.

Articles

"The Return of U.S. Currency from Abroad in the Inter-War Years: Fact or Fiction," with Richard Porter. In review.

"Are Central Bankers Currency Manipulators?" *Atlantic Economic Journal,* v. 41, no. 3, September 2013: 231-239.

"Denison's Law at Forty (or So): An Update," with William A. Bomberger. Online version 2008.

"Seigniorage, Legal Tender, and the Demand Notes of 1861," with William A. Bomberger. *Economic Inquiry,* v. 48, no. 4, October 2010: 916-932.

"The World According to Arthur Laffer, circa 1861." *Journal of Political Economy,* v. 112, no. 6, December 2004: back cover.

"Energy Independence: Would It Free the United States from Oil Price Shocks?," with Marc Labonte. *International Journal of Energy, Environment, and Economics,* v. 10, no. 3, 2001: 220-235.

"An Independent Central Bank and an Independent Monetary Policy: The Role of the Government Budget. The Case of Poland 1924-26." *Public Budgeting and Finance*, v. 21, no. 1, Spring 2001: 22-34. (Given the Jesse Burkhead Award as one of the two best articles in the journal during 2001.)

"Use of Interest-Bearing Currency in the Civil War: The Experience below the Mason-Dixon Line," with G. Thomas Woodward. *Journal of Money, Credit, and Banking*, v. 32, no. 1, February 1999: 121-129.

"Explaining Interest." *Journal of Political Economy*, v. 102, no. 6, December 1994: back cover.

"Inflation and Relative Price Variability: Parks' Study Re-examined," with William A. Bomberger. *Journal of Money, Credit, and Banking*, v. 25, no. 4, November 1993: 854-861.

"The Currency Ratios 1929-80: A Re-examination," with Mark Ladenson. *Atlantic Economic Journal*, v. 20, no. 4, December 1992: 1-9.

"A Monetary Interpretation of the Poincaré Stabilization of 1926," with G. Thomas Woodward. *Southern Economic Journal*, v. 51, no. 1, July 1989: 191-211.

"The Taiwanese Hyperinflation and Stabilization of 1945-1952," with G. Thomas Woodward. *Journal of Money, Credit, and Banking*, v. 21, no. 1, February 1989: 90-105. (Chapter 10 in this book.)

"The Demand for Money, the 'Reform Effect,' and the Money Supply Process in Hyperinflation: The Evidence from Greece and Hungary II Re-examined," with Robert B. Anderson and Willliam A. Bomberger. *Journal of Money, Credit, and Banking*, v. 20, no. 4, November 1988: 653-672. (Chapter 8 in this book.)

"The Greek Hyperinflation and Stabilization of 1943-1946: A Reply," *Journal of Economic History*, v. 48. No. 1, March 1988: 140-142.

"The Transition from Hyperinflation to Stability: Some Evidence," with G. Thomas Woodward. *Eastern Economic Journal*, v. 14, no. 1, January-March 1988: 19-26. (Chapter 9 in this book.)

"The Greek Hyperinflation and Stabilization of 1943-46." *Journal of Economic History*, v. 46, no. 3, September 1986: 795-805. Reprinted in Forrest Capie, editor, *Major Inflations in History*. North Hampton, Massachusetts: Edgar Elgar Publishers, 1991. (Chapter 7 in this book.)

"Some Anecdotal Evidence Relating to the Legal Restrictions Theory of Money," with G. Thomas Woodward. *Journal of Political Economy*, v. 94, no. 2, April 1986: 260-265.

"Inflation Uncertainty and the Demand for Money in Hyperinflation," with Willliam A. Bomberger. *Atlantic Economic Journal*, v. 13, no. 2, July 1985: 12-20. (Chapter 11 in this book.)

"The Greek Stabilization of 1944-46." *American Economic Review*, v. 74, no. 5, December 1984: 1067-1074. (Chapter 5 in this book.)

"Some Further Thoughts on the Hungarian Hyperinflation of 1945-46," with Willliam A. Bomberger. *South African Journal of Economics*, v. 51, no. 4, December 1983: 564-566. (Chapter 4 in this book.)

"The Hungarian Hyperinflation and Stabilization of 1945-1946," with Willliam A. Bomberger. *Journal of Political Economy*, v. 91, no. 5, October 1983: 801-824. Reprinted in Forrest Capie, editor, *Major Inflations in History*. North Hampton, Massachusetts: Edgar Elgar Publishers, 1991. (Chapter 6 in this book.)

"Indexation, Inflationary Finance and Hyperinflation: The 1945-46 Hungarian Experience," with Willliam A. Bomberger. *Journal of Political Economy*, v. 88, no. 3, June 1980: 550-560. Reprinted in David D. VanHoose and Roger Leroy Miller, *Modern Money and Banking*, New York: Thomson Advantage Books, 1995. (Chapter 3 in this book.)

"The Chinese Hyperinflation Re-examined," with Jarvis M. Babcock. *Journal of Political Economy*, v. 83, no. 6, December 1975: 1259-1267. (Chapter 2 in this book.)

"Hyperinflation and the Dynamics of the Money Supply," with Willliam A. Bomberger. Mimeo, 1975.

"Economic Stabilization in Wartime: A Comparative Case Study of Korea and Vietnam." *Journal of Political Economy*, v. 79, no. 6, November-December 1971: 1216-1243. (Chapter 1 in this book.)

Select Publications by William A. Bomberger

"Disagreement and Uncertainty: A Reply to Rich and Butler." *Journal of Money, Credit, and Banking*, v. 31, no. 2, May 1999: 273-276.

"Disagreement as a Measure of Uncertainty." *Journal of Money, Credit, and Banking*, v. 28 no. 3, August 1996: 381-392.

"Income, Wealth, and Household Demand for Deposits." *American Economic Review*, v. 83, no. 4, September 1993: 1034-1044.

"The Effects of Fiscal Policies When Incomes Are Uncertain: A Contradiction to Ricardian Equivalence: Comment." *American Economic Review*, v. 80, no. 1, March 1990: 309-312.

"Interest Rates, Uncertainty and the Livingston Data," with William J. Frazer. *Journal of Finance*, v. 36, no. 3, June 1981: 661-676.

"A Comment on Tobin and Buiter." In Jerome L. Stein, editor, *Monetarism*. Amsterdam: North-Holland Publishing Company, 1976.

"Wage Determination, Inflation, and the Industrial Structure: Comment." *American Economic Review*, v. 65, no. 3, June 1975: 504-506.

Select Publications by G. Thomas Woodward

"Revenue Response from a Tax Cut: The Walker Tariff of 1845." *National Tax Association Proceedings, 104th Annual Conference on Taxation*, 2011: 139-146.

"Economic Issues in Taxing the Untaxed Business Sector," with Dennis Zimmerman. *National Tax Association Proceedings, 98th Annual Conference on Taxation*, 2005: 329-335.

"The Costs of State-Sponsored Terrorism: The Example of the Barbary Pirates." *National Tax Journal*, v. 57, no. 3, September 2004: 596-612.

"Federal Revenue Policy" and "Inflation Tax." In *Encyclopedia of Taxation and Tax Policy*, 2nd edition, edited by Joseph J. Cordes, Robert D. Ebel, and Jane G. Gravelle. Washington, D.C.: Urban Institute Press, 2004.

"Interest-Bearing Currency: Evidence from the Civil War Experience: Comment." *Journal of Money, Credit, and Banking*, v. 27, no. 3, August 1995: 927-937.

"What Made Receipts Boom and When Will They Go Bust?" with Richard A. Kasten and David J. Weiner. *National Tax Journal*, v. 52, no. 3, September 1999: 339-347.

"The Savings and Loan Debacle." In Leonard W. Levy and Louis Fisher, editors, *Encyclopedia of the American Presidency*, v. 4. New York: Simon and Schuster, 1994.

"Evidence of the Fisher Effect from U.K. Indexed Bonds." *Review of Economics and Statistics*, v. 74, no. 2, May 1992: 315-320.

"The Real Thing: A Dynamic Profile of the Term Structure of Real Interest Rates and Inflation Expectations in the United Kingdom, 1892-1989." *Journal of Business*, v. 63, no. 3, July 1990: 373-398.

"Government Sponsored Enterprises: Another View." *Public Budgeting and Finance*, v. 9, no. 3, Fall 1989: 87-93.

"Comment: 'The Real Rate of Interest: Inferences from the New U.K. Indexed Gilts.'" *International Economic Review*, v. 29, no. 3, August 1988: 565-568.

"A Factor Augmenting Approach to Studying Capital Measurement, Obsolescence, and the Recent Productivity Slowdown." In Ali Dogramaci, editor, *Developments in Econometric Analysis of Productivity*. Boston: Kluwer-Nijhoff Publishers, 1982.

Select Publications by Robert B. Anderson

"Toward Realistic Policy Design: Policy Reaction Functions that Rely on Economic Forecasts," with Jared Enzler. In Rudiger Dornbusch, Stanley Fischer, and John Bosson, editors, *Macroeconomics and Finance: Essays in Honor of Franco Modigliani*. Cambridge, Massachusetts: MIT Press, 1987.

"Interaction between Fiscal and Monetary Policy and the Real Interest Rate," with Albert Ando and Jared Enzler. *American Economic Review*, v. 74, no. 2, May 1984: 55-60.

"The Incidence and Excess Burden of a Profits Tax under Imperfect Competition," with J. Gregory Ballentine. *Public Finance / Finances Publiques*, v. 31, no. 2, 1976: 159-176.

References

Abel, Andrew, Rudiger Dornbusch, John Huizinga, and Alan Marcus. 1979. "Money Demand during Hyperinflation." *Journal of Monetary Economics*, v. 5, no. 1, January: 97-104.

Agapitides, Sotirios. 1945. "The Inflation of the Cost of Living and Wages in Greece during German Occupation." *International Labour Review*, v. 52, no. 6, December: 643-651.

Allen, S. D. 1979. "Price Uncertainty Variables in a Money Demand Function: The Case of the German Hyperinflation." University of North Carolina-Greensboro, Working Paper No. 790901, September.

Allied Mission to Observe the Greek Elections. 1946. *Report of the Allied Mission to Observe the Greek Elections.* Department of State Publication 2522, April. Washington, D.C.: Government Printing Office.

Anderson, Robert B., William A. Bomberger, and Gail E. Makinen. 1988. "The Demand for Money, the 'Reform Effect,' and the Money Supply Process in Hyperinflations: The Evidence from Greece and Hungary II Re-examined." *Journal of Money, Credit, and Banking*, v, 20, no. 4, November: 653-672. (Chapter 8 in this book.)

Ausch, Sándor. 1958. *Az 1945-1946, évi infláció és stabilizáció* (Inflation and Stabilization during 1945-1946). Budapest: Kossuth Könyvikiadó (Kossuth Publishing House).

Babcock, Jarvis M., and Gail E. Makinen. 1975. "The Chinese Hyperinflation Re-examined." *Journal of Political Economy*, v. 83, no. 6, December: 1259-1267. (Chapter 2 in this book.)

Bailey, Martin J. 1956. "The Welfare Cost of Inflationary Finance." *Journal of Political Economy*, v. 64, no. 2, April: 93-110.

Bank of China [Taiwan]. 1950-1955. *Monthly Review.* Taipei: Bank of China.

Bank of Greece. 1948. *Annual Report.* Athens: Bank of Greece.

Bank of Korea. 1962, 1963. *Economic Statistics Yearbook.* Seoul: Bank of Korea.

Bank of Korea. 1952-1955. *Monthly Statistical Review,* various issues.

Bank of Taiwan. 1955. *Taiwan Financial Statistics Monthly*, v. 40, March. Taipei: Bank of Taiwan.

Bank of Taiwan 1966. *Taiwan Statistical Data Book*. Taipei: Republic of China, Council for International Economic Cooperation and Development, June.

Barro, Robert J. 1970. "Inflation, the Payments Period, and the Demand for Money." *Journal of Political Economy*, v. 78, no. 6, November-December: 1228-63.

Barro, Robert J. 1972. "Inflationary Finance and the Welfare Cost of Inflation." *Journal of Political Economy*, v. 80, no. 5, September-October: 978-1001.

Berend, Ivan T., and Gyorgy Ranki. 1974. *Hungary: A Century of Economic Development*. New York: Barnes and Noble.

Blejer, Mario I. 1979. "The Demand for Money and the Variability of the Rate of Inflation: Some Empirical Results." *International Economic Review*, v. 20, no. 2, June: 545-549.

Bloomfield, Arthur I., and John P. Jensen. 1951. *Banking Reform in South Korea*. New York: Federal Reserve Bank of New York.

Bomberger, William A., and Gail E. Makinen. 1980. "Indexation, Inflationary Finance and Hyperinflation: The 1945-1946 Hungarian Experience." *Journal of Political Economy*, v. 88, no. 3, June: 550-560. (Chapter 3 in this book.)

Bomberger, William A. and Gail E. Makinen. 1983. "The Hungarian Hyperinflation and Stabilization of 1945-1946." *Journal of Political Economy*, v. 91, no. 5, October: 801-824. (Chapter 6 in this book).

Bomberger, William A., and Gail E. Makinen. 1975. "Hyperinflation and the Dynamics of the Money Supply." Mimeo.

Boonekamp, C. 1978. "Inflation, Hedging and the Demand for Money." *American Economic Review*, v. 68, no. 5, December: 821-833.

Bresciani-Turroni, Constantino. 1937. *The Economics of Inflation*. Translated by Millicent E. Sayers. London: Allen & Unwin, 1937. (Italian original *Le vicende del marco tedesco*, 1931.)

Bronfenbrenner, Martin, and Franklyn D. Holzman. 1963. "Survey of Inflation Theory." *American Economic Review*, v. 53, no. 4, September: 597-600.

Cagan, Phillip. 1956. "Monetary Dynamics of Hyperinflation." In Milton Friedman, editor, *Studies in The Quantity Theory of Money:* 25-117. Chicago: University of Chicago Press.

Campbell, Colin D., and Gordon Tullock. 1957. "Some Little-Understood Aspects of Korea's Monetary and Fiscal Systems." *American Economic Review*, v. 47, no. 2, June: 336-349.

Capie, Forrest. 1986. "Conditions in which Very Rapid Inflation Has Appeared." *Carnegie-Rochester Conference Series on Public Policy*, v. 24, Spring: 115-168.

Chang, Kia-ngau. 1958. *The Inflationary Spiral: The Experience in China, 1929-1950*. Cambridge, Massachusetts: MIT Press.

Chou, Shun-Hsin. 1963. *The Chinese Inflation 1937-1949*. New York: Columbia University Press, 1963.

Commercial Bank of Pest. 1947. *Survey of the Economic Situation in Hungary*. Budapest, January.

Cooley, Thomas F., and Stephen F. LeRoy. 1981. "Identification and Estimation of Money Demand." *American Economic Review*, v. 71, no. 5, December: 825-844.

Delivanis, Dimitrios, and William C. Cleveland. 1949. *Greek Monetary Developments, 1939-1948*. Bloomington, Indiana: University of Indiana Press.

Donaldson-Rawlins, E. C. 1925. *Report on the Commercial and Industrial Situation in Hungary*. London: His Majesty's Stationery Office.

Ecker-Racz, L. László. 1933. "The Hungarian Thrift-Crown." *American Economic Review*, v. 23, no. 3, September: 471-474.

Ecker-Racz, L. László. 1946a. "Hungarian Currency Stabilization, 1946." Mimeo, U.S. Legation, Budapest.

Ecker-Racz, L. László. 1946b. "Hungarian Economic Developments January 1945-June 1946." Mimeo, U.S. Legation, Budapest, July 1.

Ecker-Racz, L. László. 1954. *The Hungarian Economy, 1920-1954*. Washington, D.C.: Council for Economic and Industry Research.

Ecker-Racz, L. László. 1981. Interview, Arlington, Virginia, February 23.

Eckstein, Alexander. 1955. "National Income and Capital Formation in Hungary 1900-1950." In Simon Kuznets, editor, *Income and Wealth*, series 5. London: Bowes & Bowes.

Eckstein, Otto. 1981. *Core Inflation*. Englewood Cliffs, New Jersey: Prentice-Hall.

Eden, Benjamin. 1975. "Aspects of Uncertainty in Simple Monetary Models." Ph.D. dissertation, University of Chicago, June.

Eden, Benjamin. 1976. "On the Specification of the Demand for Money: The Real Rate of Return versus the Rate of Inflation." *Journal of Political Economy*, v. 84, no. 6, December: 1353-1359.

Fair, Ray. 1970. "The Estimation of Simultaneous Equation Models with Lagged Endogenous Variables and First Order Serially Correlated Errors." *Econometrica*, v. 38, no. 3, May: 507-516.

Falush, Peter. 1976. "The Hungarian Hyperinflation of 1945-46." *National Westminster Bank Quarterly Review*, August: 46-56.

Feldstein, Martin, Jerry Green, and Eytan Sheshinski. 1978. "Inflation and Taxes in a Growing Economy with Debt and Equity Finance." *Journal of Political Economy*, v. 86, no. 2, part 2, April: S53-S70.

Fishlow, Albert. 1974. "Indexing Brazilian Style: Inflation without Tears?" *Brookings Papers on Economic Activity*, no. 1: 261-280.

Flood, Robert P., and Peter M. Garber. 1980. "An Economic Theory of Monetary Reform." *Journal of Political Economy*, v. 88, no. 1, February: 24-58.

Flood, Robert P., and Peter M. Garber. 1983. "Process Consistency and Monetary Reform: Some Further Evidence." *Journal of Monetary Economics*, v. 12, no. 2, August: 279-295.

Frenkel, Jacob A. 1977. "The Forward Exchange Rate, Expectations, and the Demand for Money: The German Hyperinflation." *American Economic Review*, v. 67, no. 4, September: 653-670.

Frenkel, Jacob A. 1979. "Further Evidence on Expectations and the Demand for Money during the German Hyperinflation." *Journal of Monetary Economics*, v. 5, no. 1, January: 81-96.

Friedman, Milton. 1974. "Monetary Correction." In Herbert Giersch, Milton Friedman, William Fellner, Edward M. Bernstein, and Alexandre Kafka, editors, *Essays on Inflation and Indexation*. Washington, D.C.: American Enterprise Institute.

Friedman, Milton, and Anna Jacobson Schwartz. 1963. *A Monetary History of the United States, 1867-1960*. Princeton, New Jersey: Princeton University Press.

Galbraith, John Kenneth. 1975. *Money: Whence It Came, Where It Went.* Boston: Houghton Mifflin.

Garber, Peter M. 1982. "Transition from Inflation to Price Stability." *Carnegie-Rochester Conference Series on Public Policy,* v. 16, Spring: 11-42.

Goode, Richard. 1952. "Anti-Inflationary Impacts of Alternative Forms of Taxation." *American Economic Review, Papers and Proceedings,* v. 42, no. 2, May: 147-160. See also the discussion by Carl Shoup, pp. 161-165.

Gordon, Robert J. 1978. "Why Stopping Inflation May Be Costly: Evidence from Fourteen Historical Episodes." In Robert Hall, editor, *Inflation: Causes and Effects:* 11-40. Chicago: University of Chicago Press.

Graham, Frank D. 1930. *Exchange, Prices, and Production in Hyper-inflation Germany, 1920-23.* Princeton, New Jersey: Princeton University Press.

Granger, Clive W. J. 1969. "Investigating Causal Relations by Econometric Models and Cross-Spectral Methods." *Econometrica,* v. 37, no. 3, August: 424-438.

Greece. High Board of Reconstruction. 1950. *National Income and Investment in Greece during the Years 1945-49.* March. Athens.

Gurley, John. 1953. "Excess Liquidity and European Monetary Reforms, 1944-1952." *American Economic Review,* v. 43, no. 1, March: 76-100.

Hanke, Steve H., and Nicholas Krus. 2012. "World Hyperinflations." Cato Institute Working Paper, August 15.

Helmreich, Ernst C., editor. 1973. *Hungary.* Westport, Connecticut: Greenwood Press.

Ho, Samuel P. S. 1978. *Economic Development of Taiwan 1860-1970.* New Haven: Yale University Press.

Holtfrerich, Carl L. 1982. "Domestic and Foreign Expectations and the Demand for Money during the German Inflation, 1920-1923." In Charles P. Kindleberger and Jean-Pierre Laffargue, editors, *Financial Crises: History, Theory and Policy:* 117-132. Cambridge: Cambridge University Press.

Holtfrerich, Carl L. 1983. "Political Factors of the German Inflation, 1914-23." In Nathan Schmukler and Edward Marcus, editors, *Inflation through the Ages: Economic, Social, Psychological and Historical Aspects:* 400-416. New York: Brooklyn College Press.

Hu, Teh-wei. 1971. "Hyperinflation and the Dynamics of the Demand for Money in China, 1945-1949." *Journal of Political Economy,* v. 79, no. 1, January-February: 186-195.

Hu, Teh-wei. 1975. "Errata." *Journal of Political Economy,* v. 83, no. 6, December: 1268.

Humphrey, R. J. E. 1924. *Report on the Commercial and Industrial Situation in Hungary.* London: His Majesty's Stationery Office.

Hungarian General Credit Bank. 1946. *Report.* August. Budapest.

Hungary. Central Statistical Office (Office central hongrois de statistique). 1946. *Revue hongroise de statistique,* nos. 10-12, October-November.

Irvine, Reed J., and Robert F. Emery. 1966. "Interest Rates as an Anti-inflationary Instrument in Taiwan." *National Banking Review,* v. 4, no. 1, September: 29-40.

Jacobs, Rodney L. 1977. "Hyperinflation and the Supply of Money." *Journal of Money, Credit and Banking,* v. 9, no. 2, May: 287-303.

Jessen, Raymond J., and others. 1947. "On a Population Sample for Greece." *Journal of the American Statistical Association,* v. 42, no. 239, September: 357-384.

Johnson, Harry G. 1967a. *Economic Policies toward Less Developed Countries.* New York: Praeger.

Johnson, Harry G. 1967b. "A Survey of Theories of Inflation." In *Essays in Monetary Economics,* 1st edition. London: Unwin University Books.

Kaldor, Nicholas. 1946. "A Study in Inflation: I. Hungary's Classical Example" and "A Study in Inflation: II. Stabilization." *Manchester Guardian Weekly,* November 29, December 6.

Karasz, Arthur. 1981. Interview, Washington, D.C., February 15.

Kemény, Gyöögy. 1952. *Economic Planning in Hungary, 1947-49.* London: Royal Institute of International Affairs.

Keynes, John Maynard. 1923. *A Tract on Monetary Reform.* London: Macmillan.

Khan, Mohsin S. 1977. "The Variability of Expectations in Hyperinflations." *Journal of Political Economy*, v. 85, no. 4, August: 817-827.

Klein, Benjamin. 1975. "Our New Monetary Standard: The Measurement and Effect of Price Uncertainty, 1880-1973." *Economic Inquiry*, v. 13, no. 4, December: 461-484.

Klein, Benjamin. 1977. "The Demand for Quality-Adjusted Cash Balances: Price Uncertainty in the U.S. Demand for Money Function," *Journal of Political Economy*, v. 85, no. 4, August: 691-715.

Klein, Lawrence R. 1958. "The Estimation of Distributed Lags." *Econometrica*, v. 26, no. 4, October: 553-565.

Korea (Republic). Economic Planning Board, Bureau of Statistics. 1962. *Statistical Handbook of Korea*. Seoul: Bureau of Statistics.

Korea (Republic). Office of Public Information. 1955a. *A Handbook of Korea*. Seoul: Ministry of Information.

Korea (Republic). Office of Public Information. 1955b. *Korean Report. Volume 2, 1952-53*. Seoul: Ministry of Information.

Kuo, Shirley W. Y. 1983. *The Taiwan Economy in Transition*. Boulder, Colorado: Westview Press.

LaHaye, Laura. 1985. "Inflation and Currency Reform." *Journal of Political Economy*, v. 93, no. 3, June: 537-560.

Lee, H. B. 1968. *Korea: Time, Change and Administration*. Hawaii: East-West Center.

Liu, Fu-chi. 1970. *Studies in Monetary Development of Taiwan*. Taipei: Academia Sinica, October.

Lucas, Jr., Robert E. 1973. "Some International Evidence on Output-Inflation Tradeoffs." *American Economic Review*, v. 63, no. 3, June: 326-334.

Makinen, Gail E. 1986. "The Greek Hyperinflation and Stabilization of 1943-46." *Journal of Economic History*, v. 46, no. 3, September: 795-805. (Chapter 7 in this book.)

Makinen, Gail E. 1984. "The Greek Stabilization of 1944-46." *American Economic Review*, v. 74, no. 5, December: 1067-1074. (Chapter 5 in this book.)

Makinen, Gail E. 1981. *Money, Banking, and Economic Activity*. New York: Academic Press.

Makinen, Gail E., and G. Thomas Woodward. 1988. "The Transition from Hyperinflation to Stability: Some Evidence." *Eastern Economic Journal*, v. 14, no. 1, January-March: 19-26. (Chapter 9 in this book.)

Makinen, Gail E., and G. Thomas Woodward. 1989a. "The Taiwanese Hyperinflation and Stabilization of 1945-1952." *Journal of Money, Credit and Banking*, v. 21, no. 1, February: 90-105. (Chapter 10 in this book.)

Makinen, Gail E., and G. Thomas Woodward. 1989b. "A Monetary Interpretation of the Poincaré Stabilization of 1926." *Southern Economic Journal*, v. 56, no. 1, July: 191-211.

Makinen, Gail E., and G. Thomas Woodward. 1990. "Funding Crises in the Aftermath of World War I." In Rudiger Dornbusch and Mario Draghi, editors, *Public Debt Management: Theory and History:* 153-183. Cambridge: Cambridge University Press.

Mao, Songian. 1967. "The Activities of the Bank of Taiwan in the Past 20 Years." *Bank of Taiwan Quarterly*, v. 18, no. 1, March: 56-90. (In Chinese.)

McCabe, Ralph. 1954. *Army Payments in Korea: An Inquiry into the Financing of Military Procurement.* Baltimore: Operations Research Office, Johns Hopkins University.

McKinnon, Ronald I. 1973. *Money and Capital in Economic Development.* Washington, D.C.: Brookings Institution.

Mitzakis, Michel G. 1926. *Le relèvement financier de la Hongrie et la Société des nations.* Paris: Presses Universitaires de France.

Musgrave, Richard. 1959. *The Theory of Public Finance.* New York: McGraw-Hill.

National Bank of Hungary. 1945-1948. *Monthly Bulletin.* Budapest: National Bank of Hungary.

National Bank of Hungary. 1946, 1947a. *Annual Report.* Budapest: National Bank of Hungary.

National Bank of Hungary. 1947b. *Hungary in Statistical Tables.* Budapest: National Bank of Hungary.

National Bank of Vietnam. 1965-1967. *Annual Report.* Saigon: National Bank of Vietnam.

New York Times. 1946a. June 28: 6.

New York Times. 1946b. July 7: 4.

New York Times. 1946c. July 27: 1, 11.

New York Times. 1946d. July 31: 15-18.

New York Times. 1946e. August 7: 7.

New York Times. 1948. September 12: 16.

New York Times. 1949. February 8: 14.

New York Times. 1969a. June 9: 1.

New York Times. 1969b. September 22: 1.

Nichols, Donald. 1974. "Some Principles of Inflationary Finance." *Journal of Political Economy,* v. 82, no. 2, part 1, March-April: 423-430.

Nogaro, Bertrand. 1948. "Hungary's Recent Monetary Crisis and Its Theoretical Meaning." *American Economic Review,* v. 38, no. 5, September: 526-542.

Okun, Arthur. 1978. "Efficient Disinflationary Policies." *American Economic Review,* v. 68, no. 3, May: 348-352.

Okun, Arthur. 1978. "Efficient Disinflationary Policies." *American Economic Review,* v. 68, no. 2, May: 248-352.

Patterson, Gardiner. 1948. "The Financial Experiences of Greece from Liberation to Truman Doctrine (October 1944-March 1947)." Ph.D. dissertation, Harvard University.

Patterson, Gardiner. 1983. Interview, Washington, D.C., July 10.

Pautler, Paul A. 1981. "Uncertainty in the Demand for Money during Hyperinflation." *Economic Inquiry,* v. 19, no. 1, January: 165-172.

Pou, Pedro. 1976. "The Variability of the Rate of Inflation, Risk, and the Demand for Money." Discussion Paper, Center for Latin American Monetary Studies, Mexico City.

Protopapadakis, Aris. 1983. "The Endogeneity of Money during the German Hyperinflation: A Reappraisal." *Economic Inquiry,* v. 21, no. 1, January: 72-92.

Riegg, Nicholas H. 1978. "The Role of Fiscal and Monetary Policies in Taiwan's Economic Development." Ph.D. dissertation, University of Connecticut.

Sargent, Thomas J. 1983. "Stopping Moderate Inflations: The Methods of Poincaré and Thatcher." In Rudiger Dornbusch and Mario H. Simonsen, editors, *Inflation, Debt, and Indexation:* 54-96. Cambridge, Massachusetts: MIT Press.

Sargent, Thomas J. 1977. "The Demand for Money During Hyperinflations Under Rational Expectations: I." *International Economic Review*, v. 18, no. 1, February: 59-82.

Sargent, Thomas J. 1982. "The Ends of Four Big Inflations." In Robert Hall, editor, *Inflation: Causes and Effects:* 41-93. Chicago: University of Chicago Press.

Sargent, Thomas J., and Robert E. Lucas. 1978. "After Keynesian Macroeconomics." In *After the Phillips Curve: Persistence of High Inflation and High Unemployment,* Federal Reserve Bank of Boston, Conference Series No. 19, June: 49-73. Boston: Federal Reserve Bank of Boston.

Sargent, Thomas J., and Neil Wallace. 1973. "Rational Expectations and the Dynamics of Hyperinflation." *International Economic Review*, v. 14, no. 2, June: 328-350.

Sargent, Thomas J., and Neil Wallace. 1981. "Some Unpleasant Monetarist Arithmetic." Federal Reserve Bank of Minneapolis *Quarterly Review*, Fall: 1-17.

Sargent, Thomas J., and Wallace, Neil. 1982. "The Real-Bills Doctrine versus the Quantity Theory: A Reconsideration." *Journal of Political Economy*, v. 90, no. 6, December: 1212-1236.

Schuker, Stephen A. 1978. "Finance and Foreign Policy in the Era of the German Inflation: British, French, and German Strategies for Economic Reconstruction after the First World War." In Otto Busch and Gerald D. Feldman, editors, *Historische Prozesse der deutschen Inflation, 1914-1924:* 343-371. Berlin: Colloquium-Verlag.

Sims, Christopher A. 1972. "Money, Income, and Causality." *American Economic Review*, v. 62, no. 4, September: 540-552.

Smirlock, Michael. 1982. "Inflation Uncertainty and the Demand for Money." *Economic Inquiry*, v. 20, no. 3, July: 355-364.

Spulber, Nicolas. 1973. "National Income and Its Distribution." In Ernst C. Helmreich, editor, *Hungary*. Westport, Connecticut: Greenwood Press. (Original printing New York: Frederick A. Praeger, 1957.)

Stroup, Robert H., and William J. Frazer, Jr. 1969. "The Demand for Money by Households in South Vietnam: The Evidence from Cross-Section Data." *Journal of Political Economy*, v. 77, no. 4, July-August: 489-493.

Taiwan (Republic of China). Directorate-General of Budget, Accounting and Statistics. 1975. *Statistical Yearbook of the Republic of China*. Taipei.

Taiwan (Republic of China). Directorate General of Budgets, Accounts and Statistics, Executive Yuan. 1968. *National Income of the Republic of China*, October. Taipei: Directorate General of Budgets, Accounts and Statistics, Executive Yuan.

Taiwan (Republic of China). Economic Research Center, Council for U.S. Aid. 1966. *Taiwan Statistical Data Book*. Taipei: Economic Research Center, Council for U.S. Aid.

Tang, De-Piao, and Teh-Wei Hu. 1983. "Money, Prices, and Causality: The Chinese Hyperinflation, 1945-49." *Journal of Macroeconomics*, v. 5, no. 4, Fall: 503-510.

Teichova, Alice. 1983. "A Comparative View of the Inflation of the 1920s in Austria and Czechoslovakia." In Nathan Schmukler and Edward Marcus, editors, *Inflation through the Ages: Economic, Social, Psychological and Historical Aspects*: 531-567. New York: Brooklyn College Press.

Tobin, James. 1980. "Stabilization Policy Ten Years After." *Brookings Papers on Economic Activity*, v. 11, no. 1: 19-72.

Tobin, James. 1971. "An Essay on the Principles of Debt Management." In *Essays in Economics, Volume I: Macroeconomics*: 378-455. Chicago: Markham.

Tsiang, S. C. 1985. "Monetary Reform China: Comments." In John Williamson, editor, *Inflation and Indexation: Argentina, Brazil, and Israel*: 148-151. Washington, D.C.: Institute for International Economics.

United Nations Relief and Rehabilitation Agency (UNRRA). 1947. *Economic Rehabilitation in Hungary*. London: UNRRA European Regional Office, May.

United Nations Statistical Office. 1947. *Monthly Bulletin of Statistics*, no. 6, June.

United States Agency for International Development (USAID). 1966-1968. *Annual Statistical Bulletin*. Washington, D.C.: Government Printing Office.

United States Armed Forces Far East. 1953a. *Civil Affairs Activities in Korea*, March. Washington, D.C.: Government Printing Office.

United States Armed Forces Far East. 1953b. *Monthly Civil Affairs Summary for Korea*, December. Washington, D.C.: Government Printing Office.

United States. Department of State. 1952. "Agreement on Economic Coordination between the Unified Command and the Republic of Korea, Pusan, May 24, 1952." In *United States Treaties and Other International Agreements, III*. Washington, D.C.: Government Printing Office.

Varga, Stephen. 1949. "Hungary's Monetary Crisis: Comment." *American Economic Review*, v. 39, no. 5, December: 951-960.

Vietnam (Republic). National Institute of Statistics. 1966-1968. *Vietnam Statistical Yearbook*. Saigon: Directorate General of Planning.

Walré de Bordes, J. van. 1924. *The Austrian Crown*. London: P. S. King.

Webb, Steven B. 1983. "Money Demand and Expectations in the German Hyperinflation: A Survey of the Models." In Nathan Schmukler and Edward Marcus, editors, *Inflation through the Ages: Economic, Social, Psychological and Historical Aspects*: 435-449. New York: Brooklyn College Press.

Webb, Steven B. 1985. "Government Debt and Inflationary Expectations as Determinants of the Money Supply in Germany 1919-23." *Journal of Money, Credit, and Banking*, v. 17, no. 4, November, part 1: 479-492.

Winkle, F. F. 1947 "Some Aspects of the Recent Inflation and Stabilization of the Hungarian Currency." *South African Journal of Economics*, v. 15, no. 3, September: 178-191.

Witt, Peter-Christian. 1983. "Tax Policies, Tax Assessment and Inflation: Toward a Sociology of Public Finance in the German Inflation, 1914-1923." In Nathan Schmukler and Edward Marcus, editors, *Inflation through the Ages: Economic, Social, Psychological and Historical Aspects*: 137-160. New York: Brooklyn College Press.

Index

www.ingramcontent.com/pod-product-compliance
Lightning Source LLC
Chambersburg PA
CBHW050457190326
41458CB00005B/1320